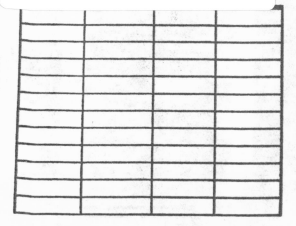

JOSEPH SHUMAN
JOURNALISM COLLECTION

POINT PARK COLLEGE

MEDIATIONS

MEDIATIONS

Essays on Brecht, Beckett, and the Media

MARTIN ESSLIN

Louisiana State University Press   Baton Rouge

DESIGNER: Joanna Hill
TYPEFACE: VIP Sabon
TYPESETTER: G & S Typesetters, Inc.
PRINTER: Thomson-Shore
BINDER: John Dekker & Sons

LIBRARY OF CONGRESS CATALOGING IN PUBLICATION DATA

Esslin, Martin.
  Mediations: essays on Brecht, Beckett, and the media.

  Bibliography: p.
  Includes index.
    1. Literature, Modern—20th century—History and criticism—Addresses, essays, lectures. 2. Brecht, Bertolt, 1898–1956—Criticism and interpretation—Addresses, essays, lectures. 3. Beckett, Samuel, 1906– —Criticism and interpretation—Addresses, essays, lectures. 4. Broadcasting—Addresses, essays, lectures. 5. Drama—20th century—History and criticism—Addresses, essays, lectures. I. Title.
  PN771.E77   1980   809.2′04   80-16076
  ISBN 0-8071-0771-9

Contents

MEDIATIONS

Introduction: A Personal Aside

A collection of writings on a variety of topics, gathered together from the periodicals or the volumes of papers by divers hands in which they first appeared, must have some connecting link. I have always found in reading such books that the strongest and most basic, most evident connecting link is, in fact, the person of the author; hence, perhaps a few remarks on how the pieces in this volume hang together might be justified, even in what otherwise should be regarded as a fairly serious book on a number of serious topics.

In one respect, I see myself as a very typical child of this century, which has been a century of violent upheavals characterized by vast movements of refugees across national frontiers, a century in which, as Brecht put it, people "changed their countries oftener than their shoes." I became a refugee before I reached the age of two, when my parents, after the collapse of the short-lived Hungarian Soviet republic, in which one of my uncles held a high government post, moved to Vienna; and a second time, before I was twenty, when German troops occupied Austria. That is how, after a year of hardship in Belgium, I finally got to England. At present I divide my time between England and the United States, still changing countries halfway through each year.

In my youth, in Vienna, I became passionately interested in the theatre. I wrote, and occasionally published, poems from the age of sixteen. I wanted to become a playwright and director. And I actually succeeded in getting into Max Reinhardt's famous theatre academy, the Reinhardt Seminar, where each semester, out of several hundred, only about twenty new students passed the entrance examination. I did well at the Reinhardt Seminar: in the summer of 1937, with other students, I appeared in small parts at the Salzburg Festival in Reinhardt's production of Goethe's *Faust*; all seemed set fair for a good career in my chosen sphere. And then, from one day to the next, in March, 1938, it was all lost. How could one hope to work as a director, a playwright, let alone a poet, outside one's own language? I had read English at the University in Vienna, parallel with my studies at the theatre academy, but, when I arrived in England I felt woefully insecure in the language, and what was even worse, woefully ignorant of the whole cultural milieu: its manners and customs as well as the complex pattern of literary references which constitute the ambience of people claiming to be educated, in any country.

When the war broke out I was very fortunate in finding work in which my background could be of some use. The BBC took me on as a translator in the department that listened in to foreign broadcasts, and a year later I succeeded in getting transferred into the section which broadcast in German to Germany and was, in fact, the very fascinating front line of the psychological and propaganda battle with the Goebbels propaganda machine. That is how, as a professional listener to political broadcasts, and as a director and scriptwriter producing such broadcasts, I became interested and absorbed in the problems of the electronic media as instruments of persuasion and communication. I spent twenty years of my life in the BBC's overseas broadcasting service, working first in German, then in English as a director, writer, and finally, as a planner and executive. It was interesting work; it took me to east and central Africa to prepare features on colonial policy; it made me something of an expert in European politics and economics, and in the cold war period, on the philosophy and practice of Marxism. But I was still yearning for my original goal in life: the theatre. When Brecht died I felt there was a need for a book investigating the strange paradox of a political poet whose work seemed to contradict his professed ideology. And so, combining my political and my theatre background, I wrote my first book.

One of the effects of the success of that venture was that the BBC realized that I knew something about drama. And so, after twenty years I was offered a post in the radio drama department. It was in my capacity as assistant head and, from 1963 onwards, head of that department that I frequently came into contact with Samuel Beckett, whom I had first met shortly before my move when I was researching my second book on drama, *The Theatre of the Absurd*.

Here, then, is the connecting thread that links the elements that make up this volume: Brecht and Reinhardt (in whose theatre Brecht learned much of the craft of directing and against whom he reacted when developing his own style of drama in theory and practice); Beckett; and the whole fascinating and, in my opinion, in our century, all-important impact, the aesthetics, and the deeper nature of the electronic mass media. Moreover, it is through the often almost miraculously lucky accidents of my "translations" from one country to another that I came to occupy a position between different cultural spheres, the German, the French, and the Anglo-Saxon, which made it possible for me to see myself as a sort of mediator between them.

No one who has not experienced such a "translation" in the full sense of the word can realize how widely divergent the cultural atmospheres in the various national spheres of the West have become. Where once, till the end of the nineteenth century, there had been a unified culture, based on a common familiarity with Latin, Greek, Italian, and French and the mythology, philosophy, and imagery that went with those languages and literatures, since the gradual decline of those common *linguae francae* and the growing nationalistic emphasis of the respective educational systems, the gaps of incomprehension have become ever wider. As the links are increasingly broken, as the narrow national meanings of concepts harden, the possibility even of translations of texts decreases. Words like liberty, beauty, justice can still be translated into their equivalents, but the cluster of associations deriving from the way these concepts are actually used is different in each sphere and incapable of being translated. I realized that very strongly when, on arrival in England, I noticed that, for example, the criteria by which a work of literature was judged were entirely different here from what they had been in the German cultural milieu in which I had grown up in Austria: in England elegance, brevity, urbanity were high values; in the German cultural sphere the high values were monumentality, ruggedness, wildness, exuberance, fragmentariness. Since the Second World War the line of division between Western and Communist countries has added another element of disruption. Even within Germany itself, the dialogue between the western and eastern halves is becoming increasingly difficult, let alone that between Russians, Rumanians, Bulgarians and the West. Here too the need, during my long spell with the BBC, to understand the Marxist ideology, coupled with my knowledge of Hungarian, which had remained with me from my childhood, made me perhaps more capable of following those lines of thought than people without those experiences. Hence, rightly or wrongly, I have always seen it as one of my tasks in life to act as something like a mediator between these centrifugal cultural areas, as, indeed, also between the areas within our own local culture that also are moving apart: the areas of high culture and popular culture. Here my work in radio, which covered the entire field of drama from the most popular entertainment to the most esoteric experimentation, also forced me into the stance of someone with one foot in either camp.

The articles and papers in this volume reflect, so at least I hope, some of these preoccupations. Max Reinhardt, a man of the theatre who also felt that his work should embrace the whole gamut from farce and operetta to the most highbrow experimentation, was just the right model for me to emulate in my work in the mass media. Brecht also, a great writer and poet, so German that he has been more misunderstood than any other writer in the English-speaking world, followed a similar ideal; his work also embraces the whole spectrum from the most popular forms such as a musical like *Threepenny Opera* to the austere intellectualism of his didactic plays. And to understand Brecht one must also be able to straddle the chasm between his Western artistic roots and his Marxist, Eastern ideology.

The section on Brecht, as that on Beckett, should perhaps also be read as a supplement to the books in which I have dealt with these great dramatists earlier and at greater length. The articles on Beckett, in particular, should be put side by side with the chapter on his plays in my book *The Theatre of the Absurd*, which, after almost twenty years, still seems to be found useful by many students and readers. In the present volume they can find more about Beckett's novels, his work for radio and television, and the plays of his most recent, most compressed and enigmatic phase.

The chapter on Beckett's work for broadcasting leads over into the section dealing with problems of the mass media, radio and television. Here too, the circumstance that I am occasionally asked to review German books on this subject has given a perhaps slightly unusual slant to an article dealing with the general social and cultural impact of the media. And the paper on the television serial, in turn, highlights my conviction that the areas of popular and high art, separated as they seem to be by light-years of distance, ultimately are bound to converge and to be seen as part and parcel of one complex cultural whole.

One's personality is the product of one's destiny. One's misfortunes, if one is lucky enough to survive them, sometimes turn into advantages. My fate, which expelled me from two well-protected and cozy cultural nests and made me a wanderer between national spheres, just happened to give me a peculiar point of view. I make no special claim for this, except that perhaps it can present certain subjects from a slightly different angle, that it enables me to mediate between different national outlooks, between different media.

The articles, book reviews, and essays in this volume originated over a period of almost two decades. Some were written for publication in Britain, some for readers in the United States. I have not tried to revise them so as to blur those distinctions. After all, the English-speaking world is becoming so closely knit as far as the interchange of books, periodicals, and television programs is concerned that such an exercise in regionalism seems pointless. To those Americans who may not recognize the titles of radio and television programs from Britain, to those people in Britain who may be in the unlikely position of not recognizing the names of American television programs (and there are few of them they are not being shown anyway), I offer my apologies. Nor have I tried to update these articles too violently. The dates of their origination can easily be found in the Note on Sources, which begins on page 243. All translations from the French, German, or other languages are my own unless otherwise indicated.

In their essentials these articles have not, I believe, lost their relevance. I have avoided including book reviews, which do tend to date more radically, with two exceptions: one because I feel that far too little has been written in English on Brecht's poetry and on the problems of its translation; the other because I feel that the deplorable Beckett biography that will be on library shelves should have an antidote equally accessible in volume form. In fact, in this last case, I am responding to something like a demand from quite a number of sides.

BRECHT AND HIS BACKGROUND

Reinhardt—Creator of
the Modern German Theatre

In her memoirs the great Austrian actress Elisabeth Bergner describes an incident during the rehearsals for Brecht's adaptation of *The Duchess of Malfi* in Boston in the 1940s; Brecht was directing a scene with Bergner:

> The highly pregnant Duchess is in the garden with her lady-in-waiting. Suddenly Brecht says: "You cannot sit down on that bench again."
> I: "Why not?"
> He: "Because you have just got up from it."
> I: "What does that matter?"
> He: "You cannot possibly go back to the same place from which you got up two minutes ago."
> I: "I don't get that."
> He: "But Be*rr*gner! What would Max say to such a thing?"
> I say "Max, what has Max to do with it?"
> He: "But Be*rr*gner! It always was a deadly sin for Max, when an actor returned to a position from which he had got up five minutes earlier—except if the text explicitly required it."
> I was astonished. Firstly because in the three big productions I had been in with Max I had never encountered this rule of his; but I was even more astonished about Brecht, about the loyalty with which he defended the things he had learned from Reinhardt.[1]

1. Elisabeth Bergner, *Bewundert viel und viel gescholten. . . .* (Munich: Bertelsmann, 1978), 224–25.

Brecht's theory and practice of epic theatre is, rightly, regarded as a re-action against the naturalistic and neoromantic theatre for which Max Reinhardt's name usually stands. Yet Brecht, who had spent some time on the staff of Reinhardt's theatres in Berlin in the mid-1920s, while reacting against Reinhardt, also owed a great deal to him. Reinhardt was not only one of the greatest practitioners of theatre of his and of all time, he was one of the creators of the modern concept of the direc-tor. Piscator and Brecht built on the foundations Reinhardt had laid for them.

The rise of the director is a relatively recent phenomenon, less than a hundred years old. It is connected with the development of a sense of history when the rapid industrial and technological development of the second half of the nineteenth century first made people aware of the fact that life-styles, clothes, modes of transport, and the manufacture of the articles of everyday life were subject to violent change. The same technological and technical developments also created the need to coordinate the new possibilities for the use of such things as electric light, modern stage machinery, and new types of scenery. Here, too, tradition and the stereotyped ways of producing plays by drawing on stock scenery, primitive lighting, and conventional costume suc-cumbed to the speed and scope of technical innovation. New complex-ities made a coordinating and commanding mind essential. In some ways the rise of the director in the theatre foreshadows the even more dominant role he was later to assume in the mechanized mass media—the cinema, radio, and television. They are even more complex in their technology and, therefore, wholly dependent on a director. Max Rein-hardt (1873–1943), in whose school it was my privilege to acquire the rudiments of the craft of directing, was, in the eyes of his contempo-raries, something of a magician because he was among the first to em-ploy the whole gamut of the new technical means at the disposal of the theatre.

He is often dismissed as an eclectic who took his ideas from others and dabbled in all forms of theatre for the sake of personal commer-cial success. While there is a grain of truth in this view, it nevertheless completely misrepresents one of the greatest personalities in the the-atre of this or any other age. Reinhardt's eclecticism is merely an as-pect of the universality of his commitment to the theatre—theatre in all its forms, the more theatrical the better. And if he achieved—at the peak of his career—international successes that verged on a Barnum-and-Bailey type of showmanship, that was merely an expression of his deep conviction that the theatre is a showman's medium and that its ability to give pleasure to thousands can only be put to the proof if tens and hundreds of thousands of people actually are drawn magnetically to the theatre.

Reinhardt's roots are deeply embedded in the theatrical tradition of Vienna, a city always fanatically devoted to the theatre, idolizing its actors, dedicated to sensual enjoyment, broad humor, and glittering spectacle. The Viennese folk theatre of the eighteenth and nineteenth centuries was an amalgam, on the one hand, of the spectacular scenic effects of the Italian operas and *trionfi* by which the Hapsburg court entertained its guests at the height of the Austrian baroque period—giving immense opportunities to great designers like the members of the Galli-Bibiena clan—and, on the other, of the coarsely drastic *Hanswurst* theatre of the outer suburbs, theatre that derives directly from the Italian *commedia dell'arte*. By the end of the eighteenth century this tradition had consolidated itself into a form of musical and spectacular theatre in which the high-flown sentiments of Italian opera and baroque heroic drama mingled with a cast of comic characters, who grotesquely mirrored the elevated passions of their masters through the obscene sexuality and obsession with food of a large variety of servile creatures. From the elaborate machine opera these plays had inherited an addiction to spectacular scenic effects; in fact, the genre was usually called *Zauberkomödie* (comedy with magic). In the nineteenth century Ferdinand Raimund and Johann Nestroy brought this type of theatre to a peak of perfection. Its best known representative outside Austria is Mozart's *Magic Flute* with its cast of sublime good and evil spirits (Sarastro and the Queen of the Night), heroic lovers (Tamino and Pamina), and grotesquely animalistic clowns in motley (Papageno and Papagena). The genre itself, with its determination to include all kinds of theatrical effects, is eclectic, as indeed is the baroque spirit in all its manifestations; in architecture, painting (with elaborate *trompe-l'oeil* effects), music, and literature.

This is the background in which Reinhardt grew up in Vienna and without a knowledge of which his development cannot be understood. His parents, his whole family—Jewish merchants—had no artistic inclinations. But from his earliest youth, he was addicted to the theatre.

He himself once said that his birthplace as an artist was the top gallery of the Burgtheater, the old court theatre of the Hapsburgs:

> I was born on the fourth gallery. That is where I first glimpsed the light of the stage. That is where I was nurtured (for forty kreutzer of Austrian currency) with the rich artistic fare of that royal and imperial institution, that is where the famous actors of that epoch sang by my cradle their classical spoken arias. I could still reproduce the wonderful melodies from memory, if there were generally acceptable notations for the melodies of speech. The Burgtheater was full of voices which, like precious old instruments, formed an incomparable orchestra. The sound reached us, standing at the very top of the auditorium, as from afar. The words were by Shakespeare, Molière, Goethe, Schiller, Calderón, Grillparzer. We knew the plays by heart but we could see and hear them again and again.[2]

That repertoire of the Burgtheater was, indeed, comprehensive. It is significant that Calderón, whose works never reached the standard repertoire in the English-speaking world, or even Germany, held his rightful place in Vienna: the Hapsburgs, after all, had ruled over Spain as well as Austria, and Calderón's Spanish baroque spirit completely blended in with the Austrian baroque tradition, the greatest modern representative of which was Grillparzer, the Austrian classical dramatist who consciously modeled himself on the great Spaniards of the Golden Age. Even the remoteness of the gallery of the Burgtheater was, Reinhardt later felt, a productive influence on him: "Indeed, these bad acoustics forced my imagination to complement and fill in what did not quite reach me up there. I fantasized and invented the most gratifying things within myself. The ability which I acquired at that time to let my imagination collaborate in a creative manner later became of immense assistance to me. Since then I know that the poet should leave the director, the director the audience, room to collaborate" (*Schriften*, 21). But the Burgtheater was merely the high point in a city that, in itself, was theatrical through and through.

> That old Imperial Vienna was a theatre city unlike any other. . . . It was full of music. In all the innumerable taverns

2. H. Fetting (ed.), *Max Reinhardt: Schriften* (East Berlin: Henschelverlag, 1974), 22, hereinafter cited in the text as *Schriften* with page number.

and vineries immensely popular entertainers could be heard who still continued the age-old tradition of the improvising *commedia dell'arte*. On the streets and in courtyards beggars sang to their hurdy-gurdies. . . . And the actors dominated Vienna. They not only set the tone. Their way of dressing influenced the clothes of the elegant aristocracy. They occupied a high social position. If one of them drank a cup of chocolate on the stage, everyone watched breathlessly. But these were only externals; apart from them they penetrated deeply into the interior of a work of poetry. . . . And, to top it all, the public which was an integral part of this incomparable ensemble! (*Schriften*, 20)

In the light of all this, it seems inevitable that Reinhardt decided to become an actor. At the age of seventeen he began to frequent a theatre school and to take private lessons. At nineteen he landed his first professional engagement in the suburbs of Vienna. It was here that Otto Brahm, the great German critic and pioneer of naturalism in Germany, by then in charge of Berlin's most prestigious theatre, the Deutsches Theater, saw him act, was impressed by him, and promised him a job. But he advised him to gain some more experience in the provinces.

Accordingly, Reinhardt went into summer stock at Pressburg (now Bratislava, the capital city of Slovakia) and then accepted an engagement as an actor for character parts at the municipal theatre of Salzburg. There he played forty-nine different parts during one season (an indication of the richness of the repertoire in one of these provincial theatres at the time) and excelled above all in the portrayal of old men, although he was only twenty years old. In the spring of 1894, Brahm came to Salzburg, saw Reinhardt act again, and contracted him to come to Berlin for the next season.

Reinhardt's ability and success as an actor is of the utmost significance for an understanding of his personality and method as a director: in his eyes the theatre was primarily an actor's medium; the literary quality of a text might well be of secondary importance, provided that it gave scope for an actor's peculiar genius. Hence Reinhardt never disdained putting his hand to material that, at first sight, was unworthy of the highest in theatrical culture—operettas, farces, pantomimes.

Moreover, Reinhardt's method as a director was essentially one of showing the actors their parts—not by fully acting them out, but by a kind of actor's shorthand, a brilliantly concise indication of the essentials of a given gesture or intonation. Being a superb character actor, Reinhardt was able to show an actor not how he, Reinhardt, would act the part, but how that particular actor or actress should do it in order to give full expression to his or her essential individuality. Watching Reinhardt at rehearsals, it was uncanny to see him turn into a given actress, say Paula Wessely, and demonstrate to her the way in which she could be *more like Wessely* as Gretchen than she had been before. The rehearsal process for Reinhardt thus developed its own peculiar dialectic. Watching a given actor, the character-actor Reinhardt learned to capture that actor's optimum personality and expressive individuality; having mastered this, he reproduced it to the actor, who was thus confronted, as it were, with his ideal self in the ideal realization of the part. Thus, Reinhardt never imposed *his* way of acting a part on the actor. He grasped *that* actor's potential and helped him to see it in watching the director. A profound belief in the miracle of human individuality and the uniqueness and richness of personality was the basis of Reinhardt's artistic creed.

Reinhardt was convinced that, in most people, and most actors, the real personality is buried deep inside under a thick layer of shyness, mannerisms, and convention. To the students who later attended his theatre schools in Berlin, Vienna, and Hollywood, Reinhardt insisted, again and again, that their real task was the discovery and gradual development of that real personality that is so deeply hidden inside us. Accordingly, his conception of the actor's task was never based on the idea that the actor is an impersonator who should assume another human being's personality. For him the actor's task was to use *his own personality* to the fullest possible extent to express the essence of the character he was portraying, building that character's personality from the richness of his own experience and profound nature.

All the many great actors who passed through Reinhardt's theatres and were shaped by his influence were characterized by this quality of strength of personality. Each of them—and many reached worldwide fame: Alexander Moissi, Albert Bassermann, Emil Jannings, or Elizabeth Bergner, to name but a few of the best known—was unmistakably a Reinhardt actor, yet each had his own unmistakable personal quality. For Americans the best demonstration of this aspect of Reinhardt's approach is the film of *A Midsummer Night's Dream* he made for Warner Brothers in 1935. As a piece of cinema the production is now somewhat dated, but was James Cagney ever more like James Cagney and yet, at the same time, an ideal Bottom the Weaver? Was Mickey Rooney ever more like Mickey Rooney and yet, at the same time, an ideal Puck? The performances Reinhardt elicited from these actors, whose experience had lain anywhere but in the classical repertoire, are an eloquent proof of his magic quality as a director of actors.

But to return to Reinhardt's rise to his commanding position as a director: For seven years he acted at the Deutsches Theater and became one of the pillars of its famous ensemble. Brahm, who had started out as a critic, had been almost compelled by his championship of naturalism—Ibsen, Strindberg, and Gerhart Hauptmann—to enter the practical world of the theatre. As director of the Deutsches Theater, he perfected the naturalistic style of acting and production. Reinhardt contributed many impressive achievements to the triumph of this meticulously realistic style. But the times were changing, and he had become bored with the dryness and shabbiness of the world that dominated the naturalistic stage.

To diversify his activity, Reinhardt and a group of other like-minded actors of the Deutsches Theater formed a group that originally gave cabaret performances late at night. Here, in songs and parodistic and satirical sketches, they could let their imaginations and exuberant spirits run riot. Here, colorful costumes, grotesque makeup, elaborate fooling, and wild exaggeration—all taboo on the naturalistic stage—could be given free rein. The Paris cabaret was a dominating influence, and so was Frank Wedekind, the German playwright who had been influential in starting artistic cabaret in Munich, where he sang his wild and frivolous satirical songs. He became an important contributor to the group's work, which in 1901 finally consolidated itself in more permanent form under the title *Schall und Rauch* (Sound and Smoke) and acquired its own small theatre, called simply, Kleines Theater (Little Theatre) from August, 1902, onwards. The Kleines Theater presented not only cabaret but also full-length plays. Reinhardt was still under contract to Brahm till the end of that year and, thus, was not officially the director of the new theatre. But on January 1, 1903, he severed his connection with Brahm and became the leading spirit of the new enterprise. The first decisive success of this undertaking was a production of Gorky's *Lower Depths* that caused an immense stir and attracted large crowds. (Reinhardt appeared in it as the old pilgrim Luka; the play was directed by Richard Vallentin.) So great was the success of this performance that the group acquired a second house, the Neues Theater am Schiffbauerdamm (today the home of Brecht's Berliner Ensemble).

In these two theatres the new company, among whom Reinhardt soon became the unchallenged dominating influence, cultivated a new repertoire representative of the reaction against the pure naturalism practiced by Brahm. The later and more expressionist Strindberg; the gentle, impressionistic Chekhov; the grotesquely protoexpressionist Wedekind; the neoromantic Austrian poet Hugo von Hofmannsthal and his countryman, the subtly psychological Arthur Schnitzler; the artificial but brilliantly witty Oscar Wilde with his *Salome*—these were the mainstays of the new venture, together with a new approach to the classical authors of the German repertoire of Lessing, Goethe, Schiller, and above all, Shakespeare. So overwhelming was the response, that Reinhardt was offered the directorship of the bastion of naturalism itself, the Deutsches Theater. On August 31, 1905, he entered the theatre where he had earned his early laurels as an actor, as its artistic director. He was not yet quite thirty-two years old.

Reinhardt's ideas had consolidated themselves ever since he had started the cabaret group five years earlier. His ambitions were huge and his path fully mapped out from that time onwards. In a programmatic declaration that dates from 1901, Reinhardt was extremely specific.

> What I have in mind is a theatre that will again bring joy to people, that leads them out of the grey misery of everyday life, beyond themselves, into a gay and pure atmosphere of beauty. I can feel that people are fed up with finding their own misery again in the theatre and that they are longing for brighter colors and a heightened sense of life.
>
> This does not mean that I want to renounce the great achievements of the naturalistic technique of acting, its never heretofore attained truth and genuineness! That I could not do, even if I wanted to. I have passed through this school and am grateful for

having had the opportunity. That strict education to merciless truth can not possibly be omitted from our development . . . but I should like to carry this development further, to apply it to other things than the mere description of situations and environments, take it beyond the stale smell of poor people and the problems of social critique; I should like to obtain the same degree of truth and genuineness in the depiction of the purely human in a deeper and more subtle psychological art; and I want to show life from another side than that of merely pessimistic negation, yet equally true and genuine in its gaiety, filled with color and light. (*Schriften*, 64–65)

Reinhardt then affirmed his belief in the writers who had transcended naturalism—among them Tolstoy, Strindberg, Hamsun, Maeterlinck, Wilde, Hofmannsthal, and Wedekind—and declared his readiness to do his best for them and others who experimented in new forms. But, very characteristically, he added:

However, to me the theatre is more than an auxiliary to other arts. There is only one objective for the theatre: *the theatre*; and I believe in a theatre that belongs to the actor. No longer, as in the previous decades, shall literary points of view be the decisive ones. This was the case because literary men dominated the theatre. I am an actor, I feel with the actor and for me the actor is the natural focal point of the theatre. He was that in all great epochs of theatre. The theatre owes the actor his right to show himself from all sides, to be active in many directions, to display his joy in playfulness, in the magic of transformation. I know the playful, creative powers of the actor and I am often sorely tempted to save something of the old *commedia dell'arte* in our overdisciplined age in order to give the actor, from time to time, an opportunity to improvise and to let himself go. (*Schriften*, 65)

Ideally, Reinhardt declared in that early manifesto of 1901, he wanted two theatres: an intimate one for the modern subtly psychological chamber play and a larger one for the classics. Then, anticipating a much more distant future, he added:

And actually—don't laugh—one ought to have a third theatre as well. I am quite serious about that and I already see it in front of my eyes: a very large theatre for a great art of monumental effects, a festival theatre detached from everyday life, a house of light and solemnity in the spirit of the Greeks, but not merely for Greek works, but for the great art of all epochs, in the shape of an amphitheatre, without curtain or sets, and in the center, totally relying on the pure effect of personality, totally focused on the word, the actor, in the middle of the audience, and the audience itself, transformed into the people, drawn into, become a part of, the action of the play. (*Schriften,* 67)

Thus Reinhardt, as early as 1901, enunciated a program for a great spectacle stage: "For me the frame that separates the stage from the world, has never been essential; my imagination has only reluctantly obeyed its despotism; I regard it merely as a necessary tool of the illusionistic stage, the peep show concept of theatre that emerged from the specific requirements of the Italian opera and is not valid for all time; and everything that breaks that frame open, strengthens and widens the effect, increases contact with the audience, whether in the direction of intimacy or monumentality, will always be welcome to me. As everything is welcome to me that is apt to multiply the undreamt-of-potentialities of the theatre" (*Schriften,* 67).

There could be no more brilliantly argued, intelligent, and prophetic profession of faith in the theatrical theatre than this manifesto of a man of twenty-eight. Once he had, four years later, assumed the leadership of Germany's most prestigious theatre, he resolutely went about putting these plans into practice, making these dreams concrete reality. The first step was to create the intimate theatre that, Reinhardt felt, was needed to bring the psychological subtlety of postnaturalistic drama to its full effect. It was Strindberg who had postulated a chamber theatre for his chamber plays. Reinhardt realized this concept by the building of a second house adjoining the Deutsches Theater in the Schumannstrasse. Here the rigid division between the auditorium and the stage was broken down by letting the architectural treatment of the auditorium carry across onto the stage and by lowering the stage so that it was only a small step above the level of the auditorium. The four hundred or so spectators in this intimate theatre, the Kammerspiele, thus could have the illusion of being almost in the same room with Strindberg's or Chekhov's characters.

18

The Kammerspiele was opened on November 8, 1906, with a performance of Ibsen's *Ghosts,* with sets designed by Edvard Munch by which the masterpiece of the old naturalism was moved into an area of expressionistic transcendence of mere social realism, into a world of nightmare and depth psychology.

Yet this work on the postnaturalists could still be viewed as a direct continuation of a previous trend. The real breakthrough that established Reinhardt as the leading theatre man in Germany, a world figure—almost the first generally recognized representative of a new kind of artist, the director—was his treatment of the classical repertoire at the Deutsches Theater. Here he continued a line of approach he had first tried out at the Schiffbauerdamm with a production of *A Midsummer Night's Dream.* (It remained his favorite play, to which he returned again and again throughout his career—on the stage, in the open air, and in the cinema—precisely because this play, with its intermingling of the supernatural, the heroic, and the coarsely comical, represents the baroque idea of a mingling of worlds and styles.) Kleist's *Käthchen von Heilbronn* (October, 1905) was followed by a triumphant *Merchant of Venice* (November, 1905), *The Winter's Tale, Romeo and Juliet, Twelfth Night,* and Schiller's *Robbers.*

These productions were unprecedented in their abandonment of flat, painted scenery, which was replaced by three-dimensional and solid constructions, sometimes by an ingenious use of solid elements (like towers or arches that could be moved into different positions to indicate changes of scenes), but above all, by the free and imaginative use of the revolving stage, which not only served to produce quick changes of this solidly constructed scenery, but also was used, in its motion, as a strong theatrical effect in itself, enabling the audience to follow characters passing from an interior into the open street or the forests. The productions also made bold and brilliant use of the new possibilities of a refined lighting technology. To achieve this, Reinhardt had developed the concept of the director as the head and coordinator of a team of artists and technicians, each of whom had his distinct and original contribution to make but always under the dominant influence of the director's overall conception. Great designers like Ernst Stern and Alfred Roller (who had already revolutionized scenography in the Viennese opera with Gustav Mahler) and brilliant technicians fused their talents under Reinhardt's liberal but firm direction. For each production an overall concept was worked out, through suggestions from all sides, and then agreed on: the flow of movement that dictated the spatial formation of the stage, a dominant color scheme that was strictly adhered to, the use of music and song, the creation of atmosphere by color. It was Reinhardt who insisted, in the wake of the impressionist painters, that the lighting designer was in fact a painter using not a brush but light itself for the creation of his pictorial effects.

With all these instruments at his disposal, Reinhardt increasingly allowed the director's imagination to supplement the text. In his *Merchant of Venice*, for example, the revolving stage contained a three-dimensional structure representing different nooks and crannies of Venice with a canal crossed by a bridge as a central feature. As the stage revolved, the bridge appeared from different angles, suggesting different locations. Before the first words of the text were spoken, Reinhardt painted a loving picture of Venice arousing itself from the slumbers of the night: distant songs could be heard as the sun was slowly rising; gradually people emerged from the houses, putting up the shutters of their shops; a gondola passed on the canal as the gondolier's song could be heard, and only after the background of Venice with its teeming life and trade had been sketched in, did the action naturally arise from this background. This painting of the mood and background became one of Reinhardt's main devices in years to come. It made the director something like an autonomous artist, able to create a living image of a whole environment, a world.

In due course this preoccupation with the director's imagination as an autonomous element in the theatre logically led to Reinhardt's series of *Pantomimen* (mime plays, in which there was a minimum of text and the director merely filled a brief scenario outline with movement, dance, color, gesture, music, and light). *Sumurun*, an oriental extravaganza from the *Arabian Nights*, was the first of these. It used an approach to the stage over a bridge through the audience, based on the "flower path" of the Japanese Kabuki stage, and involved intrigue in a harem, with lovers and intruders hiding in trunks and cupboards in a spectacle half-farcical, half-poetic. So great was the success of the Berlin production (in the Kammerspiele, April, 1910) that Reinhardt was invited to produce the mime play in London (at the Coliseum, February, 1911), New York (Casino Theatre, January, 1912) and Paris (Vaudeville Theatre, May, 1912). With this, Reinhardt had arrived as an internationally famous creator of spectacular effects. No wonder he acquired the reputation of something like a circus showman. His subtle use of language, his delicate handling of chamber plays, his brilliant direction of actors in works of high literary quality could not readily be transplanted abroad; his magicianship with light and scenery, his handling of crowd scenes and spectacular lighting effects was exportable.

Having established another bridgehead in a new theatrical field, opera, with his triumphant direction of the world premiere of Richard Strauss's *Rosenkavalier* (with Reinhardt's intimate collaborator, the Austrian neoromantic poet, Hugo von Hofmannsthal, as the author of the masterly libretto) in January, 1911, Reinhardt returned to the international scene with his most spectacular production of all, *The Miracle*, at the Olympia Exhibition Hall in London. Here the theatre was at last liberated from the theatre building itself. To stage the simple story of the nun who is enticed into the world with all its lusts and tribulation but whose place in the convent is taken by the madonna herself, who descends from her place over the altar to cover up her disappearance—the neoromantic poet Karl Vollmöller had written the short scenario on which the mime play was based—Reinhardt transformed the vast exhibition hall into a full-scale cathedral in which the spectators were occupying the side naves while the action took place in the center. After the nun had left the cathedral, the stained-glass windows faded away, and the acting area became the scene of her adventures in the world, where she passed from highborn lover to lowborn companions and experienced all the sinfulness and tribulation of life. Then, for her return, the cathedral magically reappeared. There was much music and dance in *The Miracle* and an immense amount of pageantry. The costumes were sumptuous and designed to enlarge the actors' gestures through long trains and spectacularly high headgear. So great was the success of the London production, watched as it was by thousands of spectators at each performance, that further productions followed the original London one (which opened on December 23, 1911—a true English Christmas

21

pantomime event): in Vienna (in the Rotunde Exhibition Hall, September, 1912); Berlin (in the Zirkus Busch, April, 1914); and later, at New York (Century Theatre, 1924). For the American production, which toured the United States in the following two years, Norman Bel Geddes did the designs; Reinhardt enthusiastically hailed him as a scenic artist after his own heart.

It is characteristic of Reinhardt and his determination to use all possible theatrical means of expression that, quite in keeping with his early declaration of his aims and simultaneously with his experiments in the most extravagant use of scenic effects, he also actively explored methods of staging with a minimum of scenery. As early as September, 1910, Reinhardt had produced an austere *Oedipus* in an exhibition hall in Munich, and this production later transferred to circus buildings in Vienna and Berlin, where it drew large crowds to the Zirkus Schumann. What interested Reinhardt in these experiments was the use of large numbers of extras as a substitute for scenery. In his *Oedipus*, for example, the stage at the opening of the play was bare, but faint cries of distress could be heard from the distance; the cries swelled up and suddenly, like a tidal wave, the people of Thebes, in their hundreds, burst upon the open arena from all sides, so that finally a sea of outstretched arms greeted the king as he stepped from his palace.

Reinhardt liked the Zirkus Schumann so much that he staged another austere spectacle, Hofmannsthal's adaptation of the English medieval mystery play *Everyman*, there in December, 1911. The building suited Reinhardt so well that he decided to make it the third cornerstone of his permanent theatrical establishment, exactly as he had outlined it ten years earlier. He obtained the financial backing to transform the Zirkus Schumann into his "theatre of the five thousand." The architect Hans Poelzig was entrusted with the task of creating a magical environment: from relatively low-ceilinged foyers, the audience was to be led, with a sudden shock, into the vast arena that opened up like a giant fairy castle bathed in light. The open arena stage allowed the action to be taken right into the center of the auditorium. It took a long time for the transformation of the building to be completed—the First World War intervened—but on November 29, 1919, the Grosses Schauspielhaus (Great Spectacle House, if the name is translated in its literal meaning) was opened with a performance of the *Oresteia* of Aeschylus.

Thus, Reinhardt had achieved his objective of possessing three theatres to allow for the staging of intimate plays, full-scale colorful productions of the classics in a proscenium-arch setting, and a vast open arena. The various requirements of the Berlin theatrical scene added a number of other theatres to this empire; their number fluctuated in the ups and downs of an ever changing situation.

The venture with the Grosses Schauspielhaus, however, never quite succeeded artistically or, indeed, with the public. The critics accused Reinhardt of turning the theatre into a circus and using large crowds and spectacular and sensational elements like live horses merely because a circus arena required circus effects even where they were inappropriate. But Reinhardt, after having reached his first goals, had already turned toward new fields of experiment. It was not enough to have taken drama out of the conventional theatre building. He now wanted to take it into the open air.

Ever since that first hectic season as a character actor with its municipal theatre, Salzburg had been one of Reinhardt's favorite cities. And it is, indeed, one of the world's most beautiful places, both architecturally and in its situation on the banks of a fast flowing river beneath a castle high upon the rocks with a backdrop of the majestic Alps. Of all cities in the German-speaking world, it is the most Italianate. Having been ruled by sovereign archbishops for centuries, it has been embellished with innumerable churches and boasts some of the most brilliant examples of Austro-Italianate baroque. And it is the birthplace and hometown of the genius who most perfectly blended Austrian carnality with Italianate grace—Mozart.

The cathedral square of Salzburg is completely enclosed: the road passing through it enters and leaves by way of two arcaded archways that blend into the architectural ensemble. The facade of the cathedral fills one side, its entrance adorned by large baroque statues of saints. So enclosed is this square that it gives the impression of being no more than a large room. Reinhardt and Hofmannsthal both realized the potential of this venue for an open-air presentation of a religious play, while Reinhardt was still bent on implementing that part of his original program that called for theatre as more than just a casual entertainment, but wanted to make it a truly unique, solemn, and festive experience. That is how, in the last years of the First World War, among the agonies of the dying Austro-Hungarian Empire, Reinhardt began to urge the authorities to make Salzburg a festival city. When the war was over and the tiny remnant of the large empire, the little state of Austria, was looking for tourist attractions to prop up its ailing economy, Reinhardt's dream was realized. The Salzburg Festival was opened on August 22, 1920, with an open air presentation of *Everyman* (first staged by Reinhardt at the Zirkus Schumann nine years earlier) on the cathedral square. This production became the classic among Reinhardt's works. It was restaged regularly at Salzburg until 1937 (the last year before the takeover of the country by Hitler) and resumed again after the war.

Here, Reinhardt succeeded in further enlarging the scope of theatre by involving the whole city of Salzburg and its natural and architectural setting in total environmental theatre. The scenery was minimal: no more than a platform raised to be on a level with the entrance into the cathedral. The large baroque statues of the cathedral facade dominated it. The play opens with the voice of God, who complains about the sinfulness of mankind and summons his servant Death to bring him the rich Everyman to render account of his life on earth. After the prologue had been spoken, calling upon the audience to be attentive, the voice of the Lord resounded mightily from high up inside the cathedral. When the figure of Death appeared to acknowledge his summons, it was as though one of the statues adorning the facade had come to life. And when, during a rumbustious banquet on the platform, Everyman was being summoned, the voices calling him came from all sides, echoing and reechoing from the towers of the many churches of Salzburg (where indeed they had been posted). There they came—some from nearby, some from afar, some loud and thunderous, some faint and distant. There was even one actor stationed on the walls of Salzburg castle, high above the town. (I remember, as a student of the Reinhardt Seminar, serving as the link between that actor and the performance: I was stationed in the castle and had to watch for a white cloth to be waved from the tower of the cathedral to pass the cue on to the actor who was waiting, megaphone at his lips.)

When the time had come for Everyman to die, dusk was falling upon the city (the time of the start of the performance varied to allow for the sunset to happen on cue), and the figures of Faith and Good Works, dressed in white and blue, that appeared to assist the dying man on his path to Eternity, seemed again to be no more than the statues of the facade miraculously come to life. When Everyman's soul was finally received into paradise, the interior of the cathedral lit up, the massive gates opened, organ music and hymns resounded from inside, and all the bells of the city's numerous churches began to peal. By this time night had fallen, and the only light came from the dazzlingly lit marble-and-gold interior of the great baroque church.

In keeping with the character of the play, which Hofmannsthal adapted into an angular rhymed doggerel verse in the style of sixteenth-century German morality plays, and with the vastness of the auditorium, Reinhardt had given the production a rugged, larger-than-life style of gesture and speaking. The vocal line was extremely clear and required the actors to pass from high clarion notes to deep bass tones, from fast syncopated passages to solemn and slow rhythms. All this was faithfully noted down in the *Regiebuch* (production book) that Reinhardt prepared in 1920; until 1937 it was faithfully used by his assistants in the restaging each year in preliminary rehearsals, until the great man himself appeared a week or so before the opening, looked at what had more or less mechanically been put together and began to work on it, adapting the style to that of individual actors new to the cast and infusing the cold outline with new vigor and life.

The *Regiebuch*—the book in which the printed or typed text of the play had been rebound, interleaved with empty pages—was the essential basis of every Reinhardt production. He himself has described the process of work that led to a production as follows:

> One reads a play. Sometimes it clicks immediately. So great is one's excitement that one has to stop. Visions chase each other. Sometimes one has to read a play several times before a way to do it becomes visible. Sometimes none appears. Then one has to think of the casting of the big and small parts, and one recognizes where the essentials lie. One sees the environment, the ex-

ternal appearance, the milieu. Sometimes the actor must be adapted to the role, if that is possible. Sometimes the role to the actor. There never is an absolute congruence between the play as read and the play as acted. The ideal case is the one where the playwright is writing for his actors, writes them roles to fit them like a glove. Shakespeare, Molière (writing parts for himself), Nestroy. . . . In the end one has the complete optical and acoustical vision. One sees every gesture, every step, every piece of furniture, the light; one hears every intonation, each crescendo, the musicality of the speech pattern, the pauses, the different tempi. One feels every inward emotion, knows when to conceal, when to reveal it; one hears every intake of air, every breath. The way the partner listens, every noise effect offstage. The influence of the light. And then one writes it down, the complete optical and acoustic visualization, just like a musical score.

One can hardly keep up with it, it presses so powerfully, so mysteriously, without having to think, without laboring. The rational explanations come later. One writes it down, in the main, for oneself. One does not know why one hears this or that this way and not in any other way. It is difficult to write down. There are no notations for speech music. The good actor, whom one knows, is standing before one's eyes. One composes him into the picture; one knows what he can do and how he can do it, and what he cannot do. One plays all the parts. Then, before the rehearsal, one reads through what one has written, alters this or that, adds this or that. But that usually does not amount to much.

One speaks with the actors about their parts, tells them the essentials. Then comes the first read-through. One does not tell details, only to those one knows well. But one communicates enthusiasm to them. The cardinal point is they must be happy, glad, hopeful, they must believe in themselves and their parts— even the one who has the smallest part. One listens, one gets new ideas; many a chance plays its role. Some actors are angry, furious about their parts. Some laugh and cry outside their parts. One watches them, fishes for hints, fixes them in the memory. That's how they must shout, be silent, boil over in this or that scene, exactly as they did it now, when they were complaining about their part. One retains intonations, movements, spies upon them. (*Schriften*, 257)

That is how Reinhardt acquired his uncanny ability to show the actor how the actor himself would have ideally acted a part. He listened to the suggestions of the actors, allowed himself to be persuaded by them to adopt their views of the part. And sometimes he even used what they had offered. Then came the blocking rehearsals with the actors still reading their text from the page.

Some have to keep reading for a long time; they find it hard to learn the words. One tells them their positions, talks about the author's intentions, fixes the tempo, the general outline. Then it is best to leave some rehearsals to an assistant. That is good. The actor feels freer, less supervised. The assistant watches over the positions, the text, the main action and leaves the actors as much as possible free to run on in their own manner.

The first, second, third, fourth rehearsals are usually dull. The actors fight with the text, with their memory. Then one comes again and listens. Much has become new, interesting, individual. One alters one's original concept, rejects certain things, builds many elements anew. . . . Everything is in flux. Now the real work starts. One emphasizes details, experiments, fixes things. Enriches the intonations, the speech melody. . . . The importance of pauses: they are the most important feature of speech, just as being able to stop is the most important thing in skiing. Reining in a horse: intensification downwards. The complete dissolution of punctuation: the comma is undramatic, academic, book-bound. The dramatic thing is the full stop midway in a sentence. Thought, the formation of a thought, its genesis, the search for words, particularly when they are unusual. Listening. Eye contact. How it alters the intonation. How feet, hands, looks talk. The ability to walk in excitement, in a quiet mood. The changes of position. Playing with the props. Furniture, tables, chairs. To involve the walls as means of expression. Nothing left to chance. No piece of furniture that does not join in the acting, that remains mere decor. As every moment, every look, every walk, every pause must mean something, has to express something, there must be no accidental unmeaning looks, walks, movements, pauses.

The greatest economy with these elements as with the word, the sparseness of which is the prerequisite of drama. . . . Clarity. Plasticity. Monumentality. . . . One tries this and that, never clings stubbornly to what one has written down, one remains open for everything, to give the actor the widest possible freedom of maneuver and, above all, to make him enjoy himself, again and again. Then he will be at his best. (*Schriften*, 258–59)

The success of the Salzburg Festival and the acquisition of a stately home, the castle of Leopoldskron outside Salzburg (a gem of baroque architecture, built beside a small artificial lake by one of Salzburg's ruling archbishops for his mistress—the outside of the palace is well known to Americans through the film *The Sound of Music*), brought Reinhardt back to Austria. He was somewhat disillusioned with the workings of his Berlin empire, particularly because the success of the Grosses Schauspielhaus had been disappointing. Accordingly, in the autumn of 1920 he temporarily abandoned the direct artistic responsibility for the running of his Berlin theatres although he retained ultimate control and ownership. Reinhardt concentrated on Salzburg (where he produced Calderón's *El Gran Teatro del Mundo* in 1922 in the University Church in an adaptation by Hofmannsthal) and began to look for a theatre of his own in Vienna. This he found in one of the oldest and most beautiful of the suburban folk theatres of the heyday of the Viennese popular drama, the Theater in der Josefstadt (Theatre in St. Joseph's Suburb), a late eighteenth-century building, small but with exquisite acoustics and sumptuous foyers that once served as dance halls for the Waltz King, Johann Strauss. Reinhardt acquired this bijou house and true to his conviction that it was the actor who should dominate the theatre, named his new enterprise "The actors in the Theater in der Josefstadt under the leadership of Max Reinhardt." The opening performance on April 1, 1924 was Goldoni's *Servant of Two Masters*, freely adapted as a wild and farcical *commedia dell'arte* romp. This, too, was a programmatic choice, Reinhardt's return to the deepest roots of the theatrical. Hermann Thimig, an actor of quicksilver intelligence and dexterity of movement, played Truffaldino; his greedy devouring of a plate of spaghetti when famished stopped the show.

Having found a new venue for a wildly comedic actor's theatre— and the Theater in der Josefstadt became famous for the subtlety and inventiveness of its productions of sophisticated light comedy and the rumbustiousness of its farce—Reinhardt pursued his search for theatre outside theatre buildings. The eighteenth-century idea of the large-scale spectacle specially prepared by a prince for his invited guests in an ideal location such as the courtyard of his palace, the baroque practice of presenting spectacular events to vast crowds in public places, the concept of a performance as something unique happening for a brief time in a uniquely suitable location haunted Reinhardt for the rest of his life. Having become a secular prince himself by owning a princely palace, he staged Molière's *Le Malade Imaginaire* in the marble hall of Leopoldskron for no more than sixty carefully chosen invited guests (1923); *Twelfth Night* by the Leopoldskron lake, the shipwrecked Viola stepping out of the boat that saved her life; *A Midsummer Night's Dream* in the Boboli Gardens in Florence (1933) and later that year for the Oxford University Dramatic Society on the grounds of an Oxford College; *Danton's Death* by Büchner in front of Vienna's majestic gothic town hall (1929); and *The Merchant of Venice* on a secluded Venice square, the Campo San Trovaso (1934). It is as though the eye of the most theatrical of directors had become accustomed to looking for the theatrical space wherever Reinhardt traveled.

The twenties and early thirties were filled for him in a restless shuffle between Salzburg, Vienna, and Berlin, where, from crisis to crisis, he reassumed and rerelinquished direct responsibility for his theatres. All the international centers clamored for him. With the advent of Hitler's regime in Germany, however, Reinhardt's world narrowed. When the new anti-Semitic government divested him, the Jew, of his wide-ranging properties among the Berlin theatres, he wrote them a famous letter in which he solemnly bequeathed the Deutsches Theater not to the Nazi government but to the German people, whose national theatre and national pride it had become.

It was after 1933 that Reinhardt more and more strove to shift the focus of his activities to the United States, where he produced his film of *A Midsummer Night's Dream* and opened a theatre school in Hollywood. Various attempts to establish himself on Broadway went off at half cock or failed. He could not fit himself, with his extravagant grand-seigneurial ways, into a purely commercial mode of operation. From time to time he returned to Vienna, and of course, to Salzburg, where his production of the first part of Goethe's *Faust* (1933—1937) further widened his use of natural settings combined with large crowds.

This *Faust* was presented in the Felsenreitschule (Rock Riding School) that adjoins the large Festival Theatre in Salzburg. It is, as the name implies, an area originally designed for exercising horses and had been blasted out of the sheer rock of the mountainside that towers above Salzburg. Here, below the sheer drop of the rock face, with the trees on the top of the rock visible to the audience, Reinhardt built his *Fauststadt* (Faust city), an elaborate set containing—in analogy, perhaps, to the mansions of the medieval mystery play—a multitude of different distinct locations: Faust's study, Gretchen's house and garden, the tavern, the cathedral, a place for dancing around a linden tree by a well, and rising steeply above it all, a multitude of narrow streets and houses. Whichever locale was required for a scene lit up, and when the whole town was involved—as in the scene when, on Easter Sunday, the people flock out into the countryside on the first day of spring—the whole city came alive. The opening scene, the Prologue in Heaven, was particularly impressive. High up, on top of the rock face, the archangels who sing the praises of the Lord's creation became visible; then—far, far below—Mephistopheles, the fallen angel, presented his compliments to the Lord. And while God and the Devil bargained about Faust's soul, we could see him by the light of a candle, working quietly in his study. This was, indeed a realization of the baroque concept of the theatre as an image of the whole world on all its levels: heaven and hell and, in between, the earth, with life as an endless process of rising and falling from one sphere to the other.

This production of *Faust* (in which, as a student of the Reinhardt Seminar, I played a small speaking part in the summer of 1937, the last time that Reinhardt worked in Salzburg) was particularly brilliant in its handling of large crowds. Reinhardt's method of directing crowds was based on the conviction that every extra was an actor and must play his part as an individual, fully aware of the objectives and motivations of each of his movements and actions. To achieve this, the crowd was subdivided into smaller groups of not more than fifteen people, each under a group leader who had to oversee the performance of each extra, tell him what his function and objective was in each scene and at each moment. Thus, for the great Easter scene in *Faust*, an action was invented for each group or type of people. The students who went to seek the open air, the groups of girls who wanted to attract the students' attention, the burghers going for a walk with their numerous families, soldiers on furlough fooling around, beadles supervising the crowd, and a multitude of other highly individualized types of characters. Each group was given a carefully devised itinerary that would bring it into contact with given other groups at given points of the set, so that the students pursuing the girls would run into the thief being pursued by the beadle at an appropriate moment in the action, or that, at one point, all would converge on the well and the linden tree to listen to the music of the fiddlers and to dance. All this was completely integrated with the main action, which was Faust and his assistant Wagner's Easter promenade, in the course of which they muse on the people and their ways. The overall impression to the audience was one of teeming life, comparable to the grouping and organization of one of the paintings of peasant feasts by the Elder Brueghel.

Once this complex pattern had been carefully and painstakingly rehearsed by his assistant in accordance with Reinhardt's *Regiebuch*, he himself would appear at the last few rehearsals; and then he worked in detail on the interpretation not only of the principals, but also of the smallest character in the crowd. Gently and quietly, he would indicate the movement he wanted or speak the line in the correct intonation. The plasticity and clarity of these directions were truly astonishing. One could not but execute them to perfection, so persuasive and immediately convincing was the direction.

The outbreak of World War II trapped Reinhardt in America. His attempts, when he was nearing seventy, to set up something like an "artistic" theatre in New York were pathetic. Among his productions in America was a version of Strauss's *Die Fledermaus* on Broadway (retitled *Rosalinda*) in October, 1942, and a play by Irwin Shaw, *Sons and Soldiers*, in May, 1943. But that last production failed to become a commercial success. Max Reinhardt died in New York on October 31, 1943, aged seventy.

Reinhardt's supposed eclecticism was, it seems to me, merely an expression of his universality, the breadth of his range. Being besotted with the art of acting, every manifestation of the acting instinct, trade,

31

craft, or sublime spiritual activity fascinated him. He wanted to carry the theatre into every nook and cranny of human life, from the private performance for a handful of invited guests to the spectacle in town squares and exhibition halls that could be watched by tens of thousands. He delighted in the magical effects of color and sensational stage machinery as much as in the most austere manifestations of pure acting against blank walls or draperies. His personality as a director was that of the comedian who wants to act Hamlet; of Bottom the Weaver who wants to act all the parts in the play. He *did* act them all, in the quiet of his study when composing his *Regiebuch* in a frenzy of inspired excitement, and later, during rehearsals, as he guided his actors and demonstrated movements and melodies to them. No wonder that, however diverse all the great actors who had ever worked under Reinhardt might appear, they all seemed to have something in common: that was the imprint and impact of Reinhardt's personality, his personality as an actor. He gave them the wide and highly stylized range of tonal variation, the mastery of pausing, the economy of movement, the inner stillness that each of them developed in his own individual manner.

Reinhardt's technical achievement in the theatre—and beyond it in the development of techniques for staging outside conventional theatre buildings—is perhaps even more impressive: his innovations in the use of lighting—and he inspired technical development by giving the electrical industry the most demanding specifications—were copied all over Europe. It was Basil Dean, for example, who went to Berlin to learn from Reinhardt how to light his famous production of *Hassan* and how to use the revolve. Productions like *The Miracle*, which concentrated on technical effects and toured the world, transformed stage technology everywhere they were seen.

It was Brecht (himself for a while employed by Reinhardt as a *Dramaturg* at the Deutsches Theater, a post he mainly used to be able to spend hours watching Reinhardt rehearse) who insisted that good theatre must, above all, be quotable—that is, so perfectly, elegantly, and economically staged that words and gestures not only become unforgettable to the audience, but so clear to them that they can repeat them at will. As far as I personally am concerned, this is exactly the case with some of the great Reinhardt productions I was privileged to

32

watch and to be involved in. Forty years have passed since I heard the voice of the Lord resound from the tower of Salzburg Cathedral summoning Death—yet I can repeat every intonation of scores of speeches from that play exactly as Reinhardt had put them down in his *Regiebuch*; and the same is true of the speeches and movements in *Faust*. The art of the director is the most volatile and ephemeral of all. Yet Reinhardt succeeded in making his creations last in the minds of spectators who witnessed them and who regard the emotional experience they gave them as high points in their lives. No director can hope to achieve a success greater than this.

Brecht—The Icon and the Self-portrait

On August 14, 1956, Bertolt Brecht died in East Berlin. Much, far too much, has been written about him since then. He has become a cult figure, a badge, a symbol for a multitude of different causes, aesthetic as well as political. The adjective *Brechtian* is bandied about by people who have not the slightest idea of what it is supposed to mean. The exegesis of his aesthetic theories has become an academic growth-industry, while, in the East German DDR, where he had been under constant attack by the party as a "formalist" while he was alive and repeatedly had his productions banned, Brecht now runs athletics a close second as that dubious nation's main prestige exhibit in its struggle for recognition as a country with its own legitimate identity.

Bogus and based on ignorance and distortion the myth of Brecht may be, but it is, for that very reason, not less but *more* important. For myths and mystifications of this kind have their impact on the real world. Like the corpse in Ionesco's play, they grow ever larger and with increasingly nihilist results. The image of Brecht—like that of Antonin Artaud—has been used to create much of the highly inflammatory (and intellectually empty) emotional climate of the New Left of 1968, which has contributed to such cancerous excrescences as Baader-Meinhof terrorism. It has, in a different context, given rise to an enormous volume of useless, time-wasting and intellectually destructive scholasticism both in Germany and in the English-speaking world; much of this kind of pseudoaesthetic speculation about Brecht's theoretical writings is pursued by "scholars" who cannot read German and are therefore compelled to base their musings on the relatively small proportion of texts available in translation.

Yet surely Brecht deserves better than that. He is, after all, one of the great poets of our time as well as a personality whose well-documented life and thought epitomize a great many of the central issues of the contemporary world: the dilemmas of the intellectual between the ideologies of Right and Left, fascism and antifascism, liberalism and McCarthyism, the avant-garde and socialist realism; and all the stresses of exile and return to a destroyed homeland. Even the posthumous fate of Brecht has enormously significant implications. For the fact that he died in the DDR and left most of his papers there makes him a test case in the highly contentious question whether the complete and objective publication and study of a major literary and political figure is at all possible in a totalitarian society.

In this matter the signs are far from encouraging. Although in the twenty-one years since Brecht's death a collected edition of his works has been prepared under the auspices of the East German guardians of his archives, it does not include items that are known to exist (notably a series of erotic poems, which clearly would not meet the standards of Victorian prudery prevalent behind the Berlin Wall, as well as sundry writings critical of Stalin). The first volume of a vast complete bibliography of Brecht's publications,[1] which has recently appeared, presents the appearance of a work of formidable scholarship; but on closer inspection, it is also guilty of suppressing at least one of Brecht's works, the cantata *Herrnburger Bericht*, which he wrote (to music by Paul Dessau) for the World Youth Festival of 1951.

One must concede that this work *was* a major blunder; but for that very reason it is significant. For it shows Brecht's innocence and naïvety in the face of the East German regime and his blissful unawareness of its real nature. *Herrnburger Bericht* is a series of songs dramatizing an episode that happened in 1950 when a number of West German Communist youths who wanted to attend an East German youth meeting had been subjected to some harassment by West German frontier guards. Brecht made this very minor incident the occa-

1. Gerhard Seidel, *Bibliographie Bertolt Brecht*, Titelverzielchnis, Band 1 (Berlin and Weimar: Aufbau Verlag, 1975).

35

sion for a bitter indictment of the West German authorities who had resorted to "violent means" to block free intercourse between the two parts of a divided Germany. One can imagine the dismay with which a Stalinist government, desperately concerned with sealing off its frontiers and preventing its population from having free access to the West—Ulbricht's SED state, which eventually was planning to build a wall along the entire 116-mile length of its frontier—must have received this plea for the complete abolition of all frontier controls! No wonder the piece, which had already been rehearsed and performed at one of East Berlin's theatres, was withdrawn and every effort was made to consign it to complete oblivion—although the full text had been printed in the SED party newspaper *Neues Deutschland* and distributed in pamphlet form. And even now, more than twenty-five years later, its existence cannot be mentioned in what purports to be a scholarly publication!

Yet, if the censorship exercised in a totalitarian police state is disturbing, how much more disturbing is the self-censorship imposed upon themselves by the practitioners of the current West German new-left conformism in a society free of such drastic restrictiveness.

The way in which Klaus Völker, the author of the first full biography of Brecht, written and researched in West and East Germany, deals with this episode of the *Herrnburger Bericht* is highly symptomatic of this phenomenon. He devotes some two pages to the cantata, and he mentions the fact that it was withdrawn on the orders of the East German authorities. But he leaves the reasons for this as vague as possible, and he even implies that it was mainly because Brecht had ridiculed some West German politicians too crudely that Messrs. Pieck and Grotewohl did not want the work to be performed and that it was its form rather than its content that had offended them. This kind of crude equivocation in the cause of whitewashing the East German authorities is characteristic of Völker's whole approach.[2]

It is even more blatant in his treatment of the episode of the withdrawal of Brecht's and Dessau's opera *The Trial of Lucullus*. Here Völker manages to indicate the ban on the first version of the work merely between the lines and by implication. Having never mentioned

2. Klaus Völker, *Bertolt Brecht: eine Biographie* (Munich: Hanser, 1976), 377–78.

36

that the first version was banned, he simply states that "in the revised version [the opera] could be performed in the autumn of 1951 in the Staatsoper" (p. 376). In this way he conceals the actual performance and withdrawal of the piece in the spring of the same year (for after all, a revised version could have been made of an unperformed work as well) while reinsuring himself against the reproach that he had distorted the facts. In other words: those who know the facts will recognize what actually happened, while those who do not know them can be deceived.

And what can one make of similar tactics with regard to the treatment of Stalin and Stalinism in Völker's book? He cannot, in West Germany, completely conceal the facts; but he does his best to play them down, even at the cost of distorting Brecht's reaction to them. Brecht's Soviet friend, the writer Sergey Tretyakov, for example, was (according to Völker) "arrested, and perished in a labor camp" (p. 225). There is no word about the fact that Brecht heard that Tretyakov had been *shot* and that he devoted one of his most moving poems to the question whether Tretyakov could have been guilty of the crimes he had been accused of.

> Mein Lehrer
> Der grosse, freundliche
> Ist erschossen worden, verurteilt durch ein Volksgericht.
> Als ein Spion, sein Name ist verdammt,
> Seine Bücher sind vernichtet. Das Gespräch über ihn
> Ist verdächtig und verstummt.
> Gesetzt er ist unschuldig? [3]

> My teacher,
> My great, friendly teacher,
> Has been shot, condemned by a People's Court.
> As a spy. His name is execrated.
> His books are destroyed. Talk about him
> Becomes suspicious and is silenced.
> But what if he is innocent?

Surely Brecht's reaction to the death of a man who exercised a decisive influence on his development towards Marxism would have been relevant to his biography? But, then, to mention that people were actu-

3. Bertolt Brecht, *Gesammelte Werke* (20 vols.; Frankfurt: Suhrkamp, 1975) IV, 741.

ally shot in Soviet Russia under Stalin would appear as shocking to present-day German new-left conformism as the use of four-letter words at tea in an English vicarage garden would have appeared to a Victorian spinster. On the other hand, Völker's book is (for the first time) quite open about Brecht's notorious sexual exploits—which amounted to full-scale polygamy. This was a subject which could not previously be mentioned because, while she was still alive, Brecht's widow, Helene Weigel, would have wreaked fearful revenge against anyone who mentioned the matter.

But Völker's new-left puritanism where the realities of life under communism are concerned is by no means the greatest weakness of his biography (which had long been eagerly awaited since he had access to much material which had hitherto been unavailable). The book is without cohesion, lacks an integrating concept, and does not even attempt to see its subject whole. For this the author clearly lacks the intellectual equipment—a thorough knowledge of European history and of Marxism and its philosophical context, and psychological insight—as well as the courage to tackle the problems faced by Brecht in all their bewildering paradox and complexity, problems to which Brecht responded with his own strange blend of double-bottomed irony. When, for example, Brecht is reported to have replied to Sidney Hook, who drew his attention to the mass arrests of old Communists in the Soviet Union, "The more innocent they are, the more they deserve to die," Völker crudely asserts that he did so in order to shock and because "stupidity and intellectual limitations made him passionately unjust" (p. 241). Why, one asks, should Professor Hook's or anyone else's questions about Stalin's terror be a sign of stupidity? Here again Völker gives away his crude conformism to which every questioning of Soviet policy is a manifestation of idiocy. Yet he also misses the real implications of Brecht's remarks to which attention has more than once been drawn. For if *innocence* of plotting against Stalin is a reason for condemnation to death, the implication clearly is that *resistance to Stalin* must be regarded as a moral duty of the highest order! Brecht's remark could thus appear to have been at least a highly ambiguous and ironical one.

One of the most curious and revealing aspects of Völker's deeply disappointing book is its epigraph, a quotation from a letter Sigmund Freud wrote to Arnold Zweig in 1936: "Anyone who becomes a biographer takes upon himself an obligation to lie, to conceal, to be hypocritical, to make things look better than they are, and even to hide his own lack of understanding; for truth in biography is not to be had; and if one had it, one could not use it." Clearly, Völker was conscious of what he was trying to do by writing his biography of Brecht without letting his side down. It is, however, characteristic of Völker that here, too, he got it all wrong by overlooking the context of the quotation. For Freud was replying to a letter in which Arnold Zweig had offered to write his, Freud's, biography; and Freud did not want Zweig to write it because he felt that Zweig was not qualified to undertake such a task and that his biography should not be written while he was still alive. So, in fact, Freud's generalizations about the impossibility of writing biographies were a polite way of rejecting one particular biographer.

In striking contrast to the simplicities and simplifications of this biography, Brecht's own fragmentary journals, which have become available in the last few years, contribute far more to an understanding of his complex personality and his ideas.[4] They comprise portions of a detailed day-to-day journal of his personal life in his early twenties, occasional more personal jottings from later years, and at greater length, his "working diaries" from 1938 to 1955, a more impersonal record of thoughts and ideas in the latter period of his exile and during his years in East Berlin. While the early diaries are effusive, lyrical, and self-consciously dithyrambic, the *Arbeitsjournal* has obviously been written with caution and an eye on posterity. "In the last few days I have superficially leafed through this entire journal. Naturally it is pretty distorted, because of possible unwanted readers. And it will be difficult for me to make use of these hints. Certain limits are here maintained precisely because there are limits which must be transcended" (January 21, 1942). Some twenty years earlier Brecht had been rather more candid in revealing his basic attitude to life, an attitude in the light of which many of his subsequent actions become very much clearer. "A little feeling is growing inside me against dualities: (strong/weak; great/small; happy/unhappy; ideal/not ideal). This, in the last resort, is due to the fact that people cannot think of more than

4. Bertolt Brecht, *Arbeitsjournal, 1938–1955* (2 vols.; Frankfurt: Suhrkamp, 1973); Bertolt Brecht, *Tagebücher, 1920–1922. Autobiographische Aufzeichnungen, 1920–1954* (Frankfurt: Suhrkamp, 1975).

two things at once. More does not fit into their sparrows' brains. But the soundest attitude is simply: to trim [*lavieren*, which might also be rendered by to tack, to shift one's position according to circumstances, to twist and turn; *cf.* the title of Brecht's highly personal book of pastiche Chinese fables: *Me-ti: Buch der Wendungen*—Book of Twists and Turns]" (September 3, 1920). Much of the early diaries is taken up with a detailed and highly colored account of Brecht's stormy entanglements with a number of girls (their pregnancies, abortions, and illegitimate offspring); attempts to induce his father to take in his illegitimate son, which were rejected; and a succession of highly dramatic scenes with the elderly black marketeer who was the protector of the opera singer Marianne Zoff, Brecht's mistress, who, however, could not dispense with the older man's money (she was eventually briefly married to Brecht when, having miscarried one of his children, she became pregnant again and presented him with a daughter). The journal also throws a good deal of light on the psychological background of Brecht's Don Juan complex which led him into that wild series of simultaneous polygamous affairs with women, about which Klaus Völker does have a good deal to tell. For it shows the curiously erotic atmosphere of Brecht's relationship with the band of male school friends, which dominated his adolescence and which, although it might never have become overt, clearly bears the mark of latent homosexuality.

> Es ist besser mit einem Freund als mit einem Mädchen. Wir liegen im Wasser (20°R) und im Wald und dann im Boot, und da schwimmen wir noch einmal, wie es schon Nacht ist. Liegt man auf dem Rücken, dann gehen die Sterne mit, oben, und die Flut läuft durch einen durch. Nachts fällt man ins Bett wie eine reife Frucht: mit Wollust.

> It is better with a friend than with a girl. We lie in the water and in the forest and then in the boat and then we swim once more when it is night. If one lies on one's back, the stars follow one above and the flood flows through one's body. At night one falls into bed like a ripe fruit: voluptuously. (July 16, 1920)

It is also significant that Paula Banholzer, the mother of Brecht's first illegitimate son, Frank, when she became part of this band of brothers was given a male nickname (Paul Bittersweet, abbreviated to Bi). The

40

prevalence of homosexual themes in Brecht's early plays (*Baal, Edward II, In the Jungle of Cities*) reflects the intensity of this experience. That such preoccupations were present in Brecht's mind has long been evident from any close reading of these (and many subsequent) plays. The diary now gives full and convincing confirmation of such assumptions.

Equally revealing, and valuable for an understanding of Brecht's attempts to create a Marxist aesthetics of theatre is the evidence, which these early diaries supply, that, in fact, much of that theory which he laboriously rationalized in Marxist terminology predates his discovery of Marx and was already present in his earliest views on art simply because his natural instincts inclined him that way. As early as June, 1920, Brecht notes, "I am looking around for new forms and am experimenting with my emotions like the most up-to-date artists. But then again and again I am struck by the thought that simplicity, greatness, and emotion are the essence of art and *the essence of its form is coolness*" (June 27, 1920; italics added). Here we are at the source of the *Verfremdungseffekt* ("distanciation", alienation) long before that Marxist-sounding term was invented.

> Few sayings about art have gripped me as much as Meier-Graefe's sentence about Delacroix: "In his case a fiery heart beat inside a cold man."
>
> One great fault of other art I think I have managed to avoid in *Baal* and *Dickicht* [the early version of *Jungle of the Cities*]: its striving to grip and involve. Instinctively I leave distances here and make sure that my effects (poetical and philosophical) remain confined to the stage. The splendid isolation of the spectator is not touched; it is not *sua res, quae agitur*; he is not appeased by being invited to feel with the characters, to reincarnate himself in the hero, and, by looking at himself at the same time, to appear in two editions, unassailable and significant. There is a higher kind of interest: the interest in the metaphor, the other, the unsurveyable, the things which make you wonder." (February 10, 1922—Brecht's twenty-fourth birthday)

Here, without the aid of Marxism is the whole of epic theatre, almost fully formed, as Brecht himself clearly states, out of his own *instinct*. Far from being, as he later never tired of arguing, the fruit of the application of Marx's scientific principles to aesthetics, the Brechtian

41

theory can thus now be quite clearly seen as an ingenious rationalization of his own artistic instincts.

What part, then, did Marxism have to play in Brecht's subsequent development? In a later jotting, dating from July, 1926, Brecht put very clearly what it was he was searching for.

> If I decided to try my hand at real literature, I should have to turn "playing about" into work, and to declare my excesses to have been a vice. I should have to establish a plan and to execute it in order to get tradition into my work, inspiration through physical habit and the joy of working things out. I would have to make an effort to select a style which would enable me to find the easiest formula for what I had to develop. My appetites would have to be regulated so that the wild impulses are eradicated and my interest could be evolved over the long run, so perhaps, that I should still be capable of writing plays very rapidly, but not be compelled to do so. (end of July, 1926, p. 207–8)

Marxism—which Brecht discovered shortly after he had made this note—provided just that. It provided the discipline, the tradition, the restraint for his wild, inspirational outbursts that he was seeking. And this in spite of the fact that (as he said in a note jotted down in the following year, 1927) "I am not sitting comfortably on my backside: it is too bony. And the worst is: my contempt for the unfortunate is too strong. I distrust those who are distrustful, I have something against those who do not succeed in sleeping well."

Brecht's conversion to Marxism was wholehearted, not least because it provided the hard framework for his excessive and impulsive nature and enabled him to appear a cold man in spite of a hot heart. The view of the legend of his official hagiography—which he himself was not beyond fostering in his later years—that he had always been a man of the extreme Left, however, can hardly be maintained. Here is a diary entry (it dates from September, 1920) which describes his reaction to someone who had been extolling the Soviet system: "I am horrified not so much by the disorder which actually reigns there as by the order which is in fact being aimed at. I am now very much against bolshevism: conscription, food rationing, controls, corruption, favoritism. And besides, in the most favorable outcome: balance, gradual change, compromise" (September 12, 1920). Here we have the sources of a tremendous, creative inner tension. On the one hand, there is his distrust of an excessively ordered society, the Nietzschean individualism we find in a character like Baal (who has much of Brecht's early personality), the rejection of any too rigidly disciplined way of thinking. "I don't believe I'll ever have such a full-grown philosophy as Goethe or Hebbel had; they must have had the memory of tram conductors, as far as ideas are concerned. I forget my views again and again and cannot bring myself to learn them by heart" (August 24, 1920). On the other hand, there is his yearning for discipline, a fixed framework, a tradition with its own classics—Brecht rejected the German classics, Goethe, Schiller, and Hebbel, but later constantly referred to Marx and Engels as "the classics"—a band of brothers as closely knit and as emotionally charged as that band of brothers of his youth ("When George and Buschiri and their friends are drunk, they embrace, nonchalantly, romantically, silently, under the table" [August, 1920.])

No wonder that the dominant theme of the period of Brecht's conversion to the Marxist "tradition," the period of his *Lehrstücke* (didactic plays) is that of the reconciliation between the need for discipline—the merging of one's personality into the collective to the point of total self-abandonment—and a passion for freedom. The Young Comrade of *Die Massnahme*, the greatest of the didactic plays, is a man whose heart is too impulsive to conform to the hard requirements of Party discipline, which amount to a total erasure of one's individuality. But when he gives his consent to being killed by the Party for his breaches of discipline, he does so out of an abundance of emotion, which amounts to no less than an orgasm of masochistic love for his comrades; in fact, a nonchalant, romantic, and silent embrace, although this time not drunkenly under the table, but into the grave with a bullet in the nape of the neck.

Brecht's conversion to Marxism consolidated itself around 1930. In the following twenty-six years of his life, through exile and his life in a Communist country, he loyally clung to his belief against all odds and in the face of innumerable conflicts of principle and conscience. The *Arbeitsjournal*, which starts in the summer of 1938, contains ample evidence of Brecht's exasperation at the official Stalinist line in aesthetics, *i.e.* "socialist realism." "They talk again about realism, a term they have now succeeded in abasing in the same way in which the

Nazis have abased the term socialism" (July, 1938). The villain of the piece and Brecht's main bugbear here is Georg Lukacs, who was extolling the "realism" of the masters of the great bourgeois novel, Sir Walter Scott, Balzac, and Thomas Mann. "People like Sholokhov and Thomas Mann are being justified by the argument that they depict reality. Between the bourgeois and the proletarian realists we are told there is no difference (and indeed a glance at writers like Sholokhov seems to prove that view); nor, probably, between the bourgeoisie and the proletariat itself? How else could it be, under the banner of the Popular Front? Long live Pastor Niemöller! That realist of the purest water!" (p. 13). This is an attack against Stalin from the Left. Brecht was as distressed by the Popular Front's collaboration with the Social Democrats and Liberals as he later was about Stalin's pact with Hitler.

On the day Hitler occupied Warsaw, Brecht tried to convince himself that Stalin had had to act because the Western powers were not really willing to wage war against Nazi Germany. Nevertheless, he admitted "the Soviet Union now carries, in front of the world proletariat, the terrible stigma of having helped the Fascists, the most savage, the most anti-working-class part of capitalism. I don't think that one can, at the moment, say more than that the Soviet Union has saved itself at the cost of having left the world proletariat without a watchword, without hope and without help" (p. 62). And when, nine days later, Stalin actually grabbed half of Poland, Brecht added, "It is hard to get used to the naked reality, the tearing down of all ideological façades. There we have the fourth partition of Poland, the abandonment of the principle that 'the USSR needs not an inch of foreign soil,' and the appropriation of Fascist hypocrisies about 'our kith and kin,' the liberation of 'our brothers' (of Slav descent), the whole nationalist terminology. All this is being said with an eye towards the German Fascists, but at the same time, also to the Soviet troops" (September 18, 1939). These remarks show that Brecht, whose keen political grasp has never been in doubt, very well understood the close similarities between totalitarian systems. If, in the above passage, he realized the nationalistic aspects of Soviet propaganda, he also saw the Leninist origins of Hitlerism. While reading Boris Souvarine's biography of Stalin he noted, "The transformation of a professional revolutionary into a bureaucrat, of a whole revolutionary party into a civil service does, indeed, gain a new significance through the rise of fascism. The German petty bourgeoisie borrows, in its attempt to create state capitalism, certain institutions (complete with the relevant ideological material) from the Russian proletariat, which is trying to create a state socialism. In fascism socialism sees its distorted mirror-image, with none of its virtues, but all its vices" (July 9, 1943). No wonder Brecht was dismayed when he found that the German Communist party in Soviet-Stalinist exile was becoming more and more nationalistic (closely mirroring the Great-Russian nationalism of Moscow's wartime propaganda). When confronted with an article by Johannes R. Becher, the German ex-expressionist poet who later became cultural boss in the DDR, Brecht remarked, "This stinks of nationalism. Again Hitler's nationalism is here quite naïvely adopted. It's just that Hitler has the wrong brand; Becher has the correct one. We must 'create' the 'type' of a 'new German national literature.' . . . He demands that the 'weaknesses of so-called left-wing literature' should be overcome; these weaknesses, I suppose, are precisely its left-wing nature. This is terribly opportunistic rubbish, a reformism of nationalism" (November 10, 1943).

In the light of these misgivings it becomes quite clear why Brecht hesitated so long before he returned to Germany and even longer before he accepted the offer of a theatre of his own in East Berlin. Indeed, when he finally arrived there, to discuss the prospects of founding his own company of actors, he remained extremely cautious. "Peace demonstration of the *Kulturbund* [the Party's front organization for left-wing and "progressive" intellectuals]. [Arnold] Zweig is present and makes a speech. I myself do not speak, determined as I am to have a look round and not to make public statements" (October 24, 1948). And on the following day Brecht notes down his impressions of the situation in the Russian zone of occupation.

Still, after three years, I generally hear, the panic among the workers, caused by the looting and rapes after the conquest of Berlin, casts its ripples. In the working-class areas the liberators had been awaited with open arms, but the encounter deteriorated into a rape, which did not spare either seventy-year old women or twelve-year old girls and was carried out in open view of all. . . . After the material devastation which the Nazi armies caused in their country the Russian Communists will now also have to cope with the psychological devastation which Hitler's war of conquest has wreaked among the *muzhiks* who had just been thrown into the process of civilization after having been dehumanized by Tsarist rule. (October 25, 1948)

It is touching to see how desperately Brecht tried to defend the Soviet Union, even at the cost of his knowledge of history or, indeed, his Marxism. For the Russian soldiers who carried out these rapes surely were mostly in their twenties and had spent their entire life under the Soviet regime. If they were *still* dehumanized, that can hardly have been the fault of tsarism, considering that the achievements of the first five-year plans (which were greeted by Communists like Brecht as the establishment of a humane society from the early 1930s onwards) must have been fully enjoyed by soldiers born around 1920. But Brecht always tended to be more sympathetic towards the Russians than his German compatriots. When he was introduced to the burgomaster of East Berlin, Friedrich Ebert, his impression was far from favorable: "The *Herr Oberbürgermeister* said neither 'good day' nor 'good-bye' to me, did not even directly address me and merely uttered a sceptical sentence about uncertain projects which might impair existing things [Brecht was planning the foundation of the Berliner Ensemble]. . . . For the first time I felt the stinking breath of provincialism here" (January 6, 1949). Nevertheless Brecht did get his Berliner Ensemble. But at the height of Stalin's campaign against "cosmopolitanism" and "formalism" in the arts, the new venture went through some very hard times. Having boasted to the world about having secured the cooperation of Germany's greatest playwright the authorities could not openly close down his theatre. But they did their best to show their displeasure.

> Our performances in Berlin have almost no echo. In the press, notices appear months after the first performance, and they contain nothing but a few miserable sociological analyses. The public is the petty bourgeois public of the Volksbühne [the trade unions' organization for the sale of reduced-price tickets to blue-collar workers who wanted to better themselves intellectually], workers amount to barely 7 percent among them. Our efforts can only be regarded as not totally pointless if our style of acting might be taken up at a future point in time, *i.e.* if their instruc-

tional value can one day be realized. (March 4, 1953—the day before Stalin's death!)

When, in my book on Brecht (which was based on the evidence of his own writings and interviews with numerous close friends of his),[5] I ventured to suggest that the events of June 17, 1953, the day of the East German workers' rising, must have had a terrible impact on a man like Brecht who had structured his life around the conviction that the Communist party was the party of the workers, I was accused of wishful thinking and of vilifying a great man. Now we can read Brecht's own view of the matter: "The 17th of June has alienated the whole of existence" (August 20, 1953). A few weeks later he reports a conversation with a plumber who was carrying out some work at his country cottage in Buckow and who was complaining bitterly about the regime. "Under Hitler the bureaucracy [he said] was also inflated, but then there was more money around. The Russians were trying to impose their Asiatic culture on Europe. . . . What we needed were free elections. I said: 'Then the Nazis would be elected' " (September 12, 1953). Almost a decade after the end of the war, after many years of Communist rule, Brecht thus still felt that East Germany was a country inhabited by Nazis. And he felt that not only about the anonymous crowds of stony-faced workers in the streets but also about his closest and most enthusiastic disciples and collaborators. "The country still gives me the creeps. Recently, when I had driven to Buckow with young people from our *Dramaturgie* [the ensemble's script section] I sat in the garden room in the evening, while they were working or talking in their rooms. Ten years ago, it suddenly occurred to me, all three of them, if they had read anything I had written and I had been in their presence, would instantly have handed me over to the *Gestapo*" (July 7, 1954). This is one of the very last entries in Brecht's "working diary." The remaining two years of his life yield barely five pages of short jottings. And that silence, too, is significant.

There is little in all these diaries and, indeed, in Völker's biography (which does assemble a lot of factual information about Brecht's pri-

5. Martin Esslin, *Brecht—A Choice of Evils* (London: Eyre Methuen, 1980); U.S. edition: *Brecht—The Man and His Work* (Rev. ed.; New York: W. W. Norton, 1980).

vate life) that was not known before. When I was gathering material for my book on Brecht twenty years ago, I heard it all from the many close friends and associates of Brecht whom I questioned about him, and I used that information to the full.[6] But now the publication of the diaries has provided some documentary evidence for what emerged clearly enough from a careful reading of the plays and poems alone.

And what does that amount to? Simply to confirm that behind the icons of the saints of totalitarian religions like present-day party-line communism—those giant cardboard images carried aloft in processions between the banners bearing simpleminded slogans proclaiming tautological half-truths—that behind these inhuman images (of which Brecht's ironically has become one in the DDR) there stands, and has always stood, a human being made up of a highly differentiated composite of often contradictory reactions, vacillating opinions, mixtures of idealistic and opportunistic attitudes, hidden thoughts and deceptive public gestures. Even in his own diary (as early as 1942, when he was living in America), Brecht felt he had to present a less than wholly candid picture of his thoughts for fear of possible readers of his notes. Why? Because the concept of discipline, the need to present a monolithic front to the outside world, compels adherents of totalitarian creeds into attitudes of concealment. The need to suppress the true complexity and contradictoriness of one's daily thoughts (the old-fashioned word for it would be *hypocrisy*) becomes total in a country where the totalitarian party has become the government. Hence the resort to simplistic and Byzantine slogans, to generally agreed and recognizable formulae, which tend to dehumanize the public image of such personalities abroad, but also themselves; for it forces them into a schizophrenia of public pathos and private cynicism. When Hanns Eisler, a close associate and friend of Brecht's, a brilliant composer and a man of sharp intelligence, was once asked by

6. Recently a prominent academic, introducing a lecture of mine to a hall full of students, complimented me on my good "guesses" in the book, which by good fortune had now been proved true. There is a curious fetishism in academic circles that attaches greater value to written, documentary evidence than to firsthand oral reports—as though what is written down could not be equally false, as though a good deal of the information contained in letters, diaries, and memoirs were not, indeed, much more likely to be deliberately mendacious than oral evidence elicited under close questioning!

48

a friend who had met him in a Paris bar how life was in the DDR, he replied with a knowing wink, "Even Capitalism has its drawbacks." Such an attitude has driven more than one man of talent to drink. It cannot be healthy.

And in many cases it becomes unendurable. Many of the intellectual leaders in the DDR who were closest to Brecht—men like Hans Mayer, Peter Huchel, Ernst Bloch—eventually moved to West Germany, as did many of Brecht's disciples and admirers among his collaborators in the Berliner Ensemble (Peter Palitzsch, Carl Weber, Egon Monk, to mention but some of the most gifted among his pupils). The poet who shows the influence of Brecht most clearly and decisively among the younger generation in the DDR, Wolf Biermann, was recently expelled by the authorities.

It is idle to speculate whether Brecht, had he lived longer, might not also have reached such a breaking point—perhaps during the Hungarian uprising (October, 1956), which came a few months after he died; or when the Berlin Wall was built (1961); or after the invasion of Czechoslovakia (1968). Ernst Fischer, the Austrian Communist leader and one of the finest intellectuals of Brecht's generation, reached that point at the precise moment when Dubček's quixotic attempt at creating "Communism with a human face" collapsed. I remember a conversation with Ernst Fischer when the floodgates of long-suppressed misgivings had been swept away and the anger and disappointment of years of pretense poured out. He stressed again and again that Brecht had been in "exactly the same position." Much in the diaries and in Brecht's late poems seems to confirm this view. Yet again the need to protect his theatre, the place where one day his ideas and his practice might become the fountainhead of a new style of drama, might have persuaded Brecht to go on mouthing the ritual formulae of the Party line.

Perhaps his formidable cynicism might have enabled him to carry on even under the most unfavorable conditions. In sexual matters he had always possessed the monumental and self-ironical callousness of his first creation, the antisocial and monstrously self-indulgent poet, Baal. He retained it to the very end. Klaus Völker reports that when he fell in love with Isot Kilian in 1954, Brecht told her husband, the Marxist philosopher, Wolfgang Harich, "Get a divorce from her—you can marry her again in two years' time!" (p. 388). It was to her that he dictated his last will and testament in which he left the copyright of some of his plays to Ruth Berlau (the Danish actress who had followed him across the world to California and East Berlin) and to a number of his other mistresses and friends. This will, apparently, was not properly witnessed through an oversight. Brecht's wife, Helene Weigel, succeeded in having it ruled out of order. So, with truly Brechtian irony, bourgeois respectability triumphed and the legitimate spouse asserted her socially sanctioned superiority. A friend of Brecht's who attended his funeral once described the scene to me: "There were five widows there, all dressed in solemn mourning black. Four of them were crying. One was laughing—Helene Weigel."

Ruth Berlau (1906–1974), a brilliant actress and a beautiful woman, was the most tragic among the many women in Brecht's life. She had left her well-to-do husband and her position as a leading actress of the Copenhagen Royal Theatre in the 1930s and followed Brecht to America, always on the tacit understanding that Brecht would eventually set up house with her alone. When this hope proved illusory, she gradually deteriorated through drink and, after Brecht's death, was finally barred from the Berliner Ensemble (where she had worked as the house photographer, making a detailed record of Brecht's productions). The effects of drink and distress led to a series of nervous breakdowns. A recently published manuscript from Ruth Berlau's papers gives an insight into the realities behind Brecht's cynical polygamy. It recounts one of Ruth Berlau's dreams and deserves, I think, publication in full; it is a remarkable document.

> The roof collapses. And I notice that I am on fire. Funny, the hair around my lap was the first to catch fire. That I can extinguish— I reach there with both hands and try to smother the flames with the wetness of my lap. I raise my right hand, it burns like a torch, my right hand. I am pointing to him—for now you have joined me. You are standing a few yards away and you are talking to many people, you are looking diagonally towards me, and then continue talking. I can hear some of your sentences; for you it is a matter of life and death for your works. But I, once more, show the torch, my burning right hand and I am softly crying through the night: "Bertolt." Once more you look round and you say

menacingly: "If you turn to cold ash, it's all over. That is no use for me." I am trying to indicate to you: there is a star missing in Cassiopeia; that's what started the fire, this missing star has hit me. You shake your head; you don't even look up to the sky. I notice you think I have gone mad again, and Weigel takes your arm and says: "Get the fire brigade. Only the fire brigade is concerned with this. If there is a fire one has to get the fire brigade. You cannot help." Quickly I see how you give the order, one must call the fire brigade. At that moment a second star falls out of Cassiopeia. But the fire brigade is already here and takes me in and covers me up.[7]

This is the nightmare of a woman at the edge of madness, but it mirrors a great deal of the atmosphere of Brecht's life behind the façade of cheerful cynicism.

And there is no shortage of signs that behind the façade of political conformism also there was a much darker side. The German actor Klaus Kinski describes in his memoirs how Brecht, who had invited him to join the Berliner Ensemble, reacted to his refusal. "I myself would advise you against it. I have a fool's freedom in the East. But to deal with you one needs a great sense of humor, and that they haven't got."[8]

What relevance have such biographical details to the study of a great poet and important playwright like Brecht? Intrinsically, none whatever. The value of a poem or a play remains unaffected by the psychological background or the political attitude of its creator. After all, we do not know much about these things in the case of many great playwrights from Aeschylus to Shakespeare; and that does not impair the impact of their works one jot. Yet, in Brecht's case it is precisely the demands of totalitarian partisans and laudators of the writer that compel such biographical scrutiny. It is they who impose their monolithic façade, who try to suppress entire works—and works surely are relevant to a study of an author even if one leaves all biographical con-

7. Ruth Berlau, "Ein Traum" in *Material Brecht-Kontradiktionen, 1968–1976* (Berlin: Wolfgang Storch, 1976).
8. Klaus Kinski, *Ich bin so wild nach deinem Erdbeermund* (Munich: Rogner & Bernhard, 1975).

siderations outside the scope of one's inquiries. It is they who drag the biography—or rather the hagiographic version of the biography—into the arena of public scrutiny. A writer can be judged by his works alone; but a saint is worshiped for his total personality. And once he is worshiped for a false, distorted, mendacious image of his personality and that image used as an argument in political debate, it must surely become necessary to subject that image to a reasoned critique based on a full presentation of the evidence.

Moreover, Bertolt Brecht was a political poet, who wanted to have a political impact. Such a poet, admittedly, can and must be studied for his poetry and his aesthetic effect. But the political subject matter also imposes the duty to inquire into the truth, the correctness, of the facts, the soundness of the political ideology it propounds. Such a poet can no longer simply be subjected to the structural analysis of the *formal* aspects of his work. In Brecht's case it is precisely his partisans who should reject such a methodology as the depths of decadent formalism. Inevitably, therefore, the study and analysis of a poet like Brecht involves an examination of the public implications of his plays, poems, and novels and, consequently, also an inquiry into the genesis and real nature of his political ideas. And again, it is the totalitarian concept of politics which inevitably also politicizes the private personality and the private life of the individual involved. For if it is officially proclaimed that a good Party adherent does not want to travel to the West, the fact that someone who subscribes to the Party line makes elaborate arrangements to enable himself to travel freely (such as Brecht's acquisition of an *Austrian* passport) becomes a political act. And so does the maintenance of a harem in a society which insists that a good Party man and Marxist-Leninist socialist must be strictly monogamous. That, after all, is the reason why the sexual transgressions of parsons (who proclaim a similar organic connection between private beliefs and public actions) receive more publicity in the popular press than those of individuals not associated with propagating an ideology that claims to dominate every aspect of a person's life.

Brecht himself never tired of stressing the *scientific* nature of Marxism and its methodology and his belief that he had, in fact, supplied the foundations of a truly scientific aesthetics of drama, that he had made drama an instrument of scientific inquiry, an experimental laboratory of human social and political behavior. He thus, paradoxically, put himself outside the bounds of the purely aesthetic and New Criticism style of analysis.

Hence the absurdity of much of the current Brecht scholasticism in Germany and throughout the West. Here, Brecht's theoretical writings (which, he himself repeatedly stressed, are by no means aprioristic principles but derived, *a posteriori*, from his practice, *i.e.* his taste and inspiration of the moment) are subjected to endless scrutiny as to their sources in Hegel and Marx without anyone ever actually using an empirical method and asking the basic questions: To what extent would these foundations themselves stand up to scrutiny? and do they actually work? Do the alienation effects actually inhibit the spectator from feeling involved? Are the postulated political effects really achieved? Is the consciousness of audiences actually affected in the manner postulated by Brecht?

Here there is a vast field of inquiry, which has, as yet, hardly been approached. But here, too, the first step would be to establish how much of Brecht's theorizing was seriously meant and how much of it was merely a way of gaining philosophical respectability for what were, basically, simply his creative instincts. At this point one gets back to a critical discussion of the facts of his biography and his psychology. It was Brecht himself who put himself out of the bounds of purely literary "text-immanent" research. And that, indeed, is the reason why he is not only a purely literary figure, but one of the great paradigmatic personalities of our age.

Brecht in Chinese Garb

One of Brecht's most telling self-revelations, which casts a brilliant light on some of his political views and certain aspects, also, of his private life and is still almost totally unknown in the English-speaking world, although it has been available in German for some years, is his collection of brief anecdotes, fables, poems, and aphorisms, *Me-ti: Buch der Wendungen*.[1] The title of this literary *chinoiserie* is very difficult to translate; the nearest I can get to it is *Me-ti's Book of Twists and Turns*.

But to understand the title one has to go back to Brecht's own background, the cultural climate of Germany in the 1920s. At that period, Brecht's most formative years, there was a great vogue for Chinese classics in Germany. The great sinologist, Richard Wilhelm, published a whole series of volumes, finely bound in black and yellow cloth, ranging from Lao Tzu to Confucius. It also included the famous *I-Ching*, the *Book of Changes*, which is basically a handbook of oracles, enabling the user to predict the future from the way in which a number of shorter and longer sticks fall when thrown at random.

The *Me-ti* of the title, the imagined author of Brecht's book, is clearly derived from the philosopher Mo-ti, whose works were also published in Germany in the twenties. And the title itself is equally clearly a paraphase—and parody—of the *Book of Changes* (*Wandlungen*) to *tactical twists and turns* (*Wendungen*). For here Brecht has left us a record of his attitude to Marxism and the Communist party

1. Bertolt Brecht, *Gesammelte Werke* (8 vols.; Frankfurt: Suhrkamp, 1967).

54

from 1934–1956, the years during which, according to the editor, Uwe Johnson, he worked on the short anecdotes and aphorisms which make up the book.

Formally, these short pieces are very similar to the short anecdotes of the *Geschichten vom Herrn Keuner* (Keuner Stories), which Brecht published in groups from the 1930s onward. That Keuner, the sceptical moralist who is the hero of these anecdotes, was a self-portrait of Brecht has always been evident to anyone familiar with Brecht's own attitudes. Yet, as Herr Keuner often expressed views not entirely in accordance with official East German party orthodoxy, those like myself who made the point were furiously attacked from those quarters for attributing the views of a fictional character to its author. Now Brecht himself furnishes the proof for the correctness of the identification Keuner-Brecht. At the outset of the new book we find a key to the names mentioned in the *Book of Twists and Turns*, from which we learn that Ka-meh, for example, equals Karl Marx; Mi-en-leh—Lenin; Ni-en—Stalin; Su—the Soviet Union; Hitler—Hi-jeh, Hui-jeh (*cf.* the title, Arturo Ui), or Ti-hi; and Brecht—Kin, Kin-jeh, Kien-leh (all these are forms of the name Keuner, and in fact, in more than one of the anecdotes Brecht has not yet changed Keuner consistently to Kin-jeh or Kin, leaving the two names side by side). Keuner is both an inversion of Brecht's second Christian name, Eugen, and a pun on the German word Keiner, *i.e.*, no one.

The bulk of the book's two hundred pages is taken up by Brecht's attempts to grapple with the problem which Stalinism undoubtedly presented to a man who had come to communism above all as a pacifist and a somewhat anarchic believer in every kind of freedom—sexual, political, economic, and spiritual. It is touching to see Brecht's often almost pathetic efforts to persuade himself that Lenin's and later Stalin's terror was necessary. "After the forge-masters had been driven out, Mi-en-leh's association was violently attacked by many people, because there was not enough freedom in Su. And in fact the association everywhere, and for a long time, continued to oppress the followers of the forge-masters and also certain strata of wealthy peasants; and in order to be able to do this the association required an iron discipline among its members, so that great lack of freedom appeared to be prevalent even within the ranks of the association. Me-ti turned against all those who bewailed this lack of freedom in Su." Me-ti's arguments follow the familiar line that economic freedom is more important than political freedom.

> They [*i.e.* the members of the association] know that they, unlike the forge-masters and landowners, cannot be economically free as individuals but only in their collective totality. They have therefore organized their own liberation, and thus compulsion has arisen. Against all currents of thought, which threaten the production of goods for all, compulsion is used. It is against this compulsion that the clamor of those arises who want to be free from the point of view of organization, and who are mostly free economically; they protest against this compulsion as though it resembled the emperor's compulsion. They have not understood that the liberation is an economic task, a task that has to be organized.

Even more pitiful are Brecht's attempts to justify the Soviet forced labor camps.

> In the country of Tsen inequality has been abolished, the oppression of man by man has been made as difficult as possible. Yet there still exist some antisocial elements. They are being treated in a very peculiar manner. So as to make it impossible for them to cause further damage by individual action, they are being isolated for a time. In former times this was done by locking them into special buildings, nowadays this isolation is accomplished by a restrained behavior of all socially minded people against them. They are condemned to improve the social institutions of the country. Those against whom a law case has become necessary are turned into people conducting a law case. They have to find the reasons for their transgressions, and, if someone was guilty of causing them, to accuse him in public. They conduct lawsuits against their own teachers as well as against people who are responsible for certain social institutions. When they have either succeeded in bringing about changes or when their proposals have been proved impracticable, the period of their compulsory labor is deemed completed. In the latter case they are most frequently ordered to those activities which they have criticized. The wicked are made better, said Me-ti, by allowing them to make improvements.

This text is as confused and illogical in the original as it appears in the translation. If the period during which Brecht composed the book really started in 1934 (as is claimed by the editor, and there is no reason whatever to doubt his word), then this passage must have been written at a period when the idealistic projects for the abolition of prisons and their substitution by schools and debating societies had already long been abandoned in the Soviet Union. What we have here is, therefore, a strenuous effort on Brecht's part to persuade himself that the forced labor camps (and he *does* equate the activity of social inquiry to which his antisocial elements are condemned with *forced labor*) still somehow belonged to the world of those utopian dreams about the reeducation of criminals.

Brecht, of course, could not but be a little disturbed by the Byzantine adulation of Stalin. Yet here, too, he tried to persuade himself that it was necessary.

> Me-ti said: Ni-en's reputation is obscured by bad kinds of praise. There is so much incense, that one no longer sees the picture and that one says: here is something which is being concealed. This kind of praise tastes of bribery. It is true, however: when praise is necessary, we must get it from whatever quarter it can be got. To make them praise a good cause, bad people must be bribed. And at that time much praise was needed; for the path was obscure and the leader had no proofs. Hungry people who had never before seen a seed germinate were asked to sow. They were bound to believe that they were forced to throw their corn away by the handful and to hide their potatoes underground.

Or again:

> The adoration of Ni-en frequently assumed forms which amounted to a defamation of the man to be adored. Me-ti did not particularly worry about this. He said: Ni-en is building the great project. That is a very daring undertaking, never tried anywhere else. It needs great confidence on the part of the people. Ni-en knows how to get this. Through what else if not through production are people to become more intelligent and more self-reliant? Surely not by indoctrination alone?

It all comes down to the basic question whether Marxism itself represents an objective, scientific truth: "Me-ti was asked: How can you ask anyone to be at the same time objective and partisan? Me-ti replied: If the party is objectively right, there is no longer any distinction between the objective and the partisan." And yet it is clear that Brecht could not quite persuade himself by these strenuous arguments. "In a well-ordered state there is no need to talk continually of the individual's duty towards the state," he says in one of his aphorisms. And in the later portions of the *Book of Twists and Turns* the critical note becomes considerably harsher. There is a very open criticism of the Stalin constitution, for example:

> Me-ti turned against those who attacked the fact that the constitution of Su was linked with the name of Ni-en. He said: it is indeed a constitution for which he who has written it must assume the responsibility. The progressive people of the whole world are split into two camps. One side believes that in Su the *great order* reigns, the others that it does not. These opinions are both right and wrong. Some important features of the *great order* have been established in their foundations and are being developed. Individual ownership of the tools of work is abolished, and because the land itself is regarded as such a tool of work and the individual ownership of land is abolished, the distinction between town and country is disappearing. . . . But the new system, the most progressive in history, still works very badly and not very organically and needs so much effort and use of violence that the freedoms of individuals are very limited. As the system is being imposed by small groups of men, there is compulsion everywhere and no real rule of the people. The lack of freedom of opinion, freedom of coalition, lip service to authority and the acts of violence of the magistrates prove that all the basic elements of the *great order* are far from realized as yet, are far from being developed at the moment.

The great Moscow "Confessions" of the thirties also clearly shook Brecht's faith, although in public he seemed to support even the show trials enthusiastically. This, evidently, is how he really felt about them: "Me-ti criticised Ni-en because in his lawsuits against his enemies he demanded too much confidence from the people. He said: If I am asked to believe something which can be proved (without furnishing the proof) this is tantamount to my being asked to believe something which *cannot* be proved. I shall not believe it. Ni-en may have benefited the people by removing his enemies from the association, but he has not proved his point. By conducting a trial without proofs he has harmed the people. He should have taught the people to demand proof, and in particular from himself, who in general has been of so much service."

Among the names in the key at the beginning of the book it is also interesting to find, in the guise of Ko the philosopher, Brecht's old friend and mentor, the Marxist theoretician Karl Korsch, who had been expelled from the Communist party long before Hitler came to power. In a passage of some length Brecht gives a very interesting summary of Korsch's criticisms of Soviet policy.

According to Ko's view the struggle between the pupils of Mi-en-leh who had fallen out (Ni-en and To-tsi [*i.e.* Trotsky]) showed that Mi-en-leh's principles had been used up. Neither their actual application through Ni-en, nor their application proposed by To-tsi could bring a decisive success. According to Ko, To-tsi merely proposed certain rather doubtful reforms of the apparatus of power, which had begun to form the real obstacle to progress. The principles put forward by Ko showed a clear weakness at the very points where Mi-en-leh's principles had their strength, but he excellently pointed out the weaknesses of Mi-en-leh's principles, whom, in contrast to his pupils, he always treated with the highest respect.

Even more bitter than these criticisms of the developments within the Soviet Union, are the strictures Brecht levels against the tyranny exercised by the Soviet party against Communist parties outside Russia.

Under Ni-en's leadership, industry in Su was built up without exploiters and agriculture collectively conducted and supplied with machinery. But the associations outside Su degenerated. It was no longer the members who elected the secretaries but the secretaries who elected the members. The policies were dictated by Su, and the secretaries paid by Su. If mistakes were made, those were punished who had criticized them; but those who had made the mistakes remained in office. Soon they were no longer the best, merely the most pliable. . . . Those who issued the orders in Su itself were no longer informed, because the secretaries did no longer report anything that might not be welcome news for them. Confronted with these conditions the best were in despair. Me-ti deplored the decline of the *great method* (*i.e.* Marxism). Master Ko turned away from it. To-tsi denied all progress in Su, even the most obvious. Those who fought against Ni-en's influence on the associations outside Su soon realized they were alone; those who fought against him inside Su saw themselves ringed round by criminals and eventually committed crimes against the people themselves. In Su all wisdom was concentrated on economic construction, and banished from politics. Outside Su all those who praised Ni-en's merits, even those that were undeniable, made themselves suspect of being bribed; in Su anyone became suspect of treason who disclosed Ni-en's mistakes, even those under which Ni-en himself suffered most.

Those are strong words indeed. They suggest what really went on in the minds of sincere supporters of the Party at the height of the Stalinist terror, and surely they confirm the views of those who have maintained that Brecht's outward loyalty to the Party line in fact concealed a painful struggle with his own conscience. His public acceptance of the official line thus appears the outcome of a tragic and, in some ways, heroic inner conflict. Having committed himself, he did not want to become "a renegade," even one like Korsch (whom he greatly revered and admired), who remained a Marxist but openly attacked the post-Stalinist line and even questioned some of Lenin's conclusions. And yet Brecht had no illusions about the quality of the leadership of the party: "To break off discussion in a situation of urgency, to demand obedience instead of enthusiasm, to confound the need for speedy action with haste, to purloin responsibility: these are the hallmarks of bad leadership."

The aphorisms and anecdotes of the *Book of Twists and Turns* not only reveal a great deal of Brecht's political heart-searchings, they also provide some very illuminating insights into his personal attitudes, as embodied in the poet Kin or Kin-jeh.

The poet Kin said:
How am I to write immortal works when I am not famous?
How am I to answer when I am not asked?
Why should I lose time over writing verse, if time itself loses
    those verses?
I write my proposals in a durable kind of language
Because I am afraid it will take long till they are implemented.
To achieve great things, great changes are needed.
Little changes are the enemies of great changes.
I have enemies. Therefore I must be famous.

This is Brecht's definition of poetry itself—a *durable* language which
will preserve the blueprint of action. And beyond that, this durable
language should contain the power to evoke action directly, it should
be *gestisch*, gestural.

> Me-ti said: The poet Kin-jeh can claim to have renewed the lan-
> guage of literature. When he appeared upon the scene two main
> modes of language prevailed: a stylized mode which sounded
> stilted and written and was never actually spoken by the people
> as they went about their business or at other occasions; and a
> mode which could be heard spoken everywhere, which was a
> mere imitation of everyday speech and was not stylized at all. He
> used a mode of speech which was natural and stylized at the
> same time. He achieved this by observing the attitudes which un-
> derlay each sentence. His sentences always embodied attitudes
> and he always allowed the attitude to shine through the sen-
> tences. Such a language he called gestural, because it was no
> more than an expression of men's gestures. His sentences are
> best read if the reader accompanies his reading by certain bodily
> movements that fit in with them, movements which signify po-
> liteness or anger or the desire to persuade or mockery or trying
> to remember something or taking someone by surprise or warn-
> ing someone or inspiring fear. . . . The poet Kin recognized lan-
> guage as a tool of action and knew that one is speaking to others
> even at moments when one is speaking to oneself.

The most remarkable feature of the *Book of Twists and Turns*,
however, is the fact that here, in the guise of its thinly applied veneer
of *chinoiserie*, Brecht seems to have been able to speak about one of

61

the great loves of his life. The almost total absence of love poetry addressed to any of the women with whom he had relations of varying intensity in the course of his career has often been noted. Here one of these women does make an appearance under the name of Lai-tu. No clue is given to her identity in the key to Chinese names that opens the book, yet for anyone familiar with Brecht's life she is easily enough identified, as the Danish actress Ruth Berlau.

> The poet Kin-jeh said: It is difficult to say what Lai-tu produced. Perhaps it is those twenty-two lines about the countryside which I included in my play and which might never have been written without her. Of course, we never talked about the countryside. What she found amusing has also influenced me. It is not what other people find amusing. And of course I may also have used the way she moves in the structure of my poetry. She does a lot of other things as well, but even if she had only produced what made me produce, and allowed me to produce, she would have been worthwhile. [Kin-jeh did not suffer from undue modesty].

For Brecht erotic attachments and politics often merged. He called a common political commitment among lovers the *third thing* which built a bridge between two human beings. (There is a song about the third thing in *The Mother* where the common struggle against the exploiters is seen as the basis of the true friendship between Mother and Son.) But this doctrine of the third thing does not always seem to have worked as Brecht would have wanted it. "Lai-tu had a husband and they lived badly together because she did not enjoy sleeping with him, and, apart from some sympathy, there was nothing to bind her to him. She profited from Me-ti's doctrine concerning the third thing by suggesting to her husband that he should work for the oppressed people for whom she herself was working. Her husband agreed and Lai-tu continued sleeping with him. Me-ti chided her for this and said: What point is there in finding a third thing that unites you and to keep up another third thing that disunites you? It amounts to getting a piece of bread and washing it down with a draught of poison."

In spite of the Chinese setting, it is clearly stated at one point that Lai-tu went to Spain to report on the civil war there.

Kin-jeh's sister went to the front to make a report on the civil war. For a long time he was without news of her and could not write to her. He made the following song:
Our incessant conversation, which resembles
The conversation of two poplar trees, our conversation of many
  years
Has ceased. I no longer hear
What you say or write, nor do you hear
What I am saying.
I held you on my lap and combed your hair
I taught you the rules of warfare
I instructed you how to treat a man
How to read books and faces
How to struggle and how to rest
But now I see
How much I have not told you.
Often at night I get up, and in my throat
I am choking from useless advice.

But such tenderness and concern were most unusual for Brecht who loved to appear unconcerned, nonchalant, and tough. Hence: "After that period when his sister had been far away from him in the civil war, Kin-jeh always classed himself, because of his anxiety for her, among the cowards." For: "Kin-jeh strove to keep his equanimity, Lai-tu tried to shake him out of it. 'Is equanimity compatible with love?' asked Lai-tu. Kin-jeh replied: 'Yes.'"

In spite (or *because*) of the poet's striving for detachment, it was a stormy love affair. "Kin-jeh said to Me-ti: Lai-tu the selfless one has come with a basket and fetched away the gifts she gave me. She is telling my enemies that I am stealing from my collaborators. She is out of her mind. What am I to do? Me-ti said: She must be demented, if she acts like that, for she loves you. She is demanding too much, because she has given too much; she is heaping calumny on you because she has praised you too highly. See to it that no harm comes to her and that she has enough to eat. As she loves you, she will permit you to do that."

And so, from anecdotes and aphorisms, we get a most vivid picture of that fascinating and contradictory personality, the totalitarian democrat, the tender tough, the opportunistic idealist: Bertolt Brecht. "To earn one's supper, one needs intelligence; it may consist in being obedient to one's superiors. Intelligence of a different kind may induce one to strive to abolish the whole system of superiors and inferiors. Yet even for that enterprise one may still need intelligence of the first sort; for in order to be able to bring that great enterprise to a successful conclusion one still has to eat supper." This is the paradox of the political poet, the committed artist in our time—that all his choices are choices of evils. Brecht's Me-ti and his *Book of Twists and Turns* provide a veritable catechism of these dilemmas.

Brecht's Poetry in English—A Review of *Poems 1913–1956*

I must, at the very start, declare my interest: of the thirty-five translators who have contributed to this volume,[1] I am one; it does, indeed, contain three poems that I have translated. On the other hand, while this represents something to be quietly proud of, it does not entail any financial interest in the volume's success worth mentioning. And it might be argued that having worked on translations of this peculiarly difficult poetry and having participated in the laborious and very conscientious editorial process that preceded the birth of this volume gives one a certain authority to talk about the problems that arose in its formation and to offer an opinion on how they were tackled and, in many instances, overcome. And I hope that readers of this review will soon enough notice that, in spite of my marginal involvement, I am pretty detached in looking at it. After all, with the exception of three poems, the remaining five hundred or so, as well as the introduction and the critical apparatus, are entirely new to me.

First of all, however, it must be said loud and clear: this is a magnificent achievement, a major triumph of British publishing. Eyre Methuen deserves every conceivable praise for its courage to embark on this enterprise and doubled and redoubled plaudits for its perseverance with it over years of painful and costly birth pangs. The book is expensive—fifteen pounds is a lot even in a period of rampant inflation—

1. Bertolt Brecht, *Poems 1913–1956*, eds. John Willett and Ralph Manheim with the cooperation of Erich Fried (London: Methuen, 1976). A U.S. edition of the one-volume version of the book was issued in 1979 by Methuen, New York.

65

but it justifies its price. It is a truly precious addition to the sum total of poetry in English. (And it will be made available in three paperback volumes, at very much reduced cost—alas, without the notes and critical apparatus!).

But having said all this, I, for one, must also be critical of some aspects of the book. The introductory essay, "Disclosure of a Poet," not attributed to anyone in particular of the two-and-a-half editors mentioned on the title page, strikes me as a curious apologia, an apologia by a Brecht expert—or experts—who seems to have got it all wrong twenty years ago and now makes out a case that everybody else got it equally wrong. He starts with the statement:

> Well after his death in 1956 Brecht the poet remained like an unsuspected time-bomb ticking away beneath the engine room of literature. This aspect of his writing had long been concealed by the mass of his dramas, together with his theories about them, not to mention other people's theories about what those theories might mean. . . . Anybody who fails to see that his language was that of a poet is missing the main motive force of all his work.
>
> It is bad luck that so many of us have been led to approach Brecht from the wrong end: studying his theories first and then his plays, and only coming to the poems as a by-product of his theatre work; instead of seeing that the poems led into and permeated the plays, from which the theories in turn sprang.

Let us compare this with a paragraph from a book published early in 1959, very soon after Brecht's death in 1956:

> Brecht was a poet, first and foremost a poet. However much interest his writings may have aroused as expressions of the problems and anxieties of the age, as political pamphlets, manifestoes of stage reform, or social documents, their chief distinction lies in being 'memorable speech'. This is their primary significance. It underlies, from it derives, any other significance they may possess.
>
> Brecht's plays may be discussed and imitated as examples of a new kind of dramatic construction or stage technique. Nevertheless their main importance lies in their poetic quality. The new dramatic convention they represent lives above all through the grace of their language and the poetic vision of the world it conveys. Without the stamp of greatness impressed upon them by their poetry, these plays could never have exercised such an in-

fluence. They would not even have been noticed. And so it is with Brecht's ideas in other fields. They became important only as the ideas of a major poet.

This surely does not confirm the statement that Brecht the poet was an unsuspected, unnoticed, neglected entity. It may have been bad luck that so many of us (whoever those many might have been) were led (by whom?) to approach Brecht from the wrong end; the fact is that they seem to have paid little attention to those who *had* noticed Brecht's greatness as a poet and were shouting it from the rooftops: critics like Tucholsky or Feuchtwanger (whom the author of the introduction quotes as proclaiming Brecht a *Sprachschöpfer*, a "creator of language") or, in the English-speaking world, W. H. Auden, Eric Bentley, or Clement Greenberg, who, as early as 1941, called Brecht "the most original literary temperament to have appeared anywhere in the last twenty years." Or, indeed, the author of the lengthy passage cited above, which is to be found in my own book, *Brecht—A Choice of Evils*, which appeared in February, 1959, and was written between 1956 and 1958.

In the light of these facts it is surely naïve to claim that Brecht's greatness as a poet only emerged when his hitherto unpublished poems appeared in the late 1960s. While it is true that an enormous bulk of splendid material emerged from the hidden drawers of Brecht's writing desk, there can be no question that it disclosed no major facet of his poetic personality that had not been apparent before. Even the surprisingly surrealistic prose poems of the sequences of *Psalms* and *Visions* were known, at least in significant and characteristic part, by 1957; and the manner of his last epigrammatic, haikulike phase, was disclosed by the publication of six of his Buckow *Elegies* in the fourteenth issue of *Versuche* in 1954 and supplemented by a selection of his *Last Poems* in the special Brecht issue of *Sinn und Form* in 1957.

But even if these and many other poems, scattered in periodicals but readily available to those who wanted to look for them, had not been so accessible, the argument that Brecht's importance as a poet could not properly emerge until all his lyrical output was published falls to the ground if one merely pauses one moment to reflect that after all Brecht's *plays* not only contain a great deal of poetry of the most varied kind, but are, in fact, *all poetry*.

Nor is it less than naïve that the author—or authors—of the introduction, at least by implication, spreads the impression that it is only now, when so much of Brecht's *oeuvre* is accessible (and they admit that political as well as erotic poems by him are still being withheld and, indeed, suppressed by his literary executors) that we can see that Brecht was critical of the Stalinist regime in the Soviet Union and equally critical of the petty tyranny of the East German bureaucracy. The poem "The Solution," which the introduction calls "belatedly published" as if to give the impression that it has only recently come to light, *was* published in full in my book early in 1959 and had already extensively appeared in newspapers one or two years earlier. I personally feel highly gratified that the main drift of the argument of my own early study of Brecht has so completely been vindicated, but the authors of the introduction (one of whom doubtlessly is John Willett, who showered abuse on me for maintaining the very things that are now proclaimed as precious discoveries) might have had the grace to admit that not *everybody* was as mistaken and benighted as they now acknowledge themselves to have been.

So much for the introduction. What of the poems themselves? On the whole the standard of the translations is extremely high: it was, I feel, a good idea to ask practically everyone who had ever published a translation of Brecht to send in everything he had done, so that a selection of the most felicitous versions could be made. Other poems were translated specially for the volume to fill the gaps. This, as the editors say, made it possible to match the translators and the poems most congenial to them; everyone among them has his favorite Brecht poem which he has always longed to translate and which has gone round and round in his head over years until it has become as well polished as a jewel. One can see the love and care with which many of the poems have thus been nurtured in their translators' minds in many splendid instances in the book.

Of course, Brecht's unrhymed poetry is far easier to translate than his rhymed verse in strict meters. Here, it is a matter of matching the sense and the rhythm to the orginal and grasping the witty puns that Brecht loved so much. This has, in many instances, been achieved with considerable brilliance. Take the splendid epigram from the *Hollywood Elegies*, in which the scriptwriters and musicians of Hollywood are likened to whores:

Beneath the green pepper trees
The musicians play the whore, two by two
With the writers. Bach
Has written a Strumpet Voluntary. Dante wriggles
His shrivelled bottom.

"Strumpet voluntary" is splendid. The original has "*Strichquartett*": in German *Streichquartett* is a string quartet. By omitting one letter the word becomes *Strichquartett—Strich* meaning a whore's beat along which she solicits. So in Brecht's original one letter has been omitted to turn the musical term into a word from the prostitute's terminology; in the English version, the translator, John Willett, has achieved the same effect by *adding* a single letter.

But when it comes to the rhymed poems, which contain the same kind of witty punning ambiguity and in addition strict rhyme and meter, the matter becomes infinitely more difficult. Take the refrain of the "Ballad of Marie Sanders, the Jew's Whore," which is about the Nuremberg laws and a girl who had a Jewish lover. In German this runs:

Das Fleisch schlägt auf in den Vorstädten
Die Trommeln schlagen mit Macht
Gott im Himmel, wenn sie etwas vorhätten
Wäre es heute Nacht.

Now the first line of this recurring quatrain is brilliantly ambiguous. It can mean *the price of meat is going up in the suburbs*. The verb *aufschlagen*—literally something like beating up, or putting something on top of—can mean that something is put up or beaten up on top of an existing price tag. But—and that is the brilliance of the punning image—*aufschlagen* also means hitting the floor or a hard surface with a thud. In other words: the image of the butcher's meat going up in price, as the Nazi economic policy led to higher living costs, is here combined with the horrifying image of the dull thud of flesh striking the pavement as people are beaten up by the Nazis. Moreover, the third line does not merely rhyme with the first—"*Vorstädten-vorhätten*" constitutes an almost total assonance, only one single sound is different in the two words. (*Vorhätten* means "if they had something in mind," "if they planned something.") The English version (also by John Willet, as I now find; I had chosen the example almost at random without looking up who the translator was) makes a brave attempt at rendering this quatrain:

> The price is rising for butcher's meat.
> The drumming's now at its height.
> God alive, if they are coming down our street
> It'll be tonight.

The literal translation of the whole quatrain would be:

> The price of meat is going up in the suburbs (at the same time also: bodies are hitting the pavement with a thud in the suburbs)
> The drums are beating with might
> God in Heaven, if they had something in mind
> It would be tonight.

So you can see, the last line, "It'll be tonight," is perfectly rendered. In order to get a rhyme for it, the second line has to become the somewhat weak "the drumming's now at its height"—an awkward image that, because drums may be loud, but they are also deep and muffled, the opposite of reaching a height; Brecht merely says that they are being beaten with might, *i.e.* tremendous force. The pun of the first line, which, to my mind gives it all its brilliance and power in the original, is totally lost, and in order to achieve some sort of rhyme the third line is greatly weakened: "if they had something (obviously sinister) in mind" or "planned" now merely becomes: "if they are coming down our street." And the powerful and unexpected total assonance of the original merely becomes a feeble rhyme of "meat-street."

This is, as I say, an example picked out almost at random. It is not cited here to score a point against what is probably as good a translation as can be achieved, but merely to illustrate the fiendish difficulty of doing justice to a poet as deceptively simple—the "Ballad of Marie Sanders" seemingly has the simple artlessness of a folk song—but, in fact, as clever and complex as Brecht.

Inevitably—and all the translations in this massive volume show it—the intellectual brilliance of Brecht's mind is the element that survives translation best; the linguistic sophistication, which shines through his use of an unusual vocabulary in which regional elements are mingled with bureaucratic jargon, used satirically, and a powerful lapidary, monumental style taken from the Luther Bible, can occasionally be rendered through sheer ingenuity and perhaps luck; but the shimmering and profound ambivalence of the language is bound to escape translation altogether. We now have Brecht the poet in English, but not all of him. Yet we should be grateful for what we have.

A final word must be said for the critical apparatus with which the hard-cover edition concludes. (It will, alas, be omitted in the three paperback volumes). This comprises some 170 pages containing the main theoretical texts by Brecht on his own views of lyrical poetry; excellent notes on the various collections of poems that Brecht published in his lifetime, so that the reader can reconstruct these books from the poems in the volume before him, which, for very good and valid reasons, are arranged in purely chronological order. (This allows the hitherto unpublished poems to appear next to the ones which appear in the collections he himself put together.) There follow excellent and useful notes on individual poems; an alphabetically arranged list of all the original German titles of the poems in the volume so that one can readily find translations of poems one has been looking at in the original language; and finally a chronological list of the poems in the volume, which is more than a mere table of contents because it also refers to the position of each poem in the German collected editions and also provides the initials of the translators. I think it is an excellent idea not to print the translator's name after each poem in the book. This would distract the reader and tempt him to compare the performances of individual translators. This arrangement makes it possible to find the identity of the translators, but only if one really wants to identify them.

The critical apparatus provided by the editors is superior to anything available in the existing German editions of Brecht's poems. So, ironically enough, this edition of the translated poetry will be essential for any serious study of Brecht's poetry by German scholars as well!

As to the English-speaking reader: he can now get a good, if not perfect, idea of the work of one of the greatest poets of world literature. And in reading the poems in their chronological order, he can also learn something of the history and cultural climate of Europe in the first half of this century through the eyes of a man of towering intellect and insight who was deeply and personally involved in most of its major climacterics; a man whose path of exile and artistic struggle took him right across the globe: from Germany, via Denmark, Sweden, and Finland, through the Soviet Union to Vladivostok and across the Pacific Ocean to the United States and then back to Europe again; a man who was involved in Marxism and McCarthyism, Nazism and the West German economic miracle, in Dadaism and socialist realism, in radio and opera, films and theatre, and who looked at every element in his multifaceted existence with quizzical, ironic, infinitely understanding eyes—eyes which mostly stayed wide open and dry but from which, very occasionally, he shyly wiped a tear.

BECKETT

Beckett and His Interpreters

> We have no elucidations to offer of mysteries that are all of their making. My work is a matter of fundamental sounds (no joke intended) made as fully as possible, and I accept the responsibility for nothing else. If people want to have headaches among the overtones, let them. And provide their own aspirin. Hamm as stated, and Clov as stated, together as stated, nec tecum nec sine te, in such a place, and in such a world, that's all I can manage, more than I could.

Thus Samuel Beckett in one of his letters to Alan Schneider, which, most unusually, found their way into print in the *Village Voice* in March, 1958. No writer of our time has more consistently refused to comment on or explain his own work than Beckett. Yet no writer of our time has provoked a larger volume of critical comment, explanation, and exegesis in so short a time. It is hard, in working one's way through the numerous articles, reviews, essays, and weighty volumes of criticism that have appeared about him, to keep in mind how very recent and rapid his rise to world fame has been. It was only after the *succès de scandale* of *Waiting for Godot* that Beckett's name impinged on the consciousness of a wider public; and that play, safely established today as a contemporary classic, had its first performance in Paris no longer ago than January, 1953, opened in London in August, 1955, and reached the shores of the United States (in a disastrous tryout in Miami) at the beginning of 1956.

Beckett's reticence is no mere whim. Inevitably, there exists an organic connection between his refusal to explain his meaning ("We're not beginning to . . . to . . . mean something?" asks Hamm in *Endgame*; and Clov retorts, with a burst of sardonic laughter: "Mean something! You and I mean something! Ah that's a good one!") and the critics' massive urge to supply an explanation. Indeed, it might be argued that in that correlation between the author's and the critics' attitudes lies one of the keys to the whole phenomenon of Samuel Beckett, his *oeuvre*, and its impact.

Among Beckett's rare public utterances about general considerations underlying the work of creative artists in our time, the most important probably are the three dialogues on modern painters, which may or may not be a true record of conversations that took place between Samuel Beckett and Georges Duthuit but which, in any case, owe their present published form to Beckett. ("Would it be true to say you wrote down what had been said?" I asked him once; "I suppose you might say *down*; I'd rather say *up*," he replied.) In talking about the heroic enterprise of painters who refuse to look at the world "with the eyes of building contractors," Beckett suggests, as an alternative, "an art . . . weary of its puny exploits, weary of pretending to be able, of being able, of doing a little better the same old thing, of going a little further along a dreary road . . . and preferring *the expression that there is nothing to express, no power to express, no desire to express, together with the obligation to express* [my italics]."

Such, in fact, is the dilemma, the inevitable paradox of the artist in a world that lacks a generally accepted—and to the artist acceptable—metaphysical explanation that could give his efforts purpose and supply him with immutable standards of truth, goodness, and beauty. If, in happier periods of history, the artist could have no doubt that by his work he was exalting the glory of the Creator, that he was striving to capture a glow of those eternal canons of the beautiful, which remained pristine and unchangeable forever in some celestial sphere beyond the physical universe; today, if he has lost the faith, religious or secular, of his predecessors, he is left to fend for himself, without intelligible purpose in a world devoid of meaning. And yet the urge, the inescapable compulsion to express (but what?) remains embedded as strongly as ever in the artist's nature. It is a situation that is as absurd as it is tragic, yet for all that, a brave, an heroic position, challenging as it does the ultimate nothingness and making, to quote the Beckett/Duthuit dialogues again, "of this submission, this admission, this fidelity to failure, a new occasion . . . and of the act which, unable to act, obliged to act (the artist) makes an expressive act, even if only of itself, of its impossibility, of its obligation." Why, we must ask, if there is nothing to express, no power to express, no desire to express, is there yet this inescapable obligation to express?

In the general remarks that precede his script for *Film* (which Alan Schneider directed in the summer of 1964 with Buster Keaton in the lead), Beckett at least drops something like a hint as to the possible direction from which we might try to elicit a glimpse of an answer. Taking his cue from his fellow Irishman George Berkeley, Bishop of Cloyne, he says there: "*Esse est percipi* [To be is to be perceived]. All extraneous perception suppressed, animal, human, divine, self-perception maintains in being. Search of non-being in flight from extraneous perception breaking down in inescapability of self-perception.") That is: self-perception is a basic condition of our being; we exist because, and as long as, we perceive ourselves. If it is true that for the artist perception leads to the obligation to express what he perceives, it follows that for the artist the compulsion to express his intuition of the world is a condition of his very existence; as long as he exists he suffers the predicament of the voice that drones through *Cascando*: ". . . story . . . if you could finish it . . . you could rest . . . you could sleep . . . not before . . . oh I know . . . the ones I've finished . . . thousands and one . . . all I ever did . . . in my life . . . with my life . . . saying to myself . . . finish this one . . . it's the right one . . . then rest . . . then sleep . . . no more stories . . . no more words . . . and finished it . . . and not the right one . . . couldn't rest . . . straight away another . . . to begin . . . to finish . . ." And he suffers the predicament of the Opener in that brief but highly significant text, who opens the way for the stream of music (*i.e.* wordless self-perception) and that voice and shuts them off again: "And I close. So at will. It's my life, I live on that. . . . What do I open? They say, he opens nothing, he has nothing to open, it's in his head. . . . They say, That is not his life, he does not live on that. They don't see me, they don't see what my life is, they don't see what I live on, and they say, That is not his life, he does not live on that. I have lived on it . . . pretty long. Long enough."[1] The Opener, it might be argued, is the perceiving part of the self, while the voice and the wordless stream of emotion that is the music in *Cascando* are the part of the self that the perceiving part perceives. But the perceived portion of the self, by its very nature, is in constant flux. The voice tells a different story at any given moment, and so the artist's being itself is in constant flux; he can do no more than be true to each momentary atom of self-perception, of *Being*. "The individual," says Beckett in his essay on Proust, "is the seat of a constant process of decantation, decantation from the vessel containing the fluid of future time, sluggish, pale and monochrome, to the vessel containing the fluid of past time, agitated and multicolored by the phenomena of its hours." And the artist, to be true to his vocation, must confine himself to the faithful reflection of his changing self; to quote Beckett's essay on Proust again, what he is concerned with is the "non-logical statement of phenomena in the order and exactitude of their perception, before they have been distorted into intelligibility in order to be forced into a chain of cause and effect. . . . And we are reminded of Schopenhauer's definition of the artistic procedure as 'the contemplation of the world independently of the principle of reason.' " Hence an artist like Beckett does not concern himself with abstract and general verities, even if there were room for them in his view of the world. Hence, also, no universal lessons, no meanings, no philosophical truths could possibly be derived from the work of a writer like Beckett. And that is why, having stated the theme of his film script from Berkeley's principle that being is being perceived, he immediately adds, "No truth value attaches to above, regarded as of merely structural and dramatic convenience." (Compare this with Beckett's remark, when discussing St. Augustine's sentence about the two thieves on the cross that suggested one of the motifs in *Waiting for Godot*: "I am interested in the shape of ideas, even if I do not believe in them . . . That sentence has a wonderful shape. It is the shape that matters.") This persistent practice of instantly withdrawing any positive statement (which Beckett shares with most of his characters), it should by now be clear, is not self-conscious teasing or coyness, but

1. Quoted from the first published text of the English version in *Evergreen Review*, No. 30. The text in the version published in book form by Faber & Faber, London, is slightly different.

a fundamental, inevitable, and logical consequence of his artistic personality, his creed as a thinker and an artist.

We must accept, therefore, that he claims no validity as a general truth for the Berkeleyan basis of his film script. On the other hand, there can be no doubt that the flight from self-perception is one of the recurring themes of his writing from *Murphy* to *The Unnamable* and beyond, and that the nature of the Self, its inevitable split into perceiver and perceived, an ear that listens and a voice that issues forth from the depths, is another: we find this split in most of his narrative prose and also, perhaps less obviously, in his dramatic works, where the pairs of indissolubly linked characters (Didi/Gogo, Pozzo/Lucky, Hamm/Clov, Krapp present/Krapp past, Opener/Voice in *Cascando*) can be interpreted as aspects of the Self in this complementary relationship. Equally dominant throughout Beckett's entire *oeuvre* is the *compulsiveness* of the voice, the inescapability and painfulness—through its failure to achieve nonbeing—of the process of self-perception, which result from its being the essence and condition of the artist's existence itself.

Paradoxically, however, Beckett's refusal to be more than a painstaking recorder of his modes of existence, of his *Existenzgefühl*, his categorical refusal to allow any philosophical meaning or thesis to be attributed to his work, is precisely the aspect of his activity that lifts his precarious and perilous enterprise into a sphere of significance beyond the scope of most other artists. While Beckett's poems, prose narratives, and plays exist—and are highly successful—as mere literary creations, structures of verbal forms and images, they can, through their very uncompromising concentration on existential experience, also claim attention as human documents of great importance; for they constitute an exploration, on a hitherto almost unprecedented scale, of the nature of one human being's mode of existing and, thereby, of the nature of human existence itself. Beckett's writings, it might well be argued, are more than mere *illustrations* of the point-of-view of existentialist philosophers like Heidegger and Sartre; they constitute the culmination of existential thought itself *precisely because they are free of any abstract concepts or general ideas* and thus escape the inner contradiction of existentialist statements that are couched in the form of generalizations. In this respect, for instance, they are certainly superior to those of Sartre's works in which the philosopher has followed the logic of his own position to the point of putting his ideas into the form of fiction or drama; and this is the case not only because Beckett's work is on a higher level of artistic intensity and creativeness, but also because Sartre's narrative prose and theatre clearly bear the marks of having been preconceived as an illustration of general concepts and are therefore denied the profound, immediate, experiential validity of Beckett's writings. Beckett's rigid avoidance of comments on his work must be seen in this light, and the correctness, the inevitability, of his position will be instantly recognized.

In the relentlessness of his self-denial, the purity of his dedication to his chosen task, Beckett is akin to Kafka and Kierkegaard, who were equally committed to a life of the most uncompromising self-examination. Indeed, it is from the writings of Kierkegaard, the first and still incomparably the greatest of the existentialist thinkers, that we can, as it were, deduce the theoretical framework, the basic pattern that Kierkegaard sketched out for himself and tried to live up to but that Beckett fulfills more radically, giving it a far more satisfying artistic realization.

The parallel between Beckett and Kierkegaard is a striking one, although there is no evidence that Beckett has, in fact, been directly influenced by Kierkegaard's thought or writing. Like Beckett's trilogy, Kierkegaard's series of "pseudonymous books" (which, like Beckett, he produced in a great outburst of creative energy within the brief span 1843 to 1846) expresses a wide gamut of existential attitudes through a multitude of voices—characters that keep recurring in the various volumes partly as narrators, diarists, orators, and letter writers, partly as the supposed editors and commentators who are deemed responsible for having compiled the primary documents and put them before the public. "My relationship [to these books]," says Kierkegaard in the final explanatory note appended to his *Concluding Unscientific Postscript*, "is more far-reaching than that of a poet who invents characters, but appears himself in the preface, as the *author*. For I, in my own person or impersonally, am merely a prompter in the third person, who has, as a poet, created *authors*, whose *prefaces*, whose very *names*, in turn are entirely their own creations. Thus in the pseudonymous books there is not a single word by myself." Similarly, in Beckett's trilogy, not only is the autonomy of the voices that are heard complete, the voices themselves in turn present and invent other voices, while the author is reduced to no more than the neutral field of consciousness into which these autonomous voices emerge. Hence Beckett, like Kierkegaard, must insist that his own personality is not at issue. As Kierkegaard puts it, "Thus I am the indifferent element, i.e., it is indifferent what and how I am. . . . My facsimile, my picture, etc., like the question whether I wear a cap or a hat, could thus be the object of attention only for those to whom indifferent aspects have become important, perhaps in compensation for the fact that the important has become indifferent to them."

Unlike Beckett, Kierkegaard did feel it necessary to expound the theoretical basis of his method. In his *Concluding Unscientific Postscript* he explained the background of the pseudonymous books and laid the foundations for the existentialism of Heidegger and Sartre by showing that there can be no abstract truth divorced from the existential experience of the individual; that any abstract statement about the nature of the world, by having been abstracted from the living experience of an individual, is necessarily dead, the mere empty shell of a living truth. Thus existence precedes essence, subjective thought is of a higher order than objective thought.

> While objective thought is indifferent toward the thinking individual and his existence, the subjective thinker, as an existing being, is vitally interested in his own thought within which he exists. . . . While objective thought attaches supreme importance to results and enables all mankind to practice deceit by copying and repeating results and summations, subjective thought puts all its store on the process of becoming and omits the result, partly because this, precisely, is a matter for the thinker himself, he being the one who knows the way it is reached, partly because he is in a constant process of becoming. (Chapter II)

The analogy between this view and Beckett's, as outlined in his essay on Proust, as well as practiced in all his writing, is complete. As the individual is constantly changing and only experience is a valid basis of truth, generalized statements claiming an applicability outside the flux of time and outside the individual's shifting self-perception, must necessarily be false.

> Let us assume someone wanted to communicate the proposition: "It is not the truth that is the truth, but the way that is the truth, i.e., the truth consists in the process of becoming, in the process of acquiring it, therefore there is no result." Let us assume this person was a benefactor of mankind who felt compelled to inform humanity of it. Let us assume he adopted the excellent method of communicating it by direct advertisement in the local paper, thus winning a mass of adherents to his proposition; while, adopting the method of the artist, it would, in spite of all his efforts, remain impossible ever to decide if he had helped a single human being—what then? Well, then his direct statement would, in itself, have been a result. (Chapter II)

In a process of unending flux, each moment contains the negation of the preceding atom of time. Those who deal in abstract, unchanging verities, the positive thinkers, are therefore, by definition, wrong.

> The negative thinkers [says Kierkegaard] always have the advantage of having something positive, namely the fact that they are aware of the negative, the positive thinkers have nothing, for they are deceived. Precisely because the negative is present in existence, is present everywhere (for existence is constant becoming) the only salvation, when confronted with it, lies in constant awareness of the negative. It is precisely by being positively reassured that the individual is deceived. The negativity which is in existence, or rather the negativity of the existing subject . . . springs from the make-up of the subject, from its being an existing, infinite mind. Infinity and eternity are the only certainty, but by being within the subject they are in existence, the first expression of which is its negation and the monstrous contradiction that the eternal should be in the process of becoming, that it should come into being. Thus the existing subject must find a form for its thinking which can give expression to this state of affairs. If it expresses it by direct assertion, it is in fact saying something that is untrue; for in the direct assertion it is precisely

the negation that is omitted, so that the form of communication is in itself misleading, like the tongue of an epileptic uttering distorted words. (Chapter II)

In Beckett's work this tension between the transient, unendingly decaying nature of the material universe and the immaterial aspect of consciousness, which incessantly renews itself in ever recurring self-perception, plays an important part. Consciousness cannot conceive of itself as nonexisting and is therefore only conceivable as unlimited, without end. The more in Beckett's works the material envelope decays and is stripped away, the more painful becomes the tension between the temporal and the infinite. Beckett's characters may lose the capacity for locomotion; their senses may decay; yet their awareness of their own self continues relentlessly; and time can never have a stop: the final situations in *Waiting for Godot*, in *Endgame*, or in *How It Is* imply eternal recurrence, while in *Play* it is probably the impossibility of an extinction of consciousness through death itself that is dramatized: as the individual can never become aware of his own cessation, his final moments of consciousness must remain, as it were, eternally suspended in limbo and can be conceived as recurring through all eternity.

It was Kierkegaard also who recognized that a writer engaged in this kind of enterprise must necessarily be a comic as well as a tragic writer.

That the subjective, existing thinker is as much positive as he is negative, can also be expressed by saying that he has as much of the comic as he has of the pathetic. . . . Pathos that is not reinforced by the comic is illusion; the comic that is not reinforced by pathos is immaturity. . . . Existence itself, the act of existing, is a striving as pathetic as it is comic; pathetic, because the striving is infinite, i.e., directed towards infinity, an act of making itself infinite, which is the summit of the pathetic; comic, because such striving is self-contradictory. Seen pathetically, a second has infinite value; seen comically, ten thousand years are a mere flash of foolery like yesterday; and yet time, in which the existing individual finds himself, is made up of such parts. (Chapter II)

There is much material for detailed study in the parallel between Beckett and Kierkegaard; it could, for example, be carried into the very structure of their works. Kierkegaard's *Either/Or* and *Stages on Life's Way* resemble a book like *Molloy* in their shape and structure in that both present juxtapositions of the existential situation of different individuals, contrary but also complementary. One could also investigate the comparative treatment of concepts like nothingness by Kierkegaard and Beckett. There is, for example, a distinctly Beckettian flavor in the final words of Quidam's Diary in *Stages on Life's Way*. "Here ends the diary for this time. It deals with nothing. But not in the same sense as the diary of Louis XVI, the alternating contents of which are said to have been: one day 'at the chase'; the second day: '*Rien*'; the third day: 'at the chase.' It contains nothing; but if, as Cicero says, the easiest letter is the one that deals with nothing, it is sometimes the hardest life which deals with nothing."

Of course, we must always keep in mind in pursuing these fascinating correspondences and parallels that it is the shape of the thought, the symmetry that matters, that such enquiries must never rigidify into *results*—in Kierkegaard's sense. Altogether the need to resist the temptation of trying to reduce Beckett's work to neatly wrapped up *lessons* or *meanings* (in the spirit of that naïve young student in Goethe's *Faust* who feels that "what we have written down in black and white, we can in peace and comfort bear away") presents one of the most arduous obligations for all those who want to write about Beckett, and even for those who want to profit from such critical analyses. Lucky's speech in *Waiting for Godot*, richly interlarded with references to the results of numerous authorities like Puncher and Wattman, Testew and Essy-in-Possy (whose "unfinished labors were crowned by the Acacacacademy of Anthropopopometry") is, among other things, a salutary warning against, and savage parody of, the belief that the sum of human wisdom, of "thinking," can be increased by citing the results of established authorities.

The so-called nihilism of Beckett, the cliche tag that the popular consciousness has attached to him, can thus be seen as no more than the necessary outcome of Beckett's refusal to deal in generalizations and abstract truths. That, indeed, has always been the position of the artist whose mode of expression is the concrete rather than the abstract. Only that Beckett, in addition, like many writers and visual artists of his generation, has reached a position of doubt, of agnosticism about the external world itself, which, reflected as it must be within the existential experience of the individual, has lost its reassuringly positive and generally accepted outlines. That is why in the last resort there is *nothing* to express together with the obligation to express; the only certain evidence of being is the individual's experience of his own consciousness, which in turn is constantly in flux and ever changing and, therefore, negative rather than positive, the empty space through which the fleeting images pass. The existential experience is thus felt as a succession of attempts to give shape to the void; when nothing can lay claim to final, definitive reality, we enter a world of games, of arbitrary actions structured to give the illusion of reality. So Vladimir and Estragon think up their ways to pass the time; Murphy finds illumination in a game of chess; Hamm and Clov are pieces in such a game; Molloy painstakingly constructs a system of sucking stones; Watt works out his strings of permutations of the series of dogs, the series of men, the series of pictures, his system of the Krak!, Krek!, and Krik! of frogs. There is an infinite number of possibilities for such games and series, such patterns of experience. While none of them can lay claim to *meaning* anything beyond itself, they nevertheless are worth our attention: they may not express reality in terms of something outside itself, but they *are* reality, they *are* the world to the consciousness that has produced them and that, in turn, *is* what it experiences. And if the artist feels the obligation to *express* his experience of being, he is, necessarily, engaged in a twofold enterprise, however heavy the odds against success may appear: he is engaged in a *cognitive process*, an exploration of the possible modes of existential experience. For games, however arbitrarily their rules are drawn up, are by no means devoid of value in a cognitive process. The parallel here is with mathematics, which, dealing as it does with mere patterns of the mind, without any direct reference to observable reality, could itself be regarded as a form of intellectual game, and while attaching, itself, considerable importance to the theory of games, yet serves to provide a key to reality, actual and potential, theoretical and practical. A mind that has, quite arbitrarily, constructed a space with different numbers of dimensions will, by dint of having journeyed that way, return with a firmer grasp of the two-dimensional world; in the same way Beckett's limit-situations in which man is reduced to the point of zero or, alternatively, pushed far into the limbo of infinitely continuing consciousness, could be described as a kind of differential and integral calculus of the human consciousness. Again and again Beckett plays the game of imagining the two extreme limits of the human situation itself: the position of a consciousness before the moment of birth and in the hour of death and even beyond it—on the one extreme limit, the unimaginable case of a consciousness that cannot yet conceive of the fact of its own existence; on the other, the consciousness that cannot become aware of its nonbeing.

Whether Beckett can himself remember the moment before his birth, as is sometimes suggested, whether such a memory is indeed physiologically possible, is totally irrelevant. What matters is that the process of imagining it, and the process in the consciousness of his readers of being able to experience the course of this imaginative process, is an existential experience that will reflect itself in, and changes, the vision of all those who have undergone it. It is the shape of the thought, the shape of the experience that matters, for the shape is its own significance, the experience its own meaning. It is the *quality* of the experience that, communicated (should it be communicable), can change the *quality* of another human being's experience. Beckett himself may be sceptical as to the possibility of such communication. The obligation to express is not dictated by any idea of utility to others. But the fact that the obligation is felt leaves open the possibility of genuine human communication, which could only be possible, within the terms of reference of this type of thinking, as the re-creation of the experience of self-perception in one individual through inducing a secondary and analogous process of the perception of another individual's self-perception.

But in that case—if there are no secure meanings to be established, no keys guaranteed to unlock allegorical treasure-houses to be provided; if the only chance of approaching the writer's meaning is to experience his experience—what justification can there be for any critical analysis and interpretation of such a writer's work?

There is certainly no justification for criticism that will try to deliver cut-and-dried results, such as furnishing the discovery of the identity of Godot or establishing that Hamm is James Joyce and Clov, Beckett himself; nor is there point in importing Christian theology or Zen Buddhism into the work of a man whose basic attitude can be defined as a total rejection of ideology. Yet a wide area still remains that is legitimately open for critical analysis from a variety of different motivations and standpoints.

First of all, there is the entirely justifiable approach that seeks to elucidate the numerous allusions—literary, philosophical, geographical—in the text. If a reader is to be capable of sharing in the existential experience embodied in these texts, he must have a full understanding of the references that are embedded at various levels in the complex associative pattern of these intricate verbal structures. In Beckett's case the tracking down of these numerous cross-references and allusions, puns and assonances, demands such a high degree of skill and leads into such fascinating byways of recondite erudition that it can provide all the excitement and all the culminating pleasure in having found the solution that we get from the best detective thriller. There is, however, an important caution to be kept in mind: in retracing the intricate warp and woof of verbal and conceptual allusions, hidden clues, and concealed correspondences, the critic may unwittingly suggest to the reader that the author has himself intentionally constructed his work as an intellectual puzzle. Such an intentional fallacy would inevitably induce dangerous misconceptions about the motivation of a writer like Beckett, as well as about the nature of the creative process that produces literature of this type; the writer will then appear to the reader as, above all, an intellect of almost superhuman ingenuity and calculation bent on devising superhumanly difficult conundrums for similarly ingenious and erudite intellects. Nothing could, in Beckett's case, be further from the truth. He is the least consciously intellectual of writers. His method of work is spontaneous and always has as its starting point the deeply concentrated evocation of the voice within his own depths. In this there are links between Beckett and the French surrealists of the twenties and thirties, some of whom he met during his first stay in Paris. He differs from the surrealists in that he does not, having summoned up the voices from his subconscious, merely record them in automatic writ-

87

ing. He shapes them with all the skill and sense of style of a highly conscious craftsman, using the full discriminatory faculty of a skilled literary critic. Nevertheless, it is the spontaneously emerging voice that is the raw material on which he works. Inevitably, in the case of a man of such vast and varied learning as Beckett, the voices that emerge from the depths of his subconscious speak a language that reflects his past experience and the store of associations he has acquired and will therefore be studded with allusions and a wealth of cross-references. But these are the outcome of a process that is largely subconscious and certainly wholly free of any premeditation or display of euphuistic cleverness. The intricate texture the critic has to unravel is therefore nearer, in its structural principle, to the organic associative organization of images in a dream than to the calculated pattern of a crossword puzzle. The puzzle is there, but it is an organic growth, not a deliberate artifact of mystification. And the critic can help to solve it by elucidating the strands that have contributed to its growth. But the reader, once he has grasped the full import of the allusions, must accept the text as a spontaneous flow of images and allow himself to be carried along by it with equal spontaneity.

There is also, secondly (beyond the mere elucidation of associations and allusions, the provision of an annotated glossary, as it were, of verbal meanings), a wider and even more challenging task for the critic: namely, the uncovering of the structural principles, the outline of the main design, which must be present in an *oeuvre* in which the concept of the games that the consciousness must play to fill the void is of such importance. Games have rules that can be deduced from observing the players. And only when the rules are known to the spectators can they fully enter into and share the excitement of the players. The elucidation of the structural principles governing each of Beckett's works is, therefore, another legitimate auxiliary function for the critic, which should help the reader to achieve some degree of communication with the writer and to enter into the experience he is seeking to convey. In the same sense, an art critic's explanation of the underlying pattern of design in a great painting will enhance the onlooker's ability to see it with the painter's own eyes. Moreover, in an *oeuvre* as single-minded and ruthlessly consistent with itself as Beckett's, the structural patterns thus uncovered will by no means be confined to each work by itself; it will also be possible to trace a larger pattern of design of a higher order of complexity that will emerge if all the single works are seen together as the constituent parts of the writer's total output. Here again the critic can help by allowing the reader to see the parts in their relation to the whole and in their true perspective. The gradual process of eliminating external events in Beckett's narrative prose from *More Pricks Than Kicks* to *How It Is* and the progressive concentration of the action to a static pattern in his plays from *Waiting for Godot* to *Happy Days* and *Play* are cases in point.

Then, thirdly, and above all: if it is indeed true that *esse est percipi* (and for a writer's being *as a writer* it is certainly true, for his work exists only in the minds of those who read it, and the writer's activity itself has, from Horace to Proust, been frequently regarded by the writers themselves as an attempt to achieve permanent being beyond physical death, the only effective way to reach genuine immunity from the obliterating action of time), then it must also be true that a writer's very existence as a writer will depend on the manner in which his work is perceived and experienced by his readers. And this in turn will largely be shaped by the critics, who, if they fulfill their proper function, will determine the quality and depth of this experience by their account of the impact the works in question have made on themselves. It is the critics' experience that serves as an exemplar for the reactions of a wider public; they are the sense organs of the main body of readers, the first to receive the impact of a new writer and trained to experience it. Their modes of perception will be followed by the mass of readers, just as in every theatre audience it is the few individuals with a keener than average sense of humor who determine whether the jokes in a play will be laughed at at all, and to what extent, by triggering off the chain reaction of the mass of the audience.

If this is so, then the function of criticism is of particular importance for a writer like Beckett, who is not trying to communicate anything beyond the quality of his own experience of being; the quality of such a body of work, its very existence, will be determined by the quality of its reception or by the sum total of the individual experiences it provokes in individual readers. That is why a great writer's *oeuvre* can acquire a life of its own that may well go beyond its author's conscious intentions and expand by gaining layer after layer of new meaning through the experience it evokes in the minds and emotions of succeeding generations. The richer a literary creation and the more directly derived from the depths of genuine human experience, the more varied and differentiated will be the reaction it evokes in its readers. Or to put it differently: it is the existential experience in a literary work, as distinct from its purely descriptive, ideological, and polemical content, that, in evoking a direct, existential human response in the readers, will ensure its continued impact on succeeding generations. Always, however, it will be the critics who lead the way in discovering those aspects of such a literary creation that are of particular relevance to a given epoch. And it is the critics' work which remains as the permanent record of the quality of the experience provoked by a great writer's *oeuvre* in each epoch. The critics of one generation, by provoking the dissent of the next, provide the dialectical impetus for the expanding life of a great writer's creative achievement. Such a writer's work can thus be seen as the pebble thrown into a pool; from the point of impact of which an endless growing ring of circular waves spreads across the surface of the water. If, in Kierkegaard's sense, the subjective thinker's experience can never, finally and once and for all, be reduced to an abstract, dead *result*—its meaning being coterminous with itself and with the existential experience it evokes in its audience—and if the audience's reaction must necessarily be different in quality in each individual as well as from generation to generation, it follows that the mode of existence of such an individual thinker's work will eventually be seen as the movement of a living, constantly changing organic *tradition*; and at the center of such a tradition there must necessarily be found the critics who reflect and shape the movement and the quality of the individual attitudes and experiences that constitute it.

The recognition of the fact that the very existence of such a writer's work is made up of the sum total of the reactions it evokes does not, however, imply that each and every reaction, each and every critical response, is of equal value. While the impact of a text, emotional as well as intellectual, must and will be different on different individuals at different times and in different aspects of a richly structured literary creation existing on a multitude of levels, there are nevertheless definite and effective criteria that will, if only in due time, eliminate the irrelevant, insensitive, or factually mistaken critical evaluations from the body of the organic tradition that is continually forming and renewing itself around the work of a major creative writer.

In Beckett's case, the astonishing fact is the volume, the diversity, and the quality of the body of critical work he has evoked in so short a time. This surely is a measure of his relevance, richness, and depth. It might be objected that, being a difficult and puzzling writer, the volume of critical reaction merely reflects the fact that he presents a challenge to the ingenuity of critics eager to display their own discernment or erudition. There is, no doubt, a grain of truth in this argument, but any deeper examination of the great mass of critical work on Beckett must show that the argument is superficial. For it is precisely the emotional intensity of the response, even in the work of those critics who revel in the discovery of recondite allusions, that is the most striking common feature of all Beckett criticism; there can be no doubt that these critics are, above all, responding to an overwhelming, emotional, almost a mystical, experience and that this experience has sparked their zeal to elucidate and explain their author's meaning, to make him accessible to a larger number of readers. Whether they analyze the language and structure of the texts or track down the philosophical allusions and implications or even use them as the starting point for sociological analysis, they are all clearly impelled by a profound experience of insight, which has obviously had an exhilarating effect on them. In the terms of Kierkegaard's example of the thinker who faced the dilemma of proclaiming his discovery about the nature of truth by direct advertisement in the local paper or by its indirect expression through an account of his living experience, it is this emotional impact on the critics, as the representatives and advance guard of the public, that supplies the true measure of Samuel Beckett's achievement.

It is, moreover, highly significant that this emotional impact, in apparent contradiction to the recondite intellectual content of Beckett's work, is indeed an exhilarating one. How is it that this vision of the ultimate void in all its grotesque derision and despair should be capable of producing an effect akin to the catharsis of great tragedy?

Here we find the ultimate confirmation of our initial contention that it is not the content of the work, not *what* is said, that matters in a writer of Beckett's stamp, but the *quality of the experience* that is communicated. To be in communication with a mind of such merciless integrity, of such uncompromising determination to face the stark reality of the human situation and to confront the worst without ever being in danger of yielding to any of the superficial consolations that have clouded man's self-awareness in the past; to be in contact with a human being utterly free from self-pity, utterly oblivious to the pitfalls of vanity or self-glorification, even that most venial complacency of all, the illusion of being able to lighten one's anguish by sharing it with others; to see a lone figure, without hope of comfort, facing the great emptiness of space and time without the possibility of miraculous rescue or salvation, in dignity, resolved to fulfill its obligation to express its own predicament—to partake of such courage and noble stoicism, however remotely, cannot but evoke a feeling of emotional excitement, exhilaration.

And if it is the living, existential experience of the individual that matters and has precedence over any abstract concepts it may elicit, then the very act of confronting the void or continuing to confront it is an act of affirmation. The blacker the situation and the deeper the background of despair against which this act of affirmation is made, the more complete and the more triumphant must be the victory that it constitutes. The uglier the reality that is confronted, the more exhilarating will be its sublimation into symmetry, rhythm, movement, and laughter. To attempt the impossible and to emerge having failed, but not completely, may be a greater triumph than total success in easier tasks. As Beckett himself says in a fragment of verse hidden away among the Addenda to *Watt*:

who may tell the tale
of the old man?
weigh absence in a scale?
mete want with a span?
the sum assess
of the world's woes?
nothingness in words enclose?

Beckett's Novels

If the novel is defined as a pleasant tale, spun for the amusement of the reader by craftsmen of narrative technique, adept in the invention of interesting characters and the construction of intricately patterned plots, then Samuel Beckett could not be called a novelist at all, at least as far as the books he has written in French are concerned. But if, on the other hand, it were permissible to define the novel as a work in prose in which an imaginative artist may explore, with uncompromising honesty, ruthless integrity, and utter frankness, the human condition in all its naked absurdity, then prose poets like Franz Kafka or James Joyce can be called great novelists. Then too Samuel Beckett can take his place among them as one of the most profound and most significant novelists of our time. For Beckett, like Kafka, does not write for the amusement of readers. It is doubtful if, in writing his books, he ever even thinks of readers. Beckett writes because he has to write, because he is under a compulsion to search for the nature of his own self and, thus, to explore the depths of being, the nature of the predicament of man and his existence.

A Protestant Irishman, born in Dublin, at one time *lecteur d'anglais* at the École Normale Supérieure in Paris, and later, briefly, assistant to the Professor of Romance Languages at Trinity College, Dublin, Beckett has written the bulk of his most important work in French because, as he once put it: "en Français c'est plus facile d'écrire sans style"; because, that is, when writing in a language in which he has to concentrate on saying what he wants to say, there is less temptation to be carried away by sheer virtuosity of language for its own sake. Nevertheless, Beckett's earlier writings in English and his later work in French (most of which he afterwards translates into English himself) form a single whole and cannot be separated in describing his literary personality.

Because among his earliest published writings there are essays on Proust and Joyce, and because he belonged to Joyce's circle, it has become one of the endlessly repeated clichés of literary reviewers that Beckett is a follower of Joyce or has been influenced by Proust. In fact, even a fairly casual examination of his work must show that he owes little to either of these writers. As Beckett himself once pointed out in conversation, Proust is an analyzer, Joyce a synthesizer. But if Proust dissects reality by examining it minutely, if Joyce builds a new reality by the creative use of language, Beckett does neither of these things: he is searching for the nature of reality itself by eliminating and discarding layer after layer of accidental qualities, by peeling off skin after skin of the onion to reach the innermost core, the nothingness at the center of being. For Beckett, as he says in his essay on Proust, "the artistic tendency is not expansive but a contraction. And art is the apotheosis of solitude. There is no communication because there are no vehicles of communication."[1] To Beckett, therefore, the novel is not an act of communication or storytelling; it is a lonely and dedicated exploration, a shaft driven deep down into the core of the self. It is a self-contradictory, quixotic, but because of this, an infinitely heroic and noble attempt at expressing the inexpressible, saying the unsayable, distilling the essence of being, and making visible the still center of reality of which Demokritos the Abderite, in one of Beckett's favorite apophthegms, said: "Nothing is more real than nothing."

This exploration has nothing to do with mere description, it rejects "the grotesque fallacy of realistic art—'that miserable statement of line and surface', and the penny-a-line vulgarity of a literature of notations" (*Proust*, p. 57), the efforts of "realists and naturalists worshipping the offals of experience, prostrate before the epidermis and the swift epilepsy, and content to transcribe the surface, the façade, behind which the Idea is prisoner" (*Proust*, p. 59).

Yet how is the unsayable to be said, the uncommunicable to be communicated? As Beckett himself put it in describing the difficulties

1. Samuel Beckett, *Proust* (New York: Grove Press, 1970), 47.

of one of his earlier heroes, Watt, "the only way one can speak of nothing is to speak of it as though it were something, just as the only way one can speak of God is to speak of him as though he were a man, which to be sure he was, in a sense, for a time, and as the only way one can speak of man, even our anthropologists have realized that, is to speak of him as though he were a termite." Having left the surface of reality, Beckett's later novels deal with archetypes, they take place in a "*présent mythologique*" as Molloy puts it. Beckett's later novels have no story, no beginning and no end because they examine archetypal situations that are ever-present attributes of the human condition.

Nor are Beckett's protagonists, from Belacqua, Watt, and Murphy, to Molloy, Malone, and the nameless heroes of his later works, fictional characters in the usual sense. They are emanations of his own personality who appear and reappear throughout his books. Belacqua, the main character of his earliest published work of fiction, *More Pricks Than Kicks* (1934), a sequence of stories about the same tragicomic hero, reappears in *Comment c'est* (1961), or rather is mysteriously referred to, without apparent reason or explanation.

The ten Belacqua stories, picaresque sketches of the life of impecunious Irish intellectuals haunting the pubs of Dublin, already contain a good deal of the essential Beckett. Belacqua himself has the difficulty of locomotion that afflicts so many of Beckett's characters: "a spavined gait, his feet were in ruins, corns, hammer-toes." (*More Pricks Than Kicks*, p. 10). Even more characteristically, he has prenatal memories: "I want very much to be back in the caul on my back in the dark forever." (*ibid.*, p. 32). That Beckett himself retains what he believes to be a memory of his prenatal life in his mother's womb is an established fact. Peggy Guggenheim, who confesses in her memoirs that she was at one time "terribly in love" with Beckett, a "very fascinating, lanky Irishman with green eyes and a thin face and a nose like an eagle," also reports that "ever since his birth he had retained a terrible memory of life in his mother's womb. He was constantly suffering from this and had awful crises, when he felt he was suffocating." [2] The terrible situation of the embryo in the womb, which Beckett himself describes as one of nameless dread, all the more horrible because it is wholly inexpressible, concerned with a situation utterly

2. Peggy Guggenheim, *Confessions of an Art Addict* (London: André Deutsch, 1960), 49.

beyond the grasp of the sufferer, a fear for which there can be no alleviation because the terrified self knows neither its own identity nor can ever know of even the possibility of help and eventual salvation—this, the most basic of all anxieties, is one of the underlying, ever-recurring motifs of Beckett's works.

If Beckett were not an artist of supreme power, however, this antenatal memory would remain a mere psychological curiosity. It is his achievement that he has transmuted it into an image of universal significance—a summing-up of the entire human condition. For, once born into our world, man ultimately remains as unable to grasp the why and wherefore of his situation, the nature of his own identity, as the fetus in the womb; and like the fetus he is utterly incapable of even trying to form a conception of the unknown dimension on the threshold of which he is perpetually balanced: death. The image of death as the unknown into which man is about to be expelled, suddenly and violently, from the warm squalor of his present state is one of the dominant themes of Beckett's novels. The helpless, mutilated, moribund old men who populate them are in fact also helpless fetuses in nameless dread of the cataclysm of such a second birth.

The eponymous hero of *Murphy* (1938), Beckett's second work of fiction (and one of the greatest comic novels in the English language), still inhabits a recognizable world: West Brompton, the World's End (on the fringes of Chelsea) and Brewery Road, between Pentonville Prison and the Metropolitan Cattle Market. Murphy is an Irishman trying to lose himself in London (as Beckett did when he threw up his post at Trinity College after a few terms of teaching), pursued by a number of others who want to bring him back to respectability. His chief pursuer however is Celia, the charming prostitute who loves Murphy, wants to marry him and is trying to make him take up work, so that she can give up her own profession. But when he finally does find a congenial job as a male nurse at the Magdalen Mental Mercy-seat, he is so enthralled by the superior state of mind of the patients that he is doubly and irrevocably lost to Celia and the world. Every hour in the wards of the mental hospital increases,

> together with his esteem for the patients [Murphy's] loathing of
> the text-book attitude towards them, the complacent scientific
> conceptualism that made contact with outer reality the index of

mental well-being. . . . The definition of outer reality, or of reality short and simple, varied according to the sensibility of the definer. But all seemed agreed that contact with it, even the layman's muzzy contact, was a rare privilege. On this basis the patients were described as "cut off" from reality. . . . The function of treatment was to bridge the gulf, translate the sufferer from his own pernicious little private dungheap to the glorious world of discrete particles, where it would be his inestimable prerogative once again to wonder, love, hate, desire, rejoice and howl in a reasonable balanced manner and comfort himself with the society of others in the same predicament. All this was duly revolting to Murphy, whose experience as a physical and rational being obliged him to call sanctuary what the psychiatrists called exile and to think of the patients not as banished from a system of benefits but as escaped from a colossal fiasco. (*Murphy*, pp. 176–78)

Playing chess with a hypomanic, Murphy has a mystical experience. He "began to see nothing, that colorlessness which is such a rare postnatal treat, being the absence (to abuse a nice distinction) not of *percipere* but of *percipi*. His other senses also found themselves at peace, an unexpected pleasure. Not the numb peace of their own suspension, but the positive peace that comes when the somethings give way, or perhaps simply add up, to the Nothing, than which in the guffaw of the Abderite naught is more real." (*ibid.*, p. 246).

Soon after this, in a gas explosion, Murphy dies. His ashes are taken back to Dublin, but before they can be disposed of in the manner willed by Murphy, they are scattered on the floor of a pub in a brawl.

In *Murphy* we can clearly discern an important element of Beckett's literary inheritance: the bitterness, the hatred of the physical side of existence, which can be traced back to that other great Protestant Irishman, Swift.

What Beckett has in common with Swift is the combination of the deepest moral earnestness and artistic integrity with what in its essence is a comic talent. However much he may appear to be exploring the depths of human squalor and degradation, Beckett always remains a master of sardonic humor. Those critics who accuse him of unrelieved gloom and pessimism merely reveal that they lack the sense organs required to see how hilariously funny much of Beckett's vision can be: the audiences who rocked with laughter at *Waiting for Godot* had a very much clearer perception of the true nature of Beckett's genius—which lies precisely in his ability to produce the liberating catharsis of laughter by confronting his public not only with the sordidness of the human condition but also with a vision of its utter pettiness and inanity: that is why Beckett calls Demokritos' saying about the reality of nothingness a guffaw. When we see that all is vanity we can laugh even at the horrors of existence.

From the real Dublin of the Belacqua stories and the real London of *Murphy*, Beckett's own progressive retreat from external reality led him into a world of myth and allegory: the world of *Watt* (written 1943–1945). Mr. Knott's farmhouse where Watt, the pathetic, ageless tramp, mysteriously finds work as a servant—only to lose it again as mysteriously when the allotted time is up—lies in a Kafka-country with an admixture of Irish colors and Irish humor. Mr. Knott is mysterious and unpredictable: his world is ruled according to iron laws that are as inexorable as they are absurd; it is a delicate mechanism each part of which is intricately geared to all others, but at its center there is complete arbitrariness and absurdity. Two dogs are kept especially to eat Mr. Knott's surplus food, for example, but sometimes there is no surplus food from Mr. Knott's table for long periods and the dogs die. Sometimes there is too much: then the dogs die from overeating. So there is a complicated and intricately organized machinery for the replacement and care of these dogs: a whole family devoted to this service. The endless permutations of Mr. Knott's systems are echoed in the permutations of Watt's own thought, always deeply preoccupied with reasoning out the changing possibilities of intricate situations. This preoccupation with permutations, of which Molloy's sucking stones are perhaps the best-known example, is a recurring feature of Beckett's mind. Molloy had sixteen stones distributed in four pockets: "Taking a stone from the right pocket of my greatcoat, and putting it in my mouth, I replaced it in the right pocket of my greatcoat by a stone from the right pocket of my trousers, which I replaced by a stone from the left pocket of my trousers, which I replaced by a stone from the left pocket of my greatcoat, which I replaced by the stone which was in my mouth, as soon as I had finished sucking it. Thus there were still four stones in each of the four pockets, but not quite the same stones." (*Molloy*, in *Three Novels*, p. 69). Such permutations (and the example quoted is only the beginning of a long and involved calculation of probabilities) are a symbol of reality in flux, at the same time being a form of compulsion neurosis and a sheet anchor of the mind. In *Watt* the universe keeps its stability through a number of such series, "the series of dogs, the series of men, the series of pictures." It is the stability of permanence through flux. "Watt had more and more the impression, as time passed, that nothing could be added to Mr. Knott's establishment, and from it nothing taken away, but that as it was now so it had been in the beginning, and so it would remain to the end. . . . Yes, nothing changed in Mr. Knott's establishment, because nothing remained, and nothing came or went, because all was a coming and a going" (*Watt*, pp. 144–145).

Watt, written while Beckett himself, hiding as a member of the Resistance, worked as a farm laborer in the neighborhood of Avignon, marks the transition from conventional narrative to the mythological present of his French novels. Among the *parerga* and addenda to *Watt*, there is a short poem in which Beckett has summed up the book as follows:

Watt will not
abate one jot
but of what

of the coming to
of the being at
of the going from
Knott's habitat

of the long way
of the short stay
of the going back home
the way he had come

of the empty heart
of the empty hands
of the dim mind wayfaring
through barren lands

of a flame with dark winds
hedged about
going out
gone out. . . (p. 276)

These verses state the themes of Beckett's subsequent work: dim minds "wayfaring through barren lands," the flame of life hedged about with dark winds—and going out.

At the end of the war, and after a brief visit to Ireland, Beckett returned to his home in Paris. He began to write in French and, between 1945 and 1950, produced the fruits of the most creative period of his life: the novels *Molloy, Malone meurt, L'Innommable, Mercier et Camier*, the three stories and thirteen fragments collected in the volume *Nouvelles et textes pour rien*, as well as three plays, *Eleutheria* (unpublished), *En attendant Godot*, and *Fin de partie*. Of these, the trilogy of novels is undoubtedly the most important, the centerpiece of Beckett's *oeuvre*.

Molloy (1951) is a curiously constructed book. It consists of two parts of almost exactly equal length. In the first, Molloy, a lame and dim-witted tramp on a bicycle, is in search of his hometown and his mother. In the second, Moran, a suburbanite bourgeois, receives the order of a mysterious organization, whose agent he is, to set out in search of Molloy. He leaves his home with his son, fails to find Molloy, and suffers a curious change: at the end when he is back home he walks on crutches like Molloy.

Molloy is a book rich in comic incident: the lame, barely conscious tramp, lost in the town he believes to be his own hometown yet cannot recognize or remember, constantly frustrated in his quest, appears as a latter-day Ulysses trying to reach the haven of his home; like Ulysses he is held captive for a while by a woman—an old lady whose dog he has run over with his bicycle and who now tries to mother the old tramp instead. There is, at the same time, a mystical, religious element in Molloy's quest: the idea of going to see his mother comes to him when he sees two men meeting at some deserted crossroads. He later refers to them as the two thieves; thus, they may represent the fifty-fifty chance of salvation which so fascinates Beckett and which also plays so important a part in *Waiting for Godot*. The origin of this pattern of thought is the saying of Saint Augustine that calls upon mankind not to despair, for one of the thieves on the cross was saved, nor to exult, for one of them was damned.

That Moran is another aspect of Molloy can hardly be doubted. When Moran receives the order, through Gaber the messenger, from Youdi the mysterious boss, to seek out Molloy, he recognizes that he knows him already, and yet "I had no information as to his face. I assume it was hirsute, craggy and grimacing. Nothing justified my doing so" (*Molloy* in *Three Novels*, p. 114). And yet Moran has been visited by Molloy: "This was how he came to me, at long intervals. Then I was nothing but uproar, bulk, rage, suffocation, effort unceasing, frenzied and vain. Just the opposite of myself, in fact. It was a change" (*ibid.*). Moreover, Moran quite clearly states, "my own natural end, and I was resolved to have no other, would it not at the same time be his?" (*ibid.*). So Moran conjures up an image of Molloy from the dark recesses of his own mind. But Molloy has multiple aspects.

> Between the Molloy I stalked within me thus and the true Molloy, after whom I was so soon to be in full cry, over hill and dale, the resemblance cannot have been great. I was annexing perhaps already, without my knowing it, to my private Molloy, elements of the Molloy described by Gaber. The fact was, there were three, no, four, Molloys. He that inhabited me, my caricature of same, Gaber's and the man of flesh and blood somewhere awaiting me. To these I would add Youdi's were it not for Gaber's corpse fidelity to the letter of his messages. Bad reasoning. For could it seriously be supposed that Youdi had confided to Gaber all he knew, or thought he knew . . . about his protégé? Assuredly not . . . I will therefore add a fifth Molloy, that of Youdi. . . . There were others too, of course. But let us leave it at that. . . . And let us not meddle either with the question as to how far these five Molloys were constant and how far subject to variation. For there was this about Youdi that he changed his mind with great facility (*ibid.*, pp. 115–16).

Is Molloy, then, the subconscious part of Moran's own personality—which is the opposite to himself and, when released, drives him to uproar and frenzy? Is it that part of himself of which he can only get a caricatured image, but which can also be perceived differently by the outside world and by God himself, who, capricious and arbitrary, can make everything change as everything receives its being by *His* be-holding it? Is the book the twofold quest of the subconscious in search of its resting place, the peace of oblivion, and the conscious mind's quest for the subconscious?

It is easy to go too far and to interpret a complex poetic image, such as is presented by *Molloy*, too closely or too literally. Let it be said that these are elements in the picture, but they are themes woven into a symphony; they sometimes rise to the surface, sometimes they are overlaid by others that belong to the pattern which constitutes the whole but must forever remain complex, ambiguous, multidimension-al, and therefore incapable of being reduced to an interpretation in purely conceptual terms. The meaning of a poetic structure of this kind is coterminous with its expression: its ambiguities, hidden paral-lelism, associations, and assonances *are* its meaning. Thus Molloy is Molloy and Moran, Moran; and yet, as Moran says, Molloy is within him.

Molloy's quest for his mother ends in a ditch. His mind goes back to his encounter with the two travelers, the two thieves. He longs to re-turn to the forest; but then he takes that statement back. "Molloy could stay, where he happened to be." In fact, he has reached his goal. For, as the opening sentence of the book informs us, he is writing his story in his mother's room.

As for Moran, his report starts with the words: "It is midnight. The rain is beating on the windows." He too is writing a report. But the last words of his section of the book return to the opening passage. They run: "Then I went back into the house and wrote, It is midnight. The rain is beating on the windows. It was not midnight. It was not raining" (*ibid.*, p. 176).

Thus, the last sentence of the book casts doubts on the veracity of Moran's whole report. Or does it? Is this not rather an indication that Molloy and Moran themselves, aspects both of one personality, are also, in the last resort, mere emanations of a third personality—Beck-ett's own . . ?

In *Malone meurt* (1951) the arbitrary nature of the names and per-sonalities in Beckett's work is even more clearly apparent. Malone, an old man lying somewhere in a hospital or asylum, is dying. He amuses himself by making up stories about people he remembers or invents.

Like Molloy and Moran, like Beckett himself, Malone, in his dying moments, is under a compulsion to write down his thoughts, his fantasies, his memories. We hear about Saposcat, the prim and proper boy, and the Lamberts, a squalid family of farmers, and MacMann, another old and infirm man in an asylum, with his keeper and later his lover, Moll—and after Moll's death Lemuel: but then "the Murphys, Merciers, Molloys, Morans and Malones" also make an appearance. Here then is Malone, making up names and characters. But he himself in exactly the same manner, is being made up by the author of the book. Moran may have been in search of his deeper, hidden self, Molloy. But so is Beckett whose own search for his self led to the creation of them all.

For it is this search for the answer to the question: "Who am I?" or "What am I saying when I say I?" that provides the impulse for Beckett's explorations. The multiplicity of Molloys that Moran was confronted with when asked by the messenger of a higher power to find him constitutes the basic problem behind this search. What is the self? It is not outward circumstance—for that can change. It is not appearance—that too can change. Is it what I believe to be myself? That may be an illusion. Is it everything that I can think of and imagine, including all the vast crowd of characters I can make up? It is to scoop up all these, in all their infinite possibility, that Beckett is compelled to write. That is why, in one of the very enigmatic and yet highly revealing *Textes pour rien*, he says of his life, "Words, mine [*i.e.* my life] was never more than that, than this pell-mell babel of silence and words, my viewless form described as ended, or to come, or still in progress, depending on the words, the moments, long may it last in that singular way. Apparitions, keepers, what childishness, and ghouls, to think I said ghouls, do I as much as know what they are, of course I don't, and how the intervals are filled, as if I didn't know, as if there were two things, some other thing besides this thing, what is it, this unnamable thing that I name and name and never wear out, and I call that words" (*Texts for Nothing*, VI). Or again, summing it all up in another passage:

> Where would I go, if I could go, who would I be, if I could be, what would I say, if I had a voice, who says this, saying it's me? . . . . He tells his story every five minutes, saying it is

not his, there's cleverness for you. . . . . . . He has me say things saying it's not me, there's profundity for you, he has me who say nothing say it's not me. All that is truly crass. If at least he would dignify me with the third person, like his other figments, not he, he'll be satisfied with nothing less than me, for his me. . . . . . . His life, what a mine, what a life, he can't have that, you can't fool him, ergo it's not his, it's not him, what a thought, treat him like that, like a vulgar Molloy, a common Malone, those mere mortals, happy mortals, have a heart, land him in that shit who never stirred, who is none but me, all things considered. (*Texts for Nothing*, IV)

Textes pour rien was to be a further and even more daring foray into the region to which Beckett had penetrated in the third novel of his great trilogy, *L'Innommable* (1953). Going to the very limits, it provides an illuminating commentary to that most elusive of Beckett's books, but also perhaps his greatest achievement.

Here it is no longer Molloy speaking or Moran or Malone: and we have also left the half-world of mythology and allegory. The voice that is now speaking is a voice that, like the one we heard in the passages from *Textes pour rien*, is unnamable because it is the voice of a self in search of its own identity. For what is the self? The part that is speaking? Or the part that is listening? There is not *one* voice in our minds, but a multitude of voices, a complex conversation of speakers, listeners, observers, critics—some vocal, some silent. It is thus as a matrix of possibilities that *we* must see our own consciousness, and the subconscious layers that lie beneath it. In *L'Innommable* it is that unnamable voice speaking, the voice of that deepest, unidentifiable self. "I am neither, I needn't say, Murphy, nor Watt, nor Mercier, not—no I can't even bring myself to name them, nor any of the others whose very names I forget, who told me I was they, who I must have tried to be, under duress, or through fear, or to avoid acknowledging me" (*The Unnamable*, in *Three Novels*, p. 328).

All these personalities, with their infirmities, their difficulty in moving about, their poverty and simplicity of mind, have only been explorations of the self, attempts to divest it of accidentals, experiments designed to see what would remain of the self if it were lame and dull-witted, without status in the world, a tramp without a home, alone, unsupported, abandoned . . . sick, dying, covered in sores, half-blind . . . What would remain? The essence and true nature of the self?

In *L'Innommable* that exploration is carried on—but now quite openly, with the cards laid on the table. "All these Murphys, Molloys and Malones do not fool me. They have made me waste my time, suffer for nothing, speak of them, *when*, in order to stop speaking, I should have spoken of me, and of me alone . . . I thought I was right in enlisting these sufferers of my pains. I was wrong. They never suffered my pains, their pains are nothing, compared to mine, a mere tittle of mine, the tittle I thought I could put from me, in order to witness it. Let them be gone now, them and all the others, those I have used and those I have not used, give me back the pains I lent them and vanish, for my life, my memory, my terrors and shames" (*ibid.*, pp. 305–306). Now therefore, if, in the course of the search, another self has to be experimented with, it is quite openly presented as a fantasy. Is this new self to be called Basil? "Decidedly Basil is becoming important, I'll call him Mahood instead, I prefer that, I'm queer. It was he told me stories about me, lived in my stead, issued forth from me, came back to me, entered back into me" (*ibid.*, p. 311).

Mahood is a limbless creature, living in a jar, on the corner of some Paris street; so far has the self now been stripped down. But even this does not go far enough. However degraded and deprived Mahood is, he is the ruin of something that had a definite shape. The time has come to go one step further and to explore the self as pure potentiality—as the unborn, not yet determined case of humanity. "Quick give me a mother and let me suck her white, pinching my tits. But it's time I gave this solitary a name, nothing doing without proper names. I therefore baptize him Worm . . . Before Mahood there were others like him, of the same breed and creed, armed with the same prong. But Worm is the first of his kind" (*ibid.*, p. 340).

But after Worm's situation has been explored, the narrator can discard him too, as he has discarded Mahood.

> Mahood, he was called Mahood, I don't see him any more. I don't know how he lived any more, he isn't there any more, he was never there in his jar, I never saw him, and yet I remember, I remember having talked about him, the same words recur and they are your memories. It is I invented him, him and so many

others, and the places where they passed, the places where they stayed, in order to speak, since I had to speak, without speaking of me. I couldn't speak of me, I was never told I had to speak of me, I invented my memories, not knowing what I was doing, not one is of me. It is they asked me to speak of them, they wanted to know what they were, how they lived, that suited me. (*ibid.*, p. 399).

The compulsion to speak. Their voices incessantly demanding to be heard. The multitude of selves that ask to speak and to be spoken of. Nothing would be easier than to present this as a clinical picture of neurosis or psychosis. Nothing could be more wrong and more misguided. These tendencies certainly are present, but—and this is the point—they have been magnificently sublimated and turned into a work of art. The wound was there, but so was the genius to heal it, to make it fruitful and a source of healing power for others. The deeper and the more real the wound, the greater the achievement of the mind that could make the aching tissues grow and close the scar. All fiction is in the last resort a matter of voices within the writer that ask to be heard, parts of his own personality that become detached and start a dialogue. But there has been no other writer so deeply possessed and compelled and, at the same time, so triumphantly detached that he could dare to face the problem of the self in all its vertigo, its infinite recession of self-reflecting mirrors.

In Beckett's great trilogy we witness the process of the exploration. We start with fiction and we end in the most ruthless self-revelation, the agony of a soul in search of its own identity. There has been speculation as to why so many of the names in Beckett's novels start with M: Murphy, Molloy, Malone, MacMann, Mahood; there have been those who thought M may have stood for *Man*. This is to underrate the subtlety and complexity of Beckett's mind—and of his real theme. In fact the M is a Greek sigma stood on its side. The sigma stands for Beckett's own first name: Sam. And so, of course, the other way about, does the W of Watt and Worm:

I thought I was free to say any old thing, so long as I didn't go silent. Then I said to myself that after all it wasn't any old thing, the thing I was saying, that it might well be the thing demanded of me, assuming something was being demanded of me. . . I did what I could, a thing beyond my strength, and often for exhaustion I gave up doing it, and yet it went on being done, the voice being heard, the voice which could not be mine, since I had none left, and yet which could only be mine, since I could not go silent, and since I was alone, in a place where no voice could reach me. Yes, in my life, since we must call it so, there were three things, the inability to speak, the inability to be silent, and solitude, that's what I've had to make the best of. Yes, *now* I can speak of my life. (*ibid.*, p. 400)

L'Innommable is thus the culminating point of a progressive exploration of the self: it reveals, in the end, that very center of nothingness, that state of pure potentiality by which Sartre defines Being-for-Itself. The multitude of characters and personalities which the narrator's voice can assume and conjure up from the void represent so many choices of being, but the core of the self is pure potentiality, *le néant*, that very nothingness that Murphy delighted in when he had escaped from all his commitments, that pure potentiality represented by Worm, man about to be born. There is no evidence to indicate, and it seems unlikely, that Beckett has ever been consciously influenced by Sartre's philosophy. His genius is far too personal, his method of creation far too compulsive, to allow him to model his writing on some philosophy he may have heard of or read about. It is all the more remarkable that, without doubt, Beckett is the greatest creative writer ever to have put this aspect of existential philosophy into the concrete shape of a work of art. It is as though by some mysterious osmosis the currents of abstract thought and creative vision in our time had interpenetrated each other.

It seemed almost impossible, after *L'Innommable*, to continue on the path of ruthless self-exploration. *Textes pour rien*, as we have already pointed out, was an attempt at going on in the same direction. It produced some of the most beautiful pieces of Beckett's prose poetry (for all of Beckett's writing, it must never be forgotten, is poetry, with sweeping rhythms and complex patterns of sound and imagery) but was doomed to stay unfinished.

After the five years of his creative frenzy that culminated in *L'Innommable* and *Textes pour rien*, there followed a period of silence in French. After the great public acclaim of his play, *En attendant*

Godot, Beckett returned to writing in English. He wrote a number of radio plays, the work on which he regarded as a relaxation, as they did not probe the depths or demand the effort that he associates with his work in French.

The novel *Comment c'est* (1961), however, does represent both a continuation of his previous efforts and a new beginning. Written without a single punctuation mark and in strophic paragraphs of varied length, this strange book fuses the mythical elements of *Watt* and *Molloy* with the *motif* of the compelling voice we find in *L'Innommable* and *Textes pour rien* in a vision of truly Swiftian bitterness.

The voice is heard by an again unnamed narrator. He is, or perhaps only tells the story of, an old man who painfully makes his way, crawling on all fours, through a sea of mud (*E fango è il mondo*—the world is mud, was the quotation from Leopardi that Beckett used as the motto for his study of Proust thirty years earlier). The little old man, who does not know how or why he got into his prostrate position, drags with him a little sack filled with tins of fish from which he derives his sustenance—thanks to his possession of a tin opener which he is in constant dread of losing. Visions from a world of light sometimes penetrate the darkness. And then, so the voice goes on, in intervals of incessant panting which pervade the whole book the wayfarer in the mud (or is it a vast sea of excrement?) suddenly touches another human figure. Is it alive? Or dead? When poked with the tin opener, it screams—or sings?—so it is alive. Another little old man, face downwards, crawling through the mud. His name is Pim. For a brief span the two prostrate figures lie alongside each other. The narrator learns that he can make Pim talk by hurting him with the tin opener, and can make him shut up by pushing his face into the mud. Having thus learned how to manipulate his partner, he makes him tell him what he remembers of his life in the world of light, memories of his wife, Pam Prim, and their loves. . . . The narrator loves Pim, who is his victim and whom he torments. He is happy, "c'était de bons moments." But then the inexorable laws of nature assert themselves. By a curious, and to himself inexplicable *tropisme*, the narrator is compelled to crawl on, pursuing a preordained course. Pim is left behind. In the third part the narrator, or the voice who speaks through the panting, speculates on the laws that govern their world. Perhaps there are hundreds of thousands crawling through the mud along a preordained route and meeting, at regular intervals, others crawling in the opposite direction. Perhaps each is destined to be executioner and victim in turn in an endless chain of fleeting relationships, between those who stick tin openers into their victims and those who are thus made to sing. . . . And that perhaps is how it is, *comment c'est*. . .

Beckett's work is entirely *sui generis*, unclassifiable, disturbing, funny, cruel, and inspiring. It defies all attempts at interpretation—like the world of atomic particles where the introduction of an observer itself changes that which is to be observed. Like Michelangelo, who chipped away the rock to reveal the delicate beauty that had always been imprisoned within it, Beckett works by discarding layer upon layer of conventional narrative material: description, character, psychology, incident, plot, to lay bare the secret workings of the human mind. But here too he can only work as it were, by measuring out the limits of the sayable so that the unsayable may be guessed, hidden behind the last, impenetrable barrier.

Beckett's novels and plays are not easily accessible. They must be approached with due humility, read more than once, wrestled with and fought for. Beckett is a poet working for his own salvation. Public relations and an easy urbanity in the presentation of his work are not included in his basic brief.

And yet, although he has made no effort at achieving fame or creating a following, he has become famous and has won relatively wide support. Perhaps the most difficult writer of his generation, he has reached his public as a dramatist, as a writer of the most poetic radio plays of his time, and as a novelist. This is a fact that goes a long way towards restoring one's faith in the power of the dedicated pursuit of truth and beauty.

Here is a poet who has never made the slightest concession, never sought acclaim, never explained himself, who has never bowed to the demands of fashion or publicity. He merely said what he felt himself compelled to say. What he had to say was difficult, obscure, repellent (for the landscapes of the mind he has revealed were bound at first to appear as horrid and frightening as the dark valleys and ravines of the Alps before their sombre beauty was accepted at large). But, because he had something real and important to say, he has not lacked those who come, eager to hear him.

Beckett's Poems—Some Random Notes

Of all of Samuel Beckett's writing, the slim corpus of his poetry contains his most directly autobiographical utterance. Which is not to say that it yields its secrets easily to all comers. Like a shipwrecked sailor who possesses only a tiny scrap of paper to entrust to the bottle he will fling into the sea and who has to fit the largest possible amount of information about his position into the smallest possible space, Beckett's poems are compressed to the point of being in code. A single line may carry multiple meanings, public and private allusions, description and symbol, topographical reference, snatches of overheard conversations, fragments in other languages, Provençal or German, the poet's own personal asides (like "main verb at last" at the end of a long sentence in *Sanies I*), learned literary allusions together with brand names of cigarettes or shop signs in Dublin. Four lines may thus require four pages of elucidation, provided, that is, that the full information were at hand, could ever be fully elicited.

Yet with the magic of all true poetry, which is mystery, incantation, miraculous pattern of wonder-working words, this poetry compels the reader to read on, to immerse himself and, having entered into the poem, find his way through its internal labyrinth; from one revealed fragment of sense to the next glimpse of meaning, until at the center of the maze, a distant vision of the ultimate pattern beckons.

Take—in Beckett's first-published and most self-consciously allusive poem, *Whoroscope*, in which, ostensibly, it is not Beckett who speaks, but Descartes—René du Perron—the lines: "So we drink Him and eat Him / and the watery Beaune and the stale cubes of Hovis."

Could there be a clearer, a more immediately concrete, sensual image of the Eucharist—with the contrast between the biblical solemnity of the first, the bathetic, descriptive objectivity of the second line, and the added irony of the calculated anachronism (for Beaune might have been marketed in 1650, though I doubt whether under that *appellation contrôlée*; Hovis most certainly was not)! Ponder those lines and gradually the whole complex structure of the poem will begin to yield its meaning . . .

Or in *Enueg I* take the image as the poet reaches Chapelizod on his walk, the lines about

> the Isolde Stores a great perturbation of sweaty heroes
> in their Sunday best,
> come hastening down for a pint of nepenthe or moly or half and
> half
> from watching the hurlers above in Kilmainham.

There is, I am told, a store dispensing drink in Chapelizod called the Isolde Stores (-*izod* in the place-name being a reference to Iseult, they were so called after the Wagnerian version of that Irish heroine's name) . . . And in the same poem the picture of "at Parnell Bridge a dying barge / carrying a cargo of nails and timber."

We were in a broadcasting studio preparing a reading of the poem in Beckett's presence. At this point he asked the reader to put a little more stress on the nails and the timber, which, after all, stood for the cross. So intimately is the descriptive linked with the symbolic in these poems! One is tempted to wonder if the proximity of Parnell's name is not also intentional, as that of another savior crucified . . .

Or in the poem entitled *Malacoda*, in which that Dantean monster stands for the undertaker who buried Beckett's father, the description of three stages of the undertaker's appearance in the house—*to measure* the body, *to coffin* it so that it can lie in state, and *to cover* it— coupled with the poet's concern to keep the proceedings from his mother, who, at the first stage, "hear she may see she need not"; at the second, "hear she must see she need not"; while at the third, "hear she must see she must." In the same poem the lines—"lay this Huysum on the box / mind the imago it is he"—can be made to yield their meaning when one realizes that the Huysum referred to is the Dutch painter Jan van Huysum (1682–1749) who specialized in pictures of flowers and butterflies, reproductions of which were placed on coffins, and that the imago here meant therefore is the butterfly in the picture (larva, pupa, and imago being the three stages of insect development) and that imago "is he"—the dead father, who has emerged from the pupal stage of life into the imago phase of death (or afterlife). Hence the poem ends with the lines:

> all aboard all souls
> half-mast aye aye
> nay

The final nay *denies* the hope of everlasting life after death. And so, incidentally, those five final lines of a poem published by 1935 contain and foreshadow the contents of an entire later novel—*Malone Dies*.

Even more astonishing in its anticipation of the future *argument* of Beckett's complete *oeuvre* to come is the six-line poem *The Vulture*, which opens the slim volume *Echo's Bones and Other Precipitates* of which 327 copies were published in 1935. For this vulture is Death, which drags its hunger through the sky of the poet's skull, that vast internal cavity, that shell which contains the whole world, the sky as well as the earth, that internal universe which also encloses those prone figures of the poet's imagination who will in his future works drag themselves through afflictions of all kind and therefore soon must take up their life and walk, mocked by the tissue of the poet's brain which may not serve as food to the vulture, Death, till that brain itself with all the hunger, all the earth and sky it contains, has died and turned into offal.

> dragging his hunger through the sky
> of my skull shell of sky and earth
>
> stooping to the prone who must
> soon take up their life and walk
>
> mocked by a tissue that may not serve
> till hunger earth and sky be offal

There seems, moreover in the image of the vulture—and here we have a measure of Beckett's learning, the richness of the store of allusions he can draw on—a definite reference to Goethe's poem *Harzreise im Winter*, which opens with the words:

> Like the Vulture
> Who, with feathery wing
> Rests on the morning's
> Heavy cloudbanks,
> Eying his victim,
> Soar up my song.

and which contains this passage about the artist as a lonely outsider who suffers the isolation and lovelessness of so many Beckett heroes:

> Easy it is to follow the chariot
> Driven by Fortune
> Like the leisurely train
> On mended roads
> Of a Prince's progress.

> But who is it that stands
> Apart?
> His path is lost in the thicket
> Behind him the bushes
> Close up,
> The grass stands again
> Deserts engulf him.

> Oh who heals the sorrow
> Of him, whose balm turned to poison?
> Who drank misanthropy
> Out of love's flood?

Beckett's poem about the vulture consists of no more than six lines. Yet these six lines open up, through allusion, a vast treasure-house of the past, while, at the same time, forecasting all of Beckett's writing which was yet to come.

> peering out of my deadlight looking for another
> wandering like me eddying far from all the living
> in a convulsive space

among the voices voiceless
that throng my hiddenness

These lines from a poem (originally written in French), dated 1948, echo not only Beckett's own verses of *The Vulture* itself, but Goethe's also. The original French text sums up Beckett's narrative writings even more clearly:

dans un espace pantin
sans voix parmi les voix
enfermées avec moi

It is in Beckett's plays, stories and novels that we hear those voices that are enclosed within the world of his skull tell the stories of those prone figures who must take up their life and walk. In his *poems*, however, we briefly hear the voice of Samuel Beckett himself. He may argue, and indeed is almost certain to argue, that those voices spring from deeper levels of experience, that the Self which we glimpse walking through Dublin, London, and Paris, over Parnell Bridge, and through Regents Park or the Rue Mouffetard, is a more superficial, external Self than that which finds expression in the unceasing drone of those voices. And while we must inevitably agree with this view and accept that, once those voices had begun to speak loudly and clearly, the private, personal, and more external poetry had to cease, we cannot but treasure Beckett's poems for the glimpses they give us of the rare, ascetic, and saintly personality from which those voices issued forth.

And indeed, all of Beckett's writing is ultimately poetry, if poetry be defined as a structure of language in which the manner of the saying is of equal importance with the matter that is said, in which, indeed, the manner of saying and the matter said completely and organically coincide. In that sense Beckett's prose and plays also are poetry: structures of words so intricately, so delicately balanced that the removal of a single one would cause the whole edifice to lose its symmetry.

When the voices asserted their right to speak, Beckett himself stopped writing verse. But occasionally the voices themselves speak in verse. And that verse is as concise, as economical, as profound and essential as Beckett's personal poetry. Can there be a more memorable summing up of that basic image of all of Beckett's *oeuvre*—the final equation of *Birth* into a world unfathomable to the frightened being on the threshold of life, and *Death*, that terrified emergence into another unfathomable, unknowable state of being—than the final poem composed by the voice called Words in *Words and Music*?

Then down a little way
Through the trash
Towards where
All dark no begging
No giving no words
No sense no need
Through the scum
Down a little way
To whence one glimpse
Of that wellhead.

A Theatre of Stasis—Beckett's Late Plays

Pozzo and Lucky are the only characters in Beckett's stage plays who move freely through the landscape. Vladimir and Estragon, with whom they are contrasted in *Waiting for Godot*, are waiting and, in that capacity, rooted to one spot. In the last two lines of the play they announce their intention to go away. But the final stage direction puts paid to that intention: "*They do not move.*" The man in *Act Without Words I*, who is flung backwards onto the stage at the start of that mime play, demonstrates one of the processes by which immobility of this kind is induced: all his attempts to reach his objective, the carafe of water with which he might quench his thirst, are frustrated; so that even when "the carafe descends from the flies and comes to rest a few feet from his body. *He does not move.*"

In *Endgame* Hamm is immobile in his chair. Clov can move, indeed he must, as he cannot sit. But he can move only within the narrow confines of the play's circular room. If he leaves, he dies. At the end of the play he is dressed to leave but does not, or cannot, go. "He halts by the door and stands there, *impassive and motionless* . . . till the end." And Nagg and Nell are confined in their bins.

Krapp moves freely within his room; but we know that he never ventures out. And he listens to his *own voice* on tapes from his past.

In *Happy Days* Winnie is rooted in the earth, like a tree and sinking deeper and deeper. The three characters of *Play* are stuck in urns, only their heads protrude from them. And the words they utter, fragments of memory and meditation, are, we gradually realize, rigidly patterned: when they have all been uttered, they are uttered again, and then, as the play closes, the whole sequence seems to start again; no doubt it will continue to be spoken in that order and in that pattern through all eternity.

Flo, Vi, and Ru, the three women in the dramaticule, *Come and Go*, seem to be able to move; each of them, in turn, leaves the stage for a moment, but the pattern of their going and coming is so rigid that there can be no doubt that it is, also, set for all time, an endless ritual permutation.

In Beckett's most recent plays, this movement to stricter and stricter patterns seems to have carried him towards a new and far more austere form of drama: not only have his plays become more and more concise, they have also shed the notion of *characters in action* which is so often regarded as the basic minimum definition of drama itself. In *Not I* our attention is focused on no more than a *mouth* from which words issue. Admittedly, there is an Auditor of indeterminate sex who listens to the mouth, and, four times, makes a "gesture of helpless compassion." But he seems almost a representative of the audience itself. In *That Time* we see no more than a face, that of a character termed by the author, "the Listener," suspended "about ten feet above stage level midstage off centre." It is the face of an old man with long white hair. Three voices—all of them the Listener's own—are heard from three distinct sources at both sides of the stage and directly above him.

A mouth without a face or body, then, on the one hand: a mouth, merely as the orifice from which a voice issues; and, on the other, a face without a body, motionless except for the eyes, listening to voices. So thoroughly has the world been reduced to the essentials of consciousness and the self. In Beckett's third recent play, *Footfalls*, the process of concentration on the minimal essentials is different, but on very similar lines. Here the audience's attention is focused on a narrow strip downstage, which allows exactly seven (in a later version, nine) steps to be taken. A woman, disheveled, gray-haired, wearing a worn gray wrap which hides her feet, is pacing up and down on this strip, making a right-about-face turn when she reaches the left extremity, a left-about-face at its right limit. The lighting is dim throughout, but relatively strongest at floor level, "less on body, least on head." So we are concentrating on the feet hidden behind the trailing wrap. The woman, May, occasionally speaks to her—unseen—mother, and finally delivers a long speech straight into the audience. The mother's voice is heard from the dark, upstage. The action of *Footfalls* is clearly divided by long pauses in total darkness into three distinct sections: first, a dialogue between May and her unseen Mother; second, the mother's voice while May is pacing up and down (In other words: May hears her mother's voice within herself. The voice clearly says: "My voice is in her mind"); third, May, facing the audience tells a fragment of a story concerning a mother and a daughter, called Amy (an anagram of May). When darkness descends for the third time and, after a pause, the lights very faintly come up on the strip, there is no trace of May. For fifteen seconds the dim light remains on the empty strip on the ground, then the curtain comes down.

All three plays are monodramas. In each of them we are inside the mind of one human being. All three focus the attention on a portion of that human being's body: mouth, eyes, feet. All three achieve total stasis (for even pacing up and down within the narrow range of seven or nine steps amounts to immobility). All three are concerned with memories of a past life, before the final state of stasis afflicted the central characters. All three are very short, which is another way of saying that they are densely concentrated images of human existence, whittled down to the barest essentials, the stream of consciousness that constitutes the self's only awareness of its own being, a stream that essentially is a sequence of words carried on an inner voice.

If we compare these to Beckett's earlier plays we can see how they condense and concentrate elements that have always been present, but in a more diffuse, more traditionally theatrical form. Nell, after all, is Hamm's mother, and he hears her voice (no doubt not literally) emerging from a dustbin. That bin is merely there as a picturesque illustrative detail. In *Footfalls* the mother's voice remains; the dustbin, and the mother's face protruding from it, have been dispensed with as inessentials. Likewise in *Krapp's Last Tape* the tape recorder merely serves as an almost naturalistic device to make us accept Krapp's experience of his former selves. In *That Time* the voices of memory are still there, but the tape recorder has been discarded, as have Krapp's clownish antics as he puts the tapes on and off, the old man's eyes, opening and closing from time to time, are sufficient to give us the full impact of his reactions to his memories.

The stasis of these plays, far from being an absence of action, can thus be seen as, on the contrary, a concentration, condensation, and therefore maximal intensification of the tensions that make conventional plays dramatic. The real world has been left behind by these characters; but having, as it were, *fallen out* of it (in the manner of the inmates of the Magdalen Mental Mercyseat who so greatly impressed and affected Murphy; or of Watt in his pavilion who so intriguingly discoursed with Sam; or—indeed—in the manner of those victims of *encephalitis lethargica* and Parkinson's disease whom Dr. Oliver Sacks so movingly describes in his great book *Awakenings*, which often seems to be about characters from Beckett's plays and prose works), having fallen out of the world these characters carry within them the encapsulated essence of their life-experience, fused into a minimal number of key images. It is because these key images fully sum up the experiences of a complete life and because their number is a bare minimum, that they arrange themselves in rigidly structured patterns; they have become, as it were, the mathematical formulae which sum up a life; they have reached their briefest and most elegant formulation and can be retained, *must* be retained, by formalized repetition, in the way in which schoolboys remember rules of grammar by enshrining them in easily memorized rhymed patterns, mnemonic verses.

The immense dramatic tension in *Not I*, for instance, issues from the mouth's refusal, or inability, to acknowledge the experience it recounts as that of its own self. The words "Who? . . . no! . . . she!" are the recurring trigger that sets off the Auditor's gesture of helpless compassion. Highly concentrated and condensed though it is, the story the mouth tells contains the substance of a whole conventional full-length play or novel; it is the story of a life without love (hence, perhaps, so passively experienced that it was never felt to be a life lived by the self, but rather something which was passively endured like someone else's experience). The degree of concentration may be judged by just one example: what, in a conventional form, detailing all accidentals, might fill several chapters, here emerges as "out . . . into this world . . . this world . . . tiny little thing . . . before its time . . . in a god-for- . . . what? . . . girl? . . . Yes . . . tiny little girl . . . into this . . .

out into this . . . before her time . . . godforsaken hole called . . . called . . . no matter . . . parents unknown . . . unheard of . . . he having vanished . . . thin air . . . no sooner buttoned up his breeches . . . she similarly . . . eight months later . . . almost to the tick . . . so no love . . . spared that." The supreme artistry behind this highly condensed form of writing lies in Beckett's ability to concentrate without ever becoming schematic or abstract. Note the way in which the place of birth is first mentioned as merely the beginning of the phrase about the "godforsaken hole," the way it is later fully uttered, only to be abandoned before the name of the place itself is pronounced. The minimalization of the actual storytelling is achieved by, as it were, deleting all but the most essentially visual portion of what might be a long descriptive paragraph ("no sooner buttoned up his trousers" is clearly the remnant of what in a more conventional genre would be a circumstantial description of the meeting, lovemaking and parting of the parents; but the six words which remain of it all clearly imply *all* the rest).

On closer examination the text of a short play like *Not I* thus unfolds like one of those Japanese paper flowers which gain form and color as they are immersed in water and soak up its expanding force. The person with whose story the mouth is concerned spent a long life, into her sixties, practically speechless, except for bouts of logorrhea in her childhood ("sudden urge to . . . tell . . . then rush out stop the first she saw . . . nearest lavatory . . . start pouring it out . . . steady stream.") Then, suddenly in her old age, words began pouring out of her. And it is this outpouring which constitutes the play.

The Listener in *That Time* hears three voices, all his own, in a steady flow, yet with each voice clearly distinguishable as slightly different: the first of these concentrates on the image of a memory of his return to a lonely ruin where he used to hide as a child; at a much later stage in his life he had returned there, from overseas ("straight off the ferry") and had almost immediately fled back to where he had come from: the second voice describes a series of flights from wandering the streets in the rain, to the National Portrait Gallery, or a public library, or a post office; the third one to be heard (B—hence, probably, the one which comes from above, center) dwells on a moment of love, the bodies of the lovers never touching, "on a stone together in the sun

121

. . . at the edge of a little wood as far as the eye could see the wheat turning yellow." The three images intertwine like the strands of melody in a symphony, recur and are varied into a tapestry with a clearly perceptible pattern of tensions, emotional colors, and structures of a life's essential experience: the child avidly reading in the old ruin as seen by the white-haired old man just off the boat, still carrying his nightbag; the sadness and bliss of the lovers in their summer landscape; and the rain outside, contrasted with the dust enveloping the library and the post office, the dark portraits staring at the fugitive from the street as he sits in the Portrait Gallery.

Compared with these clear and poetic fragments of memory the matter of *Footfalls* must appear mysterious, its message more heavily coded. Is Amy, the daughter about whom May speaks in the third section of the play (and whose mother is called Mrs. Winter), in fact the same as May herself? The story May tells in that third section is clearly a passage from a book—perhaps one that she (like Hamm in *Endgame*) is in the act of composing. And the dialogue that passage relates—to a "reader" who is directly apostrophized—culminates in Amy denying that she was present at evensong, which, however, she seems definitely to have attended in her mother's company. "I was not there," she categorically states in the story May recounts to the audience. Perhaps the emphasis here lies not so much on the word "there" as on "I"? Perhaps the phrase should be stressed: *I* was not there. In which case the name Amy might refer to the question *Am I?* And Amy's answer to her mother might simply indicate that there might have been someone there, but *Not I*. And if the name Amy might be so interpreted, might not the name May (its anagram) not also be seen as the auxiliary verb indicating potentiality or possibility of being? And then, in the second section of the play, when the mother's voice, which is in May's mind, speaks of her insistence that the carpet on the strip of floor on which she paces up and down be removed because she "must hear the feet, however faint they fall," might not that indicate that the daughter yearns for some proof of the existence of her merely potential self and can find its only concrete manifestation in hearing the rhythm of her steps on the bare floor? These are some questions the mysterious text raises; there are some deeper and more mysterious ones beneath and behind these. For something—*it*—*it all*—is occasionally referred to, which seems to have been the cause of all that pacing up and down. And in the first section the mother who is there said to be around ninety years old is clearly an invalid, requiring injections, the rearrangement of pillows, the administering of warming pans and bedpans, and the dressing of sores, sponging down and moistening of lips. For which the mother asks the daughter's forgiveness.

The key to the riddle probably lies in the recurring lines: "Will you never have done revolving it all. It? It all." It is the revolving, the incessant reliving of a traumatic key experience which clearly is the foundation of the insistent pattern of seven steps, turnabout, seven steps back, turnabout, seven steps . . . To revolve also means to turn about. The steps and turns are the expression of the event which is being turned about in May's (Amy's?) mind.

Economy—concentration upon essentials—is one of the hallmarks of supreme artistry. Throughout his life as a writer Beckett has striven to reach the utmost degree of economy and density. Dramatic forms of presentation tend to be more economical than mere narrative, for here the images, which need to be *described* in discursive prose, can be made concrete and instantly perceptible on the stage. Drama of the kind Beckett writes is poetry of concrete, three-dimensional stage images, complex metaphors communicable in a flash of visual intuitive understanding. For let there be no mistake about it: while Beckett's texts yield great insights to those who closely analyze them by repeated reading, that is not the manner in which they are meant to communicate to an audience. In plays like *Not I*, *That Time*, and *Footfalls*, it is by no means essential that the audience in the theatre should be able to decode the complex story lines and intellectual puzzles they enshrine. On the contrary, what the audience should experience and take home with them after their brief exposure to these dramatic metaphors is precisely the *overall impact* of a single overwhelmingly powerful image, composed of the startling visual element; the strange murmur of subdued voices in a dim half-light; the strange and powerful *rhythms* of both light and voices; the magical effect of the poetic phrasing and the richness of the images the language carries along on its relentless flow.

It is by making his images *unforgettable* through the startling novelty of their visual impact and the density of a multitude of linguistic, visual, and dramatic elements deployed at one and the same time at a multitude of levels, that Beckett reaches his audience. Many people who have seen *Not I* will never be able to forget the image of the mouth, a patch of light in the surrounding darkness, from which, as though it came from an unfathomable depth, the breathless hurried voice of Billie Whitelaw issued forth. Some of these may since have gone to the text and puzzled out the full story it contains. But far more important is the fact that the image of the mouth pouring out the contents of a mind has, for these spectators, crystallized and encapsulated one of the basic mysteries of human existence, the strange duality between body and mind of which the mouth is the manifest image: the mouth, which is the threshold between the material world and the immaterial world of consciousness; the mouth which thus becomes the symbol of the mystery of the self which *should* be the link between the body and its consciousness—but which, as the body is in constant change and the consciousness in constant flux, remains ever elusive.

Looked at from this point of view, Beckett's plays will appear as materializations, incarnations of some of the basic questions of our existence.

Samuel Beckett and the Art of Broadcasting

Samuel Beckett's work for broadcasting—five completed radio plays and three television plays—is a highly significant part of his *oeuvre* and far less fully discussed in the mounting literature on Beckett than his other output, far less readily available, also, in performance, which alone can bring out its full flavor. But beyond that, Beckett's experience with broadcasting, and above all radio, has played a significant and little-known part in his development as an artist.

It has become a kind of cliché of the Beckett literature that the BBC commissioned radio plays from Beckett. Even the cover of the first American publication of *All That Fall* and *Embers* in the Grove Press paperback, *Krapp's Last Tape and Other Dramatic Pieces* (1960), baldly states: "two radio plays commissioned by the BBC's Third Programme." Beckett himself has always strenuously denied that he writes plays on commission from anyone. And the truth is that he was, indeed, never commissioned by the BBC to write anything. The real story of the genesis of these radio plays is far more complex and interesting.

The first communication between Beckett and the BBC goes back to the period before his rise to fame as the author of *Waiting for Godot*. On June 1, 1952, Beckett sent P. H. Newby (then a talks producer, later to become Controller of the Third Programme, and later still, Director of Programs for Radio) the text of *Cascando*. The brief note from Beckett stands forlorn and unexplained in the file. Clearly this was not the radio play of that title, but the poem. Mr. Newby assumes that he had heard about Beckett's poetry from someone familiar with the Paris scene—possibly Christopher Logue—and asked him to send some of his poetry. Nothing seems to have come of this first contact.

It was only after the success of *Waiting for Godot* that enquiries were made about the play early in 1953 and, indeed, steps were taken to secure the rights to translate the play. On August 6, 1953, the BBC was informed that the author insisted on making his own translation. When a copy of this arrived, the producer who had been enthusiastic about the Paris production (let him remain mercifully nameless) found the translation not as good as the original. He felt that perhaps it might be made workable if the author was willing to allow improvements to be written into it. But alas, he added in a final memorandum (dated May 24, 1954), Beckett's Paris publisher had assured him that the author was "*un sauvage*" and quite unwilling to listen to reason. Nevertheless, after the success of the London performance, another producer, Raymond Raikes, warmly urged that it should be preserved for posterity by being recorded and broadcast. By December 6, 1955, the rights to broadcast the performance had been obtained, though, for some reason now impossible to ascertain, nothing came of the project.

Through all this argument and agitation Beckett's name had become familiar within the Drama Department and the Third Programme team, and John Morris (then Controller of the Third Programme) was very eager to broadcast something by him. In June, 1956, he heard rumors of a new play to be performed in Marseilles and asked the Paris representative of the BBC, Cecilia Reeves, to make inquiries. She wrote to Morris on June 21, 1956: "I have written to Beckett asking if he would write a piece for Third and if he would let us have the text of *La Fin du Jeu* [sic—either that was the title at that stage or Miss Reeves had misremembered it]. He is, as you know, an elusive character and spending much of his time outside Paris and our mutual contact Desmond Ryan has already gone South. He has however reacted amiably to the suggestion that his mime piece *Soif* [clearly the original title of *Acte sans paroles I*], also to be given at Marseilles, should be considered for television, so I imagine that his former, rather hostile, attitude to radio in general is improving." The Head of Television Drama, Michael Barry, must have met Beckett in Paris shortly afterwards to discuss the television broadcast of the mime play, for on July 4, 1956, Cecilia Reeves's assistant wrote to the Head of Radio Drama: "This is just to confirm what Mr. Barry has already told you that Beckett is agreeable, in principle, to writing a radio play for Third and that he will discuss the idea in more detail with Miss Reeves when she comes back. He says, however, that he has never written anything for radio before and will probably need a little persuasion from Miss Reeves before he actually starts working on it. As regards the play which is to be produced at Marseilles next month, Beckett has not yet finished writing it and is not yet sure about its title which is at present *Fin de Partie*. He will certainly let us have the text later on." On the same day Beckett wrote to Miss Reeves, who was on leave in England, that he had had an idea which might or might not lead to something. Within a week John Morris wrote to Beckett to tell him how excited he was to hear of this and suggested that he might meet him for lunch in Paris to discuss this and other ideas. The lunch duly took place on July 18, 1956, and John Morris wrote on the same day to the Head of Radio Drama, Val Gielgud:

> I saw Samuel Beckett in Paris this morning. He is extremely keen to write an original work for the Third Programme and has, indeed, already done the first few pages of it. I got the impression that he has a very sound idea of the problems of writing for radio and I expect something pretty good. He says his output is unpredictable. Sometimes he works slowly, at others very fast, but he does not wish to be tied down to any definite date . . . The play which was to have been done at the Marseilles festival has now been cancelled because of some sort of muddle with the organizers. . . . He has promised the Third Programme the first chance to do an English translation as soon as the French stage production is fixed up.

Beckett sent John Morris the finished manuscript of *All That Fall* on September 27, 1956. So only just over 2½ months had elapsed between the date at which Beckett first mentioned the idea and the actual completion of the play. In a brief note accompanying the manuscript Beckett stated that the play might well call for a special quality of *bruitage* and that if necessary he would let him have further details. Morris expressed his delight with the play and asked for a note on the special *bruitage*. On October 18, Beckett replied that he found it difficult to put his ideas about the sound effects on paper, and suggested that it might be best for him to meet the *bruiteur*. By return of post, on the following day, Morris responded with the news that "Donald McWhinnie who will be producing *All That Fall* is going to be in Paris for a week from Monday next, 22nd October. I think it would be very useful for you to meet him since I know he would like to discuss with you personally a number of production points." And so started the immensely fruitful relationship between Donald McWhinnie (then Assistant Head of the radio drama department, and one of the great pioneers of the art of radio) and Samuel Beckett.

The play was scheduled for the third week in January, 1957. Donald McWhinnie, having discussed the production with Beckett and finding that their ideas closely agreed, got down to work. On November 28, Beckett wrote supplying the only amendment: in the very first line of dialogue he changed the phrase which originally ran "all alone in that old crazy house" to "all alone in that ruinous old house." He later informed McWhinnie that the opening of *Fin de partie* was now planned for January 15 at the Theatre de l'Oeuvre, and that he would therefore be unable to attend the rehearsals and recording of *All That Fall* in London between January 2 and 6.

In his reply (December 13, 1956) McWhinnie expressed his regret at this decision and informed Beckett that he had decided to have all the animal noises in the script recorded by humans. He also asked for a short contribution (from five to five hundred words) for the BBC's program periodical, *Radio Times*. Beckett politely declined on his customary ground that he was incapable of writing about his own work. Nor could he see the point of having the animal noises imitated by humans. The opening of his play at the Oeuvre having been postponed, he had thought of coming to London for the production. But he had decided against it because he felt that he might be a hindrance rather than a help in the studio.

McWhinnie wrote to explain his ideas about the animal noises:

I am sorry to disturb you about the animals. Of course we have realistic recordings, but the difficulty is that it is almost impossible to obtain the right sort of timing and balance with realistic effects. By using good mimics I think we can get real style and shape into the thing. The other factor is that existing recordings are very familiar to our listeners and I do feel that without being extreme we need, in this particular case, to get away from standard realism. As far as we have got, I am very pleased with the results of this experiment; but, of course, if it should not prove right, when we have put the whole thing together, we shall have to think again.

This was on the eve of the start of rehearsals with the actors. The experiments with sound effects had been going on for some time, mainly late into the evening in drama studios vacated by their daytime users. The sound technician principally involved was Desmond Briscoe, a radio enthusiast of immense inventiveness and imagination. Beckett's script demanded a degree of stylized realism hitherto unheard of in radio drama, and new methods had to be found to extract the various sounds needed (both animal and mechanical—footsteps, cars, bicycle wheels, the train, the cart) from the simple naturalism of the hundreds of records in the BBC's effects library. Briscoe (and his Gramophone operator, Norman Baines) had to invent ways and means to remove these sounds from the purely realistic sphere. They did so by treating them electronically: slowing down, speeding up, adding echo, fragmenting them by cutting them into segments, and putting them together in new ways. These experiments, and the discoveries made as they evolved, led directly to the establishment of the BBC's Radiophonic Workshop. Beckett and *All That Fall* thus directly contributed to one of the most important technical advances in the art of radio (and the technique, and indeed technology, of radio in Britain).

The first broadcast of *All That Fall* took place on January 13, 1957. In a letter dated December 14, 1956 (although it was clearly written on January 14, 1957, the day after the broadcast) Beckett sent McWhinnie a hearty "*bien travaillé.*" The reception of the BBC's Third Programme wavelength in France had been very poor, but he had heard enough to realize that the two principals, Mary O'Farrell and J. G. Devlin, had given excellent performances, although the latter had sounded somewhat perfunctory at times. He had greatly liked the laughter with which they greeted the text of the sermon (the line from the Psalms which gives the play its title). But he still had not thought the animal noises quite right.

Donald McWhinnie has supplied a very convincing justification for the solution of the problem of the animal noises in his excellent and detailed account of the production process of *All That Fall* in his book *The Art of Radio*.[1] Recordings of actual animal sounds could never have been blended into the stylized convention of the play. The atmosphere and acoustics of the circumstances under which they were made inevitably cling to such recordings, and would have punctured the enclosed, subjective universe of *All That Fall*.

Yet it is remarkable to what extent Beckett had, in his first attempt at a radio play, intuitively grasped the specific qualities and capabilities of the medium, and how brilliantly he had seized those aspects of radio that were most germane to his own thematic and formal preoccupations.

Thematically, *All That Fall* clearly links up with Beckett's last previous work in English, *Watt*. The cast of seedy genteel Irish types, the provincial milieu, even the railway station clearly belong to the same world. But whereas *Watt* is still narrated in a clinically cool objective manner, the action of *All That Fall* is experienced by the listener subjectively from Maddy Rooney's point of view. It is precisely the nature of the radio medium which makes possible the fusion of an external dramatic action (as distinct from the wholly internalized monologues of the narrative trilogy which followed *Watt*) with its refraction and distortion in the mirror of a wholly subjective experience. In radio the dramatic action is directly placed in the listener's mind and imagination. The microphone becomes the listener's own ears. And these ears can be directed either to the outside world, or inwards to pick up an internal monologue; indeed, they can enable the listener to experience the external world *subjectively* with the ears of the character in the play.

Through the use of acoustic perspectives the radio writer and director can clearly convey to the listener with *whose* ears, from which

1. Donald McWhinnie, *The Art of Radio* (London: Faber, 1969), 133–51.

subjective viewpoint, he is witnessing the action and, indeed, inside whose mind he is supposed to be. Thus, by the use of stylized and distorted sounds, radio can create a subjective reality halfway between the objective events experienced and their subjective reflection within the mind of the character who experiences them—halfway between waking consciousness and dreamlike states, halfway between fact and fantasy, even hallucination. Just as the subject experiencing such states finds it difficult to decide whether his experience is reality or fantasy, so the radio dramatist can keep the listener in a similar state of uncertainty. In *All That Fall*, Maddy Rooney's progress towards Boghill Station has a nightmare quality; it might indeed be a bad dream. Eventually, by various subtle means, the author establishes that we are in the mind of a character to whom objective reality itself is a kind of perpetual nightmare.

Only radio among all dramatic media can create this kind of effect, this peculiar kind of dramatic suspense. Unlike a visual medium, which supplies a multitude of descriptive elements in each instantaneous picture, radio—like music—exists in the temporal dimension alone and must build its picture in a linear manner, adding one descriptive element after another. Information gradually emerges, can be withheld and then dramatically revealed.

Almost as a centerpiece to the nightmarish sequences of *All That Fall*, we are made aware of the objective reality of the place we are in and, indeed, made to see it objectively, albeit through Maddy Rooney's eyes. "The hills, the plain, the racecourse with its miles and miles of white rails and three red stands, the pretty little wayside station, even you yourselves, yes, I mean it, and over all the clouding blue, I see it all, I stand here and see it all with eyes . . . through eyes . . . oh, if you had my eyes . . . you would understand." For, far from being a blind medium, radio (*pace* Marshall McLuhan) is an intensely visual medium. The nature of man's consciousness and sensory apparatus is predominantly visual, and inevitably compels him to think and imagine in visual images. Information that reaches him through other senses is instantly converted into visual terms. And aural experiences, which include the immense richness of language as well as musical and natural sound, are the most effective means of triggering visual images. These images, moreover, being generated by each individual listener, have the advantage of being completely satisfying to him. There is no danger that the image seen will fall short of what he may have expected—as it often does in the theatre or on the screen.

Another aspect of the sound medium grasped by Beckett was its need for strict formal patterning. Because they are totally immaterial, aural art forms are in danger of becoming amorphous and demand great clarity of structure and pattern. Rhythm and rhyme, strophic forms, the patterning of music in movements, all these are devices designed to impose form on the formless. Not only is *All That Fall* very closely a three-movement structure (Maddy Rooney's anabasis, her wait at the station, her and Dan's katabasis), but it has also a very complex pattern of small-scale rhythms—the footsteps of the anabasis, the doubled footsteps and the thumping of Dan's stick in the katabasis, the rhythmic panting, etc. (That rhythmic and recurrent panting also became a feature of Beckett's *Comment c'est*.) *All That Fall* was acclaimed as a radio masterpiece; it received an enormous amount of critical attention and has established itself as one of the classics of radio drama. The original production was repeated three times in the course of 1957, and again in 1959, 1961, 1966, and 1970. A new production in stereo (again by Donald McWhinnie) was broadcast on June 4, 1972, in the course of the celebrations of the BBC's fiftieth anniversary (and repeated on December 2, 1972). The play has been translated and broadcast in many languages. It was filmed for television in France, but Beckett is supposed to have disliked the transfer of the play to another medium. When Laurence Olivier and Kenneth Tynan attempted to persuade him to allow them to mount a stage production in the British National Theatre, Beckett refused.

The tremendous success of *All That Fall* spurred the BBC to urge Beckett to write more for radio. After meeting him in February, 1957, shortly after the first broadcast of the play, McWhinnie reported that radio had obviously captured Beckett's imagination. But he was preoccupied with the plans for the stage production of *Fin de partie*, which had run into all sorts of difficulties in Paris. As it happened, the first performance of the play (in the original French) took place in London at the Royal Court Theatre, and the BBC obtained permission to broadcast it. Michael Bakewell (one of the radio drama department's most gifted young directors) undertook the task of overseeing the transfer of the production to radio; it was broadcast on May 2, 1957.

In the same month, Beckett, who had been thinking of writing a work for radio in collaboration with his cousin, the composer John Beckett, wrote to McWhinnie that he could not foresee any chance of writing an original piece for radio for a long time to come; he suggested instead that John Beckett might be asked to compose music to accompany a solo reading from one of his prose works. He was thinking of a section of *Molloy*, "from the shore to the ditch," the final section of Part One.

This idea was eagerly accepted, and John Beckett commissioned to write, the music (which eventually turned out to be for a small ensemble of nine players). To read the part of Molloy, McWhinnie cast Patrick Magee, one of the group of superb Irish actors he had assembled for *All That Fall* (Magee had played Mr. Slocum; Jack MacGowran, later to become the second of Beckett's preferred interpreters, played Tommy, the porter at Boghill Station). In November, shortly before the recording of *Molloy*, Beckett suggested another reading, of a passage from an unfinished novel, originally referred to in the BBC's records as *The Meditation*. The broadcasts of these two readings took place within the same week: *Molloy* (which ran to a length of 59 minutes, 14 seconds) on December 10 and the meditation, now retitled *From an Abandoned Work* (23 minutes, 30 seconds) on December 14, 1957.

These readings by Magee were immensely effective and successful, not least with Beckett himself, who had found an ideal interpreter. One of the consequences of this success was that George Devine, who was planning the English-language première of *Endgame* at the Royal Court, suggested to Beckett early in 1958 that he should write a stage monologue for Magee to go with the performance of *Endgame* (just as the original French performance of the play had been linked with *Acte sans paroles I*).

Beckett mentioned in a letter to McWhinnie (February 26, 1958) that he had indeed had an idea for a stage monologue for Magee, and in March informed him that he had written the piece, which involved the use of a tape recorder; he asked McWhinnie to send him operating instructions for such a machine as he had to be sure how it worked. Thus *Krapp's Last Tape* owes its existence both to Beckett's discovery of the fascinations of tape recording in the wake of the production of *All That Fall* (the reception of its second broadcast had been even worse than the first, so the tapes were sent to Beckett) and to his discovery of Magee as an ideal embodiment of characters like Molloy. Yet this play, directly inspired by Beckett's contacts with radio, is, by its very nature, incapable of being performed on radio. The effect of the play depends, above all, on the counterpoint of the powerful visual image of a man listening to his own recorded voice with his reactions to his past personality registering on his features. On radio it would be difficult to differentiate Krapp's recorded voice from his unrecorded utterance: both would be on tape, and to distort the recorded voice would be unrealistic, as tape recording only slightly distorts human speech.

The success of Magee's readings from *Molloy* and *From an Abandoned Work* led to further readings—from *Malone Dies* (with music by John Beckett; read by Magee; duration 1 hour, 11 minutes, 38 seconds) on June 18, 1958; and from *The Unnamable* (also with music by John Beckett and read by Magee; duration 1 hour, 51 seconds) on January 19, 1959.

The beginning of 1959 brought the completion of Beckett's long-awaited second original play for radio. Copyright clearance for this as yet untitled manuscript was requested on February 13, 1959. On a later memorandum a suggested title, *Ebb*, was penciled in. By April the title had definitely become *Embers*. It was in rehearsal from June 19 to 23, 1959, under Donald McWhinnie's direction; Jack Mac-Gowran was cast as Henry; Patrick Magee doubled the parts of the Music and Riding Masters. The first broadcast took place on June 24.

In *Embers* Beckett has moved further away from objective reality, closer to radio's unique ability to present an inner, wholly subjective reality. The background—a background of sound, the sea, Henry's boots on the shingle—is still real, but the voices are all internal: Henry's internal monologue as he tries unsuccessfully to conjure up

134

his dead father's presence, and later the voices of his wife and daughter and her instructors, which materialize in his memory. Apart from the basic situation, the images of an old man sitting by the sea, all the visual images built up are internal. They are all the more intense for that: like the strange, haunting scene of the two old men standing by the dying fire in the dead of night, arguing about something which never becomes wholly explicit, except that it involves an injection or shot of drugs.

If *Embers*, although its action is confined to the inner reality within its protagonist's mind, still retained the external reality of his situation within a real framework, *i.e.* on the seashore, Beckett's next two radio plays shed even that last tenuous link with the outside world.

Words and Music finally realized Beckett's long-cherished intention of collaboration on an original work with John Beckett. The decision to put this plan into practice is mentioned in a memorandum from Michael Bakewell to me (I had succeeded Donald McWhinnie as assistant head of the radio drama department) dated February 20, 1961. The completed manuscript of the play was in the hands of the BBC by the beginning of December. It was first broadcast on November 13, 1962.

Beckett's preoccupation with the process of human consciousness as an incessant verbal flow (on which the whole of his trilogy as well as *Texts for Nothing* was based) here found its logical culmination, and one which only radio could provide. For, after all, human consciousness—the self's awareness of its own existence—does not *only* consist of a constant stream of language. It has a nonverbal component as well, the parallel and no less unbroken stream of wordless consciousness of being, made up of body sensations, inner tensions, the awareness of body temperature, aches, pains, the throbbings of the flow of one's own blood: all are the multiple facets of nonverbal consciousness summed up in the overall concept of emotion. In the arts, as perhaps Schopenhauer first showed, this stream of nonverbal life-awareness, of life-force or *Will*, is the subject matter of *music* which portrays and represents the ebb and flow of the emotions. To give an adequate representation of the Beckettian exploration of the self's experience of itself, music had to be added to the verbal stream of consciousness. This is precisely what Beckett attempts in two of his later radio plays.

There are three characters in *Words and Music*: a Lord and Master, called Croak, and his two servants, Words (or Joe) and Music (or Bob), the court poet and court musician in his lordly household. In Beckett's trilogy, the self is split into a listener and a voice telling that listener stories. In this radio play the listener, Croak, commands one of his servants to regale him with a verbal, the other with a musical (*i.e.* emotional) stream of consciousness. He sets them themes on which to improvise, and if they fail to please, he silences them by thumping them on the head with his club.

The movement of the play, after unsuccessful improvisations on the themes of Sloth, Love, and Age, converges on the evocation of the features of a beloved woman—on Croak's command to his servants to improvise on Face. At one point Croak exclaims: "Lily!" Here words and music merge into song. Words' shocked exclamation: "My Lord!," the sound of the master's club which slips from his hand, and the shuffling away of slippered feet indicate that the memory of fleeting fulfillment, "one glimpse of the wellhead," has silenced Croak in total despair. The play ends with Words' attempts to make Music repeat the statement about the wellhead again and again. The last sound is a deep sigh from Words.

This short play (it ran for 27 minutes, 30 seconds) has appeared in book form; but so totally radiogenic is its very nature that the printed page cannot represent it. It exists only in sound—in radio or perhaps as a recording—for the third character, Music, in every way of equal importance with the other two, is of necessity absent on the printed page.

Cascando was an even shorter play than *Words and Music*. Beckett's work for radio echoes the tendency of all his other works to get progressively more concise—the BBC's production barely exceeded 21 minutes in duration. It was written in French in collaboration with the Rumanian composer Marcel Mihailovici—whose opera based on *Krapp's Last Tape* Beckett had greatly liked—with the French radio and Süddeutscher Rundfunk (Stuttgart) in mind. The French text reached the BBC in June, 1962, but Beckett's translation took some time to be completed; there were also fairly lengthy negotiations to obtain the tape of the music as performed in Stuttgart, so that the first broadcast of *Cascando* in English (it had been transmitted in French by ORTF on October 13, 1963) did not take place until October 6, 1964. Donald McWhinnie directed the play as guest producer.

Here again we have three characters—the Opener, a Voice which is heard when he opens one door or channel of his consciousness, and Music, which emerges if he opens the other. Occasionally he opens both (doors? channels? he never specifies what it is that he opens), and then music accompanies the voice. The Voice tells a story about the pursuit of an elusive character called Maunu in the French, Woburn in the English version (Mau-nu has suggestions of evil-born, evil-naked; Woburn of born in woe, or burning in torment). The play ends at a point where Maunu/Woburn has almost been caught, yet whether he will slip away again remains uncertain in a final silence. As in *Embers*, the action takes place in the vicinity of water. The Opener, who repeatedly mentions that people say that it is all happening in his head, might be seen as analogous to Henry who felt compelled to tell himself stories, to keep on talking all the time.

And here again the music supplies a new element, the nonverbal stream of consciousness which the Opener can evoke either by itself or in unison with the verbal flow of the voice. The outside world is again absent, except for the repeated statement by the Opener that for him it is May . . .

Besides Beckett's four original radio plays, the canon also contains a translation by him which clearly displays his great skill as a translator and is also truly creative. This is the translation of Robert Pinget's radio play *La Manivelle—The Old Tune*.

The BBC had broadcast Pinget's stage play *Lettre morte* in 1959. The script editor of the radio drama department, Barbara Bray, suggested to Pinget that he should write an original play for radio. On November 5, 1959, Pinget wrote to her: "Voici, mon enfant, grande nouvelle confirmée: Sam fait la traduction." In Beckett's translation the two old men of the original, M. Pommard and M. Toupin, became

Mr. Cream and Mr. Gorman; their ramblings, which reveal the falli-
bility of human memory, assumed a strong and very clearly Irish flavor, particularly because in Barbara Bray's production they were
played by those most Beckettian of all actors, Patrick Magee and Jack
MacGowran. Beckett's translation had its first broadcast in the Third
Programme on August 23, 1960.

Apart from works specially written for radio, the BBC has broadcast a number of Beckett's stage works. *Waiting for Godot* finally
reached the listeners of the Third Programme more than seven years
after it had first been suggested, on April 27, 1960. Patrick Magee was
cast as Estragon, Donal Donnelly as Lucky. A new production with a
different cast was broadcast in the less esoteric Home Service on February 5, 1962, in the framework of a series which surveyed the dramatic output of the previous decade under the overall title "From the
Fifties." *Endgame*, which had been discussed with Beckett since the
very first contacts between him and John Morris in 1956, did not get a
broadcast in English till May 2, 1962, (Donald Wolfit played Hamm).
This delay was partly due to scruples about the supposedly blasphemous line "The bastard, he doesn't exist."
One of the most interesting experiments in transferring a stage play
by Beckett to the radio medium, and one which revealed the workings
of Beckett's mind most clearly, was the broadcast of *Play*. The BBC's
experimental group of radio actors and directors, the Rothwell Group,
undertook (under the leadership of a young producer, Bennett Maxwell) to find a sound equivalent for the light beam, which directs the
utterance of the three characters whose heads protrude from their urns.
Maxwell had the idea that it would be possible to replace the operation
of that light by creating a continuum of sound—an endless loop of tape
of the three characters' voices saying "I," which would be abruptly
interrupted each time one of the characters was jerked into speech by
that mysterious beam of light. Beckett had categorically refused permission to broadcast *Play*, but he agreed to come and listen to a playback of this experimental production.

I remember that playback in my office very vividly. Beckett sat
through the whole play with an enigmatic and inscrutable expression

on his face. When it was over, he said: "I don't like it at all. You got it wrong."

He then proceeded to explain that the text fell into three parts: *Chorus* (all characters speaking simultaneously); *Narration* (in which the characters talk about the events that led to the catastrophe); and *Meditation* (in which they reflect on their state of being endlessly suspended in limbo). These three parts are repeated, and the play ends, as it began, with the Chorus. But, Beckett explained, there must be a clear progression by which each subsection is both faster and softer than the preceding one. If the speed of the first Chorus is 1 and its volume 1, then the speed of the first Narration must be 1 plus 5 percent and its volume 1 minus 5 percent. The speed of the following segment, the first Meditation, must then be (1 plus 5 percent) plus 5 percent, and its volume (1 minus 5 percent) minus 5 percent. The implication is quite clearly that any quantity, plus or minus, still has to be a finite quantity; however soft, however fast, the same text will go on *ad infinitum*, ever faster and ever softer without quite ceasing altogether.

Having expounded his suggested *modus operandi* Beckett had clearly become interested in the project. So when Bennett Maxwell and I asked him whether he would permit a broadcast provided we adhered to his prescription, he readily agreed, and supplied us with another modification of the text that is not apparent in its published form. In the original production at the National Theatre in London, Beckett had not merely had the whole text repeated exactly as it had been spoken the first time round; he had supplied a new way of permutating the order in which each of the three characters spoke his text. Each character spoke the same lines in the same order *within his own text*, but the order in which he was called upon to speak was different. Beckett suggested that each character's part should be recorded separately and that these permutations of exactly the same words spoken in exactly the same way be achieved by cutting the tape together like the takes of a film.

This remarkable production of *Play* was first broadcast in the Third Programme on October 11, 1966.

The tradition of readings of nondramatic texts by Beckett was kept up throughout the 1960s. Two programs of Beckett's poems, selected and introduced by John Fletcher, with the poems read by Jack Mac-

Gowran and the fine Irish actor Denys Hawthorne, were broadcast on March 9, 1966, and November 24, 1966. MacGowran also gave a stunning reading of *Imagination Dead Imagine* (March 18, 1967).

A reading that—so at least it seemed at the time—stood halfway between the mere delivery on the air of a text written for the printed page and a work which was specifically radiogenic was that of *Lessness*, Beckett's own translation of *Sans*.

Lessness is a text in which Beckett returned to his preoccupation with permutations of fixed verbal elements *ad infinitum*—a simulacrum of eternity itself, with time as an infinite combination of a finite number of basic elements. It started from six groups of statements, each containing ten sentences. The sentences within each of the six groups bear a distinct family likeness, being themselves variations on a single theme or image. Sentences from these six groups of ten—sixty in all— were then combined by Beckett at random in a given order, and subdivided into paragraphs of varying lengths containing between three and seven sentences each. Having thus arrived at a random structure, Beckett then went through the process of combining the same sentences again, using the same method of finding a new sequence and paragraph structure by random selection. It is clear that the same process could be continued indefinitely; the barren landscape with the little upright human figure can literally stretch out to the end of time, or rather to its endlessness.

The suggestion that radio might be the means of making the very complex structure of this text more clearly visible came from Beckett himself via his London publisher John Calder, who passed the structural key to the work to me. Calder and I went to Paris to discuss the production with Beckett. He read a passage of the text to me, clearly indicating the exact intervals between each sentence and the longer intervals between the paragraphs, and also specified that he wanted the voices to be distinguishable from each other although so unified in tone that they might be aspects of the same voice. As in the case of the radio production of *Play*, he wanted each group of sentences to be recorded separately by their speaker, so that the final production would consist of exactly the same sentences recombined in a different sequence by mechanical reproduction and editing, which would make it possible for the intervals of silence to be of exactly the same length, down to a tenth of a second.

For the production I tried to assemble a group of speakers whom I knew to be deeply sympathetic to Beckett's work: Nicol Williamson (who had given a breathtaking reading from *Texts for Nothing* at a Royal Court matinée some time before); Harold Pinter; Patrick Magee; Donal Donnelly; Denys Hawthorne; and Leonard Fenton. Once their recordings had been duplicated, cut up, and reassembled in their correct sequence, a strangely musical structure almost miraculously emerged.

Alas, Beckett was deeply dissatisfied with the broadcast. He felt that the voices were far too strongly differentiated, that the reading seemed too slow (we had rigidly adhered to the tempo he himself had adopted when reading a sample to me) and thus too sentimental. With his usual kindness and courtesy he took the blame upon himself and confessed that the idea of using six different voices might have been a mistake. There is certainly a dilemma inherent in this concept, for in reproducing the work in German for Westdeutscher Rundfunk (Cologne) I tried to lessen the differentiation between the voices and to speed up the tempo—and the final result was far less effective than the original English version. But *Lessness* seems to me an ideal text for radio, which alone can bring out its daring structural conception. I feel that this structure can only be made manifest by having voices as differentiated as those in our original production, and that the idea that those voices emanate from a single consciousness (which I agree is crucial to the work) does not necessarily get lost by such differentiation. After all, the Opener and the Voice in *Cascando* are very strictly differentiated and yet remain clearly within one individual's head; and this is even more the case in *Words and Music*.

Be that as it may, the broadcast (February 25, 1971) of *Lessness* on Radio 3, as the Third Programme had been renamed, had a very considerable impact on listeners—a fact attested by the unusual volume and fervor of letters of appreciation.

On Beckett's seventieth birthday, April 13, 1976, BBC Radio 3 broadcast the first performance of a further radio script by Beckett,

Rough for Radio. Harold Pinter played the part of the Animator; Billie Whitelaw, the stenographer; and Patrick Magee, Fox.

Rough for Radio, which, as the title of the English version implies, Beckett himself considers to be little more than a rough sketch, is nevertheless of very considerable interest for the light it throws on some of Beckett's recurring themes and preoccupations. The playlet, which in performance runs to about twenty minutes, is closely linked with *Words and Music* and *Cascando* as well as with an uncompleted play *Esquisse radiophonique.*

Esquisse radiophonique was published in the fifth issue of the bimonthly review *Minuit,* the literary house organ of Beckett's Paris publishers, Editions de Minuit, in September, 1973. Beckett himself dates it there as "vers 1962–63?"

Number 16 of *Minuit* (November, 1975) contains the first publication of *Pochade radiophonique* ("pochade" means a skit or sketch, hence the title of the English version, *Rough* [that is, a rough sketch] *for Radio*). This is dated by Beckett "années 60?"

Like *Words and Music* (1962) and *Cascando* (1963), these two radio pieces are concerned with aspects of the process of artistic creation, with voices and streams of music emanating from more or less mysterious sources, and the dependence of the principal characters on these and their more or less successful attempts at achieving some sort of control over them.

Esquisse radiophonique (Beckett's own translation into English gives it the title *Radio I,* while the English version of *Pochade radiophonique* carries in the typescript of the translation the title *Radio II*)[2] presents us with a man (He) who is completely dependent on one stream of music and another of words, which go on unceasingly but are made audible by turning two knobs of an apparatus reminiscent of a radio set. These voices are live (*en direct*); the use of technical language from the world of radio is significant. The sketch opens with the man being visited by a woman (She) who assumes that she has been asked to come to listen to these sounds, though the man insists that he never asks anyone to come and that he merely "suffered (her) to come" because he "meets (his) debts." The woman listens to the stream of music which emanates from the apparatus when one of the knobs is turned; she is

2. Both are contained in the volume *Ends and Odds* (New York: Grove Press, 1976) as "Radio I" and "Radio II."

surprised to find this music seems to be made by more than one instrument? person?—this remains unclear. In the French version her question as to the number of those involved is answered by the man, "Cinq . . . six." In the English version he merely agrees that there are several, but remains silent when asked "how many?" The source of the words, on the other hand, which become audible when the other knob is turned, is a solitary one. When the woman expresses her surprise that the speaker of the words is all alone, the man replies, "When one is alone one is all alone." When both knobs are turned at the same time the music and the words are heard simultaneously, but the two streams of sound nevertheless are, as the woman observes, not together. Nor as the man adds, can they see or hear each other. Asked whether he likes these sounds, the man—who never leaves the place because he has to listen to them—replies, "It's a need" (*j'en ai besoin*).

The woman leaves. The man telephones his doctor in a panic, disclosing incidentally that his, the man's, name is Macgillicuddy. Finding the doctor absent, he insists to the doctor's secretary that the matter is extremely urgent. And when, after several abortive calls, the doctor finally rings back to inquire what has happened, the man discloses in tones of extreme distress that the sounds are not only getting fainter, as though they were "ending," but they are also coming "together." It seems that the doctor's answer (which we do not hear as he is on the other end of the telephone line) indicates that this coming together of the two sources is connected with their dying, as "last gasps . . . are all alike." The doctor then, it seems, puts the receiver down. As music and voice are audibly failing, the telephone rings again, and it seems that the doctor's secretary is informing the man that the doctor cannot come to see him as he has been called to two urgent confinements, one of them a "breech" birth (*par le siège*). The doctor it seems cannot come before "tomorrow . . . noon." The sounds from the apparatus become feebler and feebler and finally cease altogether. The man is heard to whisper, "Tomorrow . . . noon."

The structure of the play, its central image, and its narrative line are fully developed. What is missing in the text is the stream of words emerging from the apparatus. This is indicated merely by a row of dots. When the play was first published, the composer Humphrey Searle, who was eager to write the musical part, suggested to the BBC that we should ask Beckett to translate it into English and to complete it. At first Beckett agreed as he was interested in collaborating with Searle; but after some months he informed me that he felt unable to proceed. When the manuscripts of both radio sketches reached me at the beginning of 1976, I felt that the play might nevertheless be produced without a text for the voice because it might be possible to treat it as no more than a faint mumbled murmur. But Beckett did not find this suggestion acceptable.

Shortly after *Pochade radiophonique* had appeared in the November, 1975, number of *Minuit*, I wrote to Beckett to ask if there was an English version of the play and whether he would agree to our producing it. He referred me to his London publishers, Faber & Faber, who had typescripts of the translations of both of the hitherto untranslated radio pieces, and agreed to a production of *Pochade radiophonique*. At that stage both pieces merely had the titles *Radio I* and *Radio II*. Because the BBC's four national radio networks are labeled Radios 1, 2, 3, and 4, it would clearly have been very confusing if Radio 3 (the network on which most of Beckett's work is broadcast) had transmitted a play called Radio II. I therefore asked Beckett whether we could not call the play *Sketch* or *Skit for Radio*. He rechristened it *Rough for Radio*.

The image of the play is that of a room containing a hooded, gagged, and blindfolded figure called Fox (in both the French and the English versions). Three other characters come to visit Fox bent on the task of extracting from him a monologue—or stream of words—to be written down. The leader of this group is called the Animator. He is accompanied by a woman stenographer and a mute figure, Dick, equipped with a whip (a bull's pizzle) and hence something like a professional torturer.

After hood, blindfold, and gag are removed from Fox and some earplugs taken out of his ears, the Animator asks the stenographer to read out the "report of yesterday's results," from which it appears that "these dicta, like all those communicated to date . . . are totally inacceptable" and, indeed, that the outlook for future results seems equally hopeless. The stenographer is then asked to read out "the exhortations" which consist of a number of points: that mere animal cries must not be recorded; that the transcript must be strictly literal; and that the subject must be completely neutralized when not in session. As the stenographer proceeds to read out a fourth point, she is stopped by the Animator who has heard enough and so we are denied knowledge of what that fourth point, or any further points, might contain. The stenographer then reads out the end of the previous day's text. This refers to an episode in which the speaker, Fox, has been washing and drying a mole he seems to have rescued in the dead of winter, after which he took the animal, with its little heart still beating, out into the blizzard and back into its chamber.

After the stenographer has shed her overalls because of the heat and glare in the room, which greatly arouses the Animator ("Ah were I but . . . forty years younger!"), and after Dick has wielded his whip on Fox's body, Fox begins to utter fragments of a monologue, interrupted by comments from the Animator and the stenographer. Fox's text is a kind of parody of the typical Beckettian interior monologue. From time to time Fox, whose vitality is low, falters and has to be recalled to his duty by the Animator impatiently knocking on his desk with his ruler and by threats of Dick's whip. Fox's monologue deals with a past life ("Live I did") and his leave-taking from the changing seasons ("such summers missed, such winters"). But he breaks down weeping when he mentions his brother, his old twin, inside him: "my brother inside me, my old twin, ah to be he and he—but no, no no. (Pause) No. No. (Silence. Ruler) Me get up me go on, what a hope, it was he, for hunger. Have yourself opened, Maud would say, opened up, it's nothing, I'll give him suck if he's still alive, ah but no, no no (Pause) No no." The mention of a woman's name, which seems to be the first instance of Fox actually naming any other character, excites the Animator: "And of a sudden, in the same sentence, a woman with Christian name to boot, and a brother. I ask you!" It seems to the Animator that they might be near their goal. He urges Dick to beat Fox into further utterance. But Fox merely screams, "Let me out! Peter out in the stones!" As so often before, Fox "has gone off again." The Animator adjures Fox to change his subject matter, to get away from rocks and rodents. "Of course we do not know, any more than you, what exactly it is we are after, what sign or set of words." He goes so far as to beg Fox to bring someone into the story, "even though it is not true!" This suggestion horrifies the stenographer.

Fox has fallen silent. As the whip no longer works, the Animator orders the stenographer to kiss him "till it bleeds! Kiss it white! . . . Suck his gullet!" Fox reacts with a howl and faints away.

There is clearly no more to be got during this session. The Animator feels that the mention of a woman might be "something at last." But when the stenographer reads the passage back to him, the Animator asks her not to omit some words. She assures him that she has omitted nothing. In spite of this—correct—assurance, the Animator orders her to insert the words "between two kisses" after the mention of Maud, thus giving the passage a spicier, erotic flavor. At this evidence of the Animator's cheating, the stenographer bursts into tears. The play ends with the Animator's consoling her, "Don't cry, Miss, dry your pretty eyes and smile at me. Tomorrow, who knows, we may be free."

Both the *Esquisse* and the *Pochade* are "*radiophonique*" in a double sense. They are not only written for radio, they also make use of radio in their imagery. In the *esquisse* sounds and words emerge from an apparatus reminiscent of the equipment of a radio studio; and they come into the apparatus *live*, that is, from somewhere like a radio studio in another, perhaps subterranean, region, a situation which frequently occurs in radio buildings, of which Beckett knows a fair number. In the *pochade* the Animator with his ruler and stenographer and additional acolyte reproduces the team of producer, secretary, and technician which Beckett must have encountered in his contacts with production teams at the BBC or the French radio. (In French *animateur* is a term used for a radio or television producer.)

That radio and its techniques has a fascination for Beckett is clear. And so are the reasons for that fascination: voices emerging from the depths, from unseen and mysterious sources, play an immense part in Beckett's imagination—the storytellers of the trilogy, the murmured voice of *Texts for Nothing*, Krapp's tape-recorded reminiscences, the three points from which the old man's voice emerges in *That Time*, the compulsive voice breaking out of the mouth in *Not I*, to mention merely the most obvious instances.

That *Esquisse radiophonique* and *Pochade radiophonique* are intimately related to *Words and Music* and *Cascando*, and are, indeed in the nature of preliminary sketches for them, seems to me fairly evident. The *esquisse*, however, is much closer to both of these than the *pochade*. In *Words and Music* and *Cascando* we encounter the same duality of the inner sounds: a strand of music, which seems to me to represent the nonverbal, nonarticulated component of human consciousness, the flow of the emotions themselves, and a strand of words, an endless interior monologue. When I once asked Beckett about his method of work, he replied that, having attained a state of concentration, he merely listened to the voice emerging from the depths, which he then tried to take down; afterward he would apply his critical and shaping intelligence to the material thus obtained. There is—and this is a frequent theme of Beckett's writings—a deep tension between his conviction that ultimately all artistic endeavor is futile and his deep need, even compulsion, to listen to his inner voice and to shape its utterance. Hence, on the one hand, the Opener's (in *Cascando*) and the Animator's (in *Rough for Radio*) hopes that one day, perhaps soon, the voice will cease and the objective of the quest be reached and, on the other, the man's alarm (in *Radio I*) that the voice and the music are ending. He has become a slave to both, cannot leave his listening post because they are continuous, and yet, as he confesses, they have become a need, a necessity for him. In *Cascando* the coming together of words and music "as though they had joined arms" is felt by the Opener (who can open both sources without having to operate knobs, the technical *accidentia* having been shed as the subject was being refined and developed) as a blessing, a sign that the quest will cease and the sounds end in silence; in the *esquisse* their ending puts him into a panic. The woman of the *esquisse* has disappeared in *Cascando*. Her role is a mysterious one. At first sign, it might seem that she is merely there to provoke a demonstration and explanation of the phenomenon by the man. Yet in a brief passage during the man's telephone conversation with his doctor there is a hint that her visit might be causally connected with the dying away of the voices: "who? . . . but she's left me . . . ah for God's sake . . . haven't they all left me? . . . did you not know that? . . . all left me." In *Words and Music* the source of the music and of the words is not, as in the *esquisse*, transmitted by mechanical means; here we are in a kind of medieval setting of a lord and his two jesters, Joe (Words) and Bob (Music). But here, too, at the climax words and music come together, and they do so in evoking the memory of a woman, a lost love. And the final silence ensues as a result of the quest having led to at least a degree of satisfaction, a longing fulfilled, a desire accomplished. It is surely not without significance that what appears as an alarming and disastrous development in the *esquisse*—the coming together and cessation of the streams of sounds—is seen as a fulfillment of sorts both in *Words and Music* and in *Cascando*, which, being finished works, clearly represent a later stage of the development of the idea.

The *pochade* varies the same theme from a slightly different and even more deeply despairing viewpoint. Here the voice (Fox surely equals *Vox*) is a somewhat comic character, his utterances are parodies of the style and subject matter of the more serious voices in Beckett's *oeuvre*. Moreover Fox's vitality is extremely low, he "goes off" again and again; and when savagely whipped by Dick, his cries of pain are faint, a sign that he has barely enough vitality even to scream out under savage torture. He responds equally feebly to the stenographer's disrobing (which excites even the Animator, who by implication is a very old man—he wishes he were forty years younger so as to be able to consummate his desire for the stenographer!) and faints away when she kisses him. The situation portrayed in the *pochade*, therefore, is far removed from that of those of Beckett's works in which we see the artist as victim of a never ending torrent of inner voices; here we have an artist who is still under the compulsion of extracting something from his inner voice, who is still hoping that one day the right word will be said which will bring release, but who is faced with a sluggish, sleepy, and feeble creative core. Hence he—the Animator, the conscious, critical part of the artist's mind—falls victim to the temptation to cheat and to insert material which is not a genuine product of his inner voice into the finished text. The *pochade* is a truly tragicomic work, for the more parodistic, the more feeble, the more comic Fox's utterances become, the more tragic is the Animator's position: he, after all, is bound to go on with his weary task until something of significance has been extracted from Fox. He is Ixion tied to a creaking, faulty wheel which increases his suffering.

If we see *Rough for Radio* as a monodrama about the artistic process in which each of the characters represents one aspect of the artist's mind, we must regard the Animator as the critical faculty trying to shape the utterances of the voice that emerges from the subconscious, while the stenographer is the recording faculty and, also, in her distress about the spurious sentence the Animator inserts in the text, the artist's conscience; Dick, the torturer, is the artist's determination to stimulate his subconscious by suffering; the stenographer's disrobing and kissing of Fox represents analogous attempts to stimulate the subconscious by erotic fantasies.

If this view of the meaning of *Rough for Radio* is correct, it must surely be regarded as one of the clearest, least "encoded" statements of Beckett's view of the artistic process or, at least, his own process of creation. He himself regards the work as unfinished, no more than a rough sketch, and felt, having heard the production, that it had "not come off." He put the blame—with his customary kindness and courtesy—on the script and thus on himself, although he felt that the production, which made the Animator and his team start briskly and become more weary and discouraged as time went on, should already have started at a high degree of weariness and despair. Yet the very roughness of the work gives it its special importance: although it may be more schematic, less refined, by dint of that very circumstance, by representing an early stage of the creative process, it allows us to see structures and methods of Beckett's technique with greater clarity, just as the first outline of a novel or the rough sketch for a painting gives us insights into the skeleton of the finished work, which, in its completed state, is hidden by the flesh and blood around it. Here the allegory is still very obvious in its rough state; in more completed works that allegorical skeleton has been concealed and refined into a far subtler organic image so that the one-to-one correspondence of allegory has become the complex allusiveness of metaphor. Croak, the lord in *Words and Music* who commands Joe and Bob to perform for him, is a far more distanced, less obvious, far more poetic concept than the Animator who whips his bound and gagged subconscious into producing a text; but the image of the Animator having Fox whipped, by being more open and more mechanical, is clearer than Croak's mysterious pursuit. Even the process of literary allusion, so beloved by Beckett, is far more openly displayed in *Rough for Radio*. When Fox sheds a tear, the Animator asks the stenographer whether she is familiar with the works of Sterne; and when she replies that she is not, he supplies the allusion: "I may be quite wrong, but I seem to remember, there somewhere, a tear an angel comes to catch as it falls. Yes, I seem to remember . . . admittedly he was grandchild to an archbishop." And at another point in the play, when Fox talks about his having lived in the past, the Animator asks the stenographer whether she is familiar with "Purgatory of the divine Florentine." And being told that she has "merely flipped through the Inferno," he informs her that, strangely, in the Purgatory the souls all sigh "I was, I was. It's like a knell. Strange, is it not?" The stenographer asks why that should be strange. The Animator replies, "Why, one would rather have expected I shall be. No?"

Technically, the greatest difficulty presented by *Rough for Radio* lies in the presence of the mute character, Dick, whose only sign of life in radio is the sound of the effort he makes when cracking his whip, followed, when he actually strikes rather than merely threatening to do so, by the impact of the bull's pizzle on Fox's flesh. Curiously enough, this difficulty would disappear if the play were performed on a stage. And indeed with its unity of place and time *Rough for Radio* would be fairly easy to produce on the stage. This is another indication of the rough state of the work. *Cascando*, which contains, in a far more refined state, many of the elements roughly present here, being more abstract in its subtlety and perfection, is essentially radiophonic. By comparison *Rough for Radio* is, if not naturalistic, at least far more earthbound, far more material, more palpable in its concept.

The four radio pieces revolving around voices and sounds are, in any case, among Beckett's most personal and revealing works. Here he deals with his own experience of the creative process both as a quest for fulfillment and release and as a form of compulsion and slavery. In *Rough for Radio* his basic concept of splitting the consciousness into distinct portions and making them into characters in a metaphorical monodrama of the mind in conflict with itself is most clearly displayed. Here we have, I feel, the key for an understanding of much that is mysterious and difficult in Beckett's other works.

Beckett's involvement with radio and his interest in the technical potential of electronic media, inevitably also led to his trying his hand at work specially written for the other electronic medium, television. In fact his first step in this direction arose directly from his relationship with one of the directors he had successfully worked with in radio, Michael Bakewell, who had been responsible for putting *Words and Music* on the air. Bakewell had become head of the play department of BBC television in 1964 and it was through his initiative that Beckett wrote his first television play for one of his favorite actors, Jack MacGowran.

This play, *Eh Joe* (first broadcast on July 4, 1966), is another proof of Beckett's appreciation of the specific capabilities of such highly technical media as radio and television, and makes masterly use of the television screen's potential, capabilities, and limitations.

The play consists of a sequence of shots of a face wordlessly listening to a woman's voice emanating from an unseen source. In the course of the play, the camera moves closer and closer to Joe's face, not in one smooth movement, but in nine clearly defined steps which stop immediately the voice resumes speaking. In the final move the camera comes so close that only Joe's eyes are visible; the next step can only be the blackness of a blank screen. It is clear that the woman's voice is in Joe's own mind, the reproachful voice of his conscience about what he had done to the woman. It also becomes clear that the camera is in some way the source from which the voice proceeds—Joe's conscience is moving in on him, until it comes unbearably close. Only in television can this technique of a camera approaching a human face in gradual steps have the desired impact. The cinema screen would be far too large, so that the ever larger close-ups of Joe's features would become disproportionate and lose all human scale.

The impact of *Eh Joe* essentially depends on the fact that television is an intimate medium, which, with its small screen, puts the spectator into intimate contact with a face that is on the same scale (in close-up) as other faces in the room. Similarly, the voice that is heard must—as in radio—be capable of being kept at a sufficiently low level to give the illusion of being inside the mind of the person whose face is observed, of being in fact an internal monologue.

It is almost impossible to find, in the vast literature of television drama, another play which is as totally conceived in terms of the small television screen and its intimate audience psychology as *Eh Joe*. Other television plays could be enlarged to the proportions of the cinema screen without too great a loss of impact. Many of them can even be effectively broadcast on radio, so much are they principally verbal rather than visual. As a demonstration of what is specifically televisual *Eh Joe* is unique and a masterpiece.

As Beckett's work became more and more concentrated and concise, the attractiveness of the intimacy and compression of the television screen, which, Beckett realized, is essentially a small-scale medium (at least in the present state of technology), increased for him. The two new plays especially written for television that were broadcast by the BBC, together with a new version of *Not I* adapted for television, under the overall title *Shades* on April 17, 1977, represent Beckett's art at a point where the distinctions between the literary and visual aspects of his work have become blurred to the extent that one can speak of these works as "visual poetic images." Here the metaphor itself has become a moving, photographically captured image; the author (who was firmly in control of the production, although a professional director, his old friend Donald McWhinnie was billed as being in charge) has turned into a painter in light and movement and image.

The translation of *Not I* into the television medium involved the elimination of the Auditor, the shadowy figure, who occasionally raises his hands in silent helplessness during a stage performance. Here the mouth, a distant point of light on the stage, is relentlessly shown in close-up throughout the entire length of the breathless monologue. While, on the stage, it is remote, here it is brutally and clinically magnified: the lips, the teeth, the tongue clearly visible inside and writhing and slithering like a snake turn into a terrifying spectacle: the voice is seen emerging from an orifice in labor. The impact of this spectacle, both awesome and obscene, is overwhelmingly powerful. Billy Whitelaw's performance is definitive.

Ghost Trio and . . . *but the clouds* . . . , the two new television plays Beckett wrote for the same program, are in a far more subdued, elegiac vein. Both are, like *Words and Music* and *Eh Joe*, concerned with the evocation of memories of a past that has become a subject of ghostly regret.

In *Ghost Trio* a female voice (Billie Whitelaw's) comments on silent action accompanied by passages from the Largo of Beethoven's fifth Piano Trio ("The Ghost"). What we see is a bare room described by the voice, in a self-ironic phrase, as "the familiar chamber" in which an old man, holding an object which later turns out to be a cassette recorder, and hence *perhaps* the source of the music, waits and occasionally gets up to ascertain whether anyone is coming to visit him. The voice makes it clear that he is waiting, or hoping for the arrival of a woman: "He will now think again he hears her." But his expectations are disappointed. But then there *is* a knock on the door. In the long corridor outside, the figure of a small boy dressed in a black oilskin hood approaches, looks upward at the old man, shakes his head, turns, and disappears again down the long corridor. The old man returns to his seat, for the first time he raises his head to the camera, for the first time the viewer can see his old, worn, despairing face.

In . . . *but the clouds* . . . we get a variation on the same theme. Here the camera concentrates on a circle of light on a bare floor, from the outer darkness we see an old man pass through that circle, in overcoat and bowler hat from one side, in a long nightshirt from the other, establishing the round of routine, everyday existence (very much on the lines of *Act Without Words II*). When at rest inside the circle, the image of a woman's face (Billie Whitelaw's) fleetingly fills the screen. The man's (Ronald Pickup's) voice sparingly evokes the memory of the woman he is thinking about and quotes the words from Yeats's poem "The Tower" which give the play its title: "but the clouds of the sky." The reference is very clear, for the context of the lines refers to the poet's preparing himself to "Make his soul . . . study," until

> The death of friends, or death
> Of every brilliant eye
> That made a catch in the breath
> Seem but the clouds of the sky
> When the horison fades:
> Or a bird's sleepy cry
> Among the deepening shades.

Hence the overall title Beckett gave the three plays as a whole.

It is a measure of Beckett's mastery of the television medium that a reading of the scripts in their published form or, indeed, descriptions of the plays as those briefly given here, cannot convey even a small portion of the impact they make when seen. Here, as in some of his radio plays, only the full performance in its recorded form—and recorded, it must be stressed, under the author's close personal guidance and supervision, so that he has become the "*auteur*" of the finished work in the sense in which that term is used in the language of film criticism—can give an adequate idea of what is involved. Here poetry, literature, has been transcended: the poet works not only in words, but in visual images, in movement, light, and color as well. (The color here being a uniform gray). Perhaps complex visual images of such a kind have existed before on the stage, in the performances of works by great poets like Shakespeare, who were also in control of the entire apparatus of their productions. But only through the electronic media's ability to preserve such performances for posterity can such works now be preserved.

Beckett's profound understanding of the highly technical electronic media springs ultimately, I think, from the meticulous craftsmanship which forms his basic attitude to his work. His contributions to a production process are always characterized by humility towards the technical side of the work, combined with a respect for the craftsmanship involved, which seems to derive from an approach similar to that of the medieval craftsmen who regarded accurate workmanship as a form of religious worship. There is an intimate connection between the highest reaches of intuitive insight (inspiration in its truest sense, the inner voice) and the need for complete mastery of the techniques—of whatever order they may be—through which that inspiration is shaped, ordered, and communicated to listeners, readers, audiences. That combination of inspiration and craftsmanship characterizes the work of a true master.

The Unnamable Pursued by the Unspeakable

"Running to 640 pages with another 80 pages of notes," said Irving Wardle in *The Times* (September 25, 1978), "the book has all the appearance of a work of scholarship and it is no pleasure to me to record that when I made a sample check with two much-quoted British sources, both vehemently dissociated themselves from it." Note: all the *appearance* of scholarship, but when a check is made, the check bounces. Yet with the customary kindness and fairness of British courtesy, Irving Wardle then breezily brushed any doubts aside: "That is worrying, but I think it is outweighed by the fact that Dr. Bair is manifestly a lover of Beckett's work and that the story she tells is too extraordinary for anyone, least of all a celebrity-hunting hack, to have invented." Note: inaccuracy of fact can be outweighed by the author of a biography seeming to like its subject. Strange logic indeed! And stranger still: an *ordinary* story could have been invented, but an extraordinary story is just too extraordinary for that. Well, let us have a look at the evidence.

Reviewing Deirdre Bair's biography, *Samuel Beckett*,[1] in the *Herald Tribune* of June 29, 1978, A. J. Leventhal, one of Beckett's oldest and closest friends wrote:

> Miss Bair tells an extraordinary story of Beckett's first meeting with the woman who was to become his wife. As the writer lay bleeding on the ground (having been stabbed in a Paris street by

1. Deirdre Bair, *Samuel Beckett: A Biography* (London: Jonathan Cape, New York: Harcourt Brace Jovanovich, 1978).

155

a pimp) a young woman appeared providentially on the scene, she "happened by" in the biographer's words. Calmly she took over from Beckett's distraught companions, pillowed the victim on a borrowed overcoat and called an ambulance. The seeds for romance were planted. So far the Myth. One that persists like the one that makes Beckett Joyce's secretary. The facts are that Beckett met Suzanne Dumesnil on a previous occasion, that the latter learned of the incident in the newspapers and hurried to the hospital to be of help.

So much for the remarkable view that the "extraordinariness" of a story is a guarantee of its truth, a view incidentally which seems to be shared by other reviewers, *e.g.* Professor Christopher Ricks who remarked in *The Sunday Times* (September 17, 1978), that the book "may be indiscriminate, chatty, sometimes inaccurate, but it does bring together an extraordinary amount of fascinating material—people, letters, incidents, mysteries." The inaccuracy of the material pales, in Professor Ricks's view, before its fascination, enabling him to conclude: "Deirdre Bair has a gripping, clawing tale to tell" (including the story of the miraculous rescue by an unknown maiden "happening by" on the scene of the stabbing, which he has swallowed hook, line, and sinker as evidenced by the fact that he singles it out for special mention).

But is this not a scholarly book, as indicated by more than eighty pages of footnotes? These, as Irving Wardle so rightly noticed, provide the *appearance* of scholarliness. But let us see how the obviously false, overromanticized story is backed up in these notes. The relevant footnote states that "among those whose interviews helped me to form an interpretation of the stabbing incident are"—and there follow seven names—"also Samuel Beckett's letters to Thomas McGreevy, George Reavey and Arland Ussher." Clearly the information supplied by these sources was wrong, or it was wrongly "interpreted." Here another observation in A. J. Leventhal's critique becomes relevant: "there are so many errors in the remarks that I myself am supposed to have made that I am driven to doubt the accuracy of other attributions."

The vast bulk of the hundreds of footnotes in the eighty pages of notes that give the book its appearance of scholarliness are in fact references to such remarks made in conversation with the author. So, in point of fact, these footnotes represent mostly hearsay evidence wrongly "interpreted" (in other words, misunderstood or otherwise distorted). I should hasten to add that I do not think that such distortions are due to any deliberate intention of the author. No. They spring from what is much worse: the lack of the necessary background to understand the implications of many of the facts she may have been told and the lack of a critical methodology that would have enabled her to sift the legends from the facts.

Any close reading of the book by someone familiar with Samuel Beckett and the intellectual climate from which he springs would be bound to reveal that Ms. Bair lacks the basic requirements for a biographer of such a man. For example: to deal with the works and to decipher the letters of a man who writes in French as well as English, and who is deeply immersed in Italian, German, Latin, and Greek, one would presuppose a minimum knowledge of these languages in the biographer. What is one, then, to think of Ms. Bair's obvious ignorance of French as shown, for example, by her seriously believing that the sentence "The bastard, he does not exist" in *Endgame*, which caused such difficulty with the British theatrical censor, was much more leniently dealt with in France (where incidentally there is no censorship of the stage: a knowledge of local theatre conditions might be another qualification for the biographer of a playwright), for, as Ms. Bair remarks, "Only in French could the deity be thus vilified" (p. 487). In fact the French expression Beckett used in this line is *salaud*—which does *not* mean bastard, is much weaker and far less, if at all, blasphemous. If this were just one isolated instance of the fact that Ms. Bair has either not looked at or not understood the French text of one of Beckett's major works, it might be the result of a simple slip. But examples of her ignorance abound. It would be tedious to list them all, but on page 493 she quotes a remark by Beckett, referring to the fact that the Irish had to become brilliant to compensate for their oppression by the English, as follows: "Il nous ailes en culer à la gloire"—a strange remark indeed, which however Ms. Bair says, "he translated immediately as 'They have buggered us into glory!' " Now this surely cannot merely be a slip in the proofreading. Even someone who has had three or four lessons of elementary French must know that *ailes* cannot possibly be a form of the verb *avoir*, and that *en culer* cannot possibly be a past participle, quite apart from all the other mistakes in that short sentence. Needless to say, there *is* a footnote, and it attributes that farrago of misunderstood French to a conversation with someone who told the story. (No doubt correctly, but if one does not know even the conjugation of *avoir* one must surely be at a disadvantage in "interpreting" such verbal information.)

Beckett knows German, and quotes German in his poems and letters. What is one to think of a biographer of a learned man who can write that "Beckett found himself fascinated by the regularity, precision and rigid structure of the German language, *so different from the Romance Languages he had studied*" (p. 54, my italics). Anyone who can make a remark like that discloses total ignorance of all the languages in question. No wonder that quotations in German in the book are grotesquely wrong. All this seems to me far removed from even a superficial appearance of scholarship. Getting to know a foreign language may well be a difficult feat, but checking a place name is surely within the range of a "scholarly" biographer. What are we to think of Beckett having "to eliminate Hellenstadt and Guedinburg from his itinerary" (p. 244) during a trip to Germany? Those cities do not exist, and are probably misreadings of Beckett's admittedly difficult handwriting for, I presume, Halberstadt and Quedlinburg. Would not a "scholar" have made *some* attempt to establish the geographical context of Beckett's remark, and at least looked at a map or a gazetteer to establish a correct reading of the letter being quoted? Needless to say, many other German place names are equally misspelled.

That classical education is, alas, no longer a requirement for being called a scholar must now be taken for granted. Nevertheless, if he or she does give classical derivations, they should be checked. Ms. Bair blithely asserts that *horo* means hour in Greek (p. 103), which it does not: the word *hora* or *hore* merely means a point in time, so both the form of the word and the translation are far off the mark. And she opines that Saposcat, the name of a character in *Malone Dies*, is derived from *Sapo* (Greek for *wisdom*). Well, search me; *sapo* never meant wisdom in my small Greek; in my little Latin the syllable *sap* was the connection with wisdom. But, then, what does the obscure difference between Latin and Greek matter?

What about our own dear *lingua franca*? Ms. Bair, who (as the blurb informs us) "teaches now in the English department of the University of Pennsylvania," is no great shakes there either. She seems to think that someone who is being taught by a tutor is a "tutee" (p. 38), that people who live alone and see few friends lead a "hermetic" life (p. 95), presumably mixing up *hermetic* (which means magical, occult) with *eremitic*. She writes that Jack McGowran had made his Beckett evening by "using a pastiche of writings to create a dramatic unity" which seems to show that she thinks *pastiche* means *collage*. Pedantic? Perhaps. Yet, le style c'est l'homme, and such solecisms do not, to me, add up to an image of "scholarship." Little slips may not destroy the substance, but they certainly destroy one's basic confidence in the author's qualifications for her task.

And when it comes to the substance, can a work undertaken with so little of the basic background yield real insights? There *is* a lot of material here. Beckett's letters to various of his friends have landed in various libraries and have become accessible; Ms. Bair has looked at all these, notably at his voluminous correspondence with Thomas McGreevy who was a close friend and confidant of Beckett in his early years. But then, to judge from Ms. Bair's attempts to summarize and review Beckett's own writings, or those accessible to her in English, she does not have any great understanding of his literary personality. The summaries she provides are utterly naïve, often inaccurate, and never rise above the level of a schoolgirl's essay. She gets as far as spotting that Beckett's relationship to his mother was important. But her amateur psychoanalyzing of that relationship is pitifully simpleminded and, moreover, shows her inability to read Beckett's own work which contains that relationship in all its complexity, love, and horror.

A book like this cannot be ignored, for it raises important issues. It is, above all, a horrifying symptom of the decline of standards in our literary culture. Ms. Bair says that she embarked on writing it because "in 1971 I was a doctoral candidate in search of a dissertation topic." That in itself seems to me to be a dismal and damaging admission. Surely a book of this ambition and bulk would have to be the result of some consuming passion, a wild enthusiasm for the author concerned, and thus spring from an intensity of initial motivations that would exclude the cool, calculated search for a Ph.D. thesis. Be that as it may, there is no indication whether the book led to a doctorate, nor is the university mentioned that might have granted it, perhaps wisely so.

For the question surely arises: can a *scholarly* biography be written about a man who is still living? Surely this is a methodological impossibility. Ms. Bair's book proves it. She herself admits that "for every person I interviewed there were at least two or three who were inaccessible." That is one difficulty, but it is by no means the worst. By the very nature of the material, Beckett's early years are more fully dealt with than the later ones. The nearer the biographer gets to the present the thinner, more scattered and haphazard, less relevant becomes the available material. As the book progresses it markedly and obviously deteriorates—until, at the end, it is reduced to mere idle gossip. That difficulty would be present even if the material were properly handled. But here, quite apart from the glaring inadequacies of the author's background knowledge, the very method of presentation is wrongheaded. All the footnotes notwithstanding, Ms. Bair adopts the storytelling method of a novelist, rather than that of a scholar. Having obtained what she (often unsoundly) regards as a fact, she begins to tell her story from Beckett's point of view. She not only reports what he did, she becomes the omniscient narrator of her subject's thoughts and feelings.

> However grateful he was for the [Nobel] prize, it was still a source of unhappiness as it exacerbated his already strained situation with Suzanne [his wife]. The greater his success and acclamation had become, the greater her discontent had grown. In the past few years she had spent money wildly on her personal adornment, and she had decorated her part of the apartment lavishly. In fact the discrepancy between her part of the apartment and his was so shocking that Beckett stopped inviting friends to visit because he could not bear their undisguised expressions of surprise. . . . The gulf between her ornamentation and his simplicity was indicative of more than their decorating tastes: it represented a chasm in their relationship which they no longer cared to bridge. She resented his fame and felt that he should have made a more public acknowledgement of her important role in bringing it about. . . . He felt he had demonstrated his

gratitude to her by marrying her when both considered the cere-
mony a mockery. (p. 533)

How can Ms. Bair *know* what Beckett thinks, what his wife thinks,
and whether he considers his marriage a mockery? Not a thousand
footnotes can excuse this style of storytelling. In fact the only footnote
referring to this passage says: "The following information is from
Jean Martin, Roger Blin, Josette Hayden, A. J. Leventhal, Marion
Leigh and others" (p. 710). A. J. Leventhal for one insists that he has
been misrepresented. And how can Jean Martin and Roger Blin, excellent actors though they are but by no means omnipresent in Mme.
Beckett's boudoir, know what she thinks about her husband's feelings
about her? Of course, they *may* have talked about it to our charming
biographer in those terms (I doubt it); but even if they did, what
would it have amounted to? Nothing but gossip.

One can imagine how such a passage comes about. Someone may
have overheard a husband telling his wife that something she wanted
to buy was too expensive. That person may have reported such a remark to the biographer. Now, in true scholarly method, all that biographer could write would be: *XYZ* reported an incident in which *A*
said to *B*: "Don't buy it! It is too expensive." But in Ms. Bair's methodology this becomes: "*A* hates *B* because he deeply resents her terrible extravagance. *B* hates *A* because he is so mean to her." No wonder
the informants whose conversations have thus been transmuted are
upset and hasten to assure the world that they never said such things.
Again I should like to stress that I don't attribute to Ms. Bair any desire to misrepresent. She is merely using an unacceptable methodology. A method in fact which leads a newspaper like *The Observer* (to
its shame) to advertise extracts from this "scholarly" doctoral dissertation as THE SECRET LIFE OF SAMUEL BECKETT, including "his *vie de
Bohème* of penury and love affairs in pre-war Paris." The "scholarly
doctoral thesis" has been transmuted into the worst kind of Sunday
newspaper sensationalism.

This, then, raises a final issue which goes much beyond mere methodology and the difference between real and pseudoscholarship. What
are the ethics of such a biography? Is it permissible to publish the feelings (real or imaginary) of a living person towards the wife with

whom he has to live for better or worse? Is it permissible to reveal to the subject of this exposure the names of his friends, probably innocent purveyors of the raw material for this deadly kind of gossip, in footnotes? And how can all this deliberately be done to a man who is known as a person morbidly averse to having his private life exposed to public curiosity? What recourse does the victim of such an assault against his privacy have? Is he to put advertisements into the newspapers proclaiming that he is *not* irritated by his wife's spending of his money? That all this should have happened to Samuel Beckett is the final Swiftian, the final Beckettian irony. It would be funny if it were not so terribly sad.

But what of the "scholarly biographer's" ultimate argument: that Beckett had actually helped her, that he had supplied her with some material? "We met in November 1971, with Beckett stressing how important his privacy is to him, but at the same time urging me to follow my inclinations. He would not help me he said, but he would not hinder me either. I told him it would be impossible for me to undertake such a massive project on the strength of that statement; as a scholar, I needed to have access to family records, correspondence, manuscripts, and had to be able to conduct interviews. He repeated that he would neither help nor hinder me and I was free to do as I wished in the matter" (p. xi). Beckett is a man of a sensitive disposition and much subtlety; that perhaps makes it difficult for him to communicate to academics with less sensitivity. Could Beckett *hinder* anyone who wanted to write about him? Surely not. Once a writer is in the public eye he cannot forbid any discussion. The statement surely merely meant that he did not want to help. Yet he did write some letters asking people to assist Ms. Bair. "Samuel Beckett was kind enough to see me whenever I went to Paris, even though I soon realized how much pain and embarrassment my questions caused him. He introduced me to his family and wrote letters on my behalf and all the while I am sure he did not want this book to be written and would have been grateful if I had abandoned it" (p. xii). Pain, embarrassment, the wish that the project should be abandoned—and yet, with the sensitivity of a pachyderm, the intrepid explorer went on. One can only surmise why Beckett actually gave some assistance. I should hazard the guess that, once he realized that nothing could deter Ms. Bair, he felt that at least some basic points should be accurate in the book. Or was it merely his unfailing kindness and old-world courtesy which made it difficult for him to say no to such insistent demands? Perhaps he thought that the kinder he showed himself the likelier it would be that sheer sympathy for him might get the better of his biographer's relentless determination to expose his "secret life." But this is only speculation; and to go on would perpetuate Ms. Bair's basic error of pretending to know what Samuel Beckett thought or felt.

What is, however, the book's final irony is precisely the fact that Ms. Bair's pages abound in examples of Beckett's really extreme aversion to any probing into his private affairs. There is, to give but one instance, the story of Harold Hobson and Samuel Beckett going to a cricket match at Lord's together.

> Beckett was disconcerted several days later to see an article in the *Times* [she means *The Sunday Times*] in which Hobson had related most of their luncheon conversation. Even though it dealt entirely with cricket, Beckett was still unhappy because it was about his personal life, not about his work. . . . During lunch [*i.e.* in Paris some time later] he found the opportunity to ask Hobson for more discretion in writing about personal matters, to which Hobson readily agreed, expressing regret that he had unknowingly violated Beckett's confidence. Beckett assured Hobson that his integrity as a journalist had never been in question, but a personal idiosyncrasy compelled him to avoid the spotlight whenever possible. (p. 537–38)

Imagine, if you can, the degree of insensitivity required to relate this story about the *suffering* caused to a man of Beckett's morbid shyness by the mere reporting of a few remarks of his about cricket by one of the most gentlemanly, discreet, and kindly journalists, in the framework of a book containing the most vulgar novelistic probings into Beckett's marriage, health, love life, and relationships to his mother and brother!

A few pages later the matter becomes even more glaringly manifest. For here Ms. Bair describes the genesis of one of the finest—and truly scholarly—books about Beckett—by Lawrence Harvey, who was

writing about Beckett's poetry and criticism. Beckett agreed to give
Harvey some assistance with biographical material.

> True to his promise, Harvey submitted the entire manuscript to
> Beckett in 1969, before it was published but Beckett discovered
> that he was unable to bring himself to read it. The experience
> was too unnerving; he simply could not deal with it. He was
> shocked by his inability to control himself, but he recoiled from
> the manuscript with horror, as if he were Dorian Grey, looking
> into the mirror of his own imperfect self. He insisted that all but
> the barest details of his father's death and his mother's illness be
> excised completely. He removed all the names of persons who
> had been important to him. Then he gave the typescript to A. J.
> Leventhal and asked him to read it carefully and remove all fur-
> ther biographical references. (pp. 546–47)

So says the good lady who has just treated us to all the details, the
more morbid the better, of Beckett's father's and mother's illnesses, his
anal cysts and pus-filled boils and sundry titbits more, over a stretch of
almost six hundred pages! The degree of insensitivity must be called
monstrous, unspeakable.

What justification can there have been for perpetrating a book
which was bound to cause its subject and victim untold embarrassment and real suffering without any chance of retaliation or refuta-
tion? Ms. Bair has the answer at hand.

> I wrote the biography of Beckett because I was dissatisfied with
> existing studies of his writing. I felt that critics tended to try so
> hard to place Beckett in whatever particular theory or system
> they espoused that they ignored those works that did not fit,
> thus creating unexplainable gaps and blatant flaws. It seemed to
> me that many of the leading Beckett interpreters substituted
> their own brilliant intellectual gymnastics for what should have
> been solid, responsible scholarship; that they created studies
> that told more about the quality of the authors' minds than
> about Beckett's writings. This exasperating situation made me
> aware of the need for a factual foundation for all subsequent
> critical exegesis. (p. xii)

So the book was written to provide a solid foundation for criticism. It provides no such thing, because its facts are highly suspicious and, where they can be checked, unreliable.

I personally have been involved in about half-a-dozen events involving Beckett and the BBC that are mentioned in the book; in each particular instance Ms. Bair's account is inaccurate and bears little resemblance to what actually happened. Other friends and associates of Beckett's who figure in the book have similarly found that episodes in which they were involved are misrepresented. Moreover, the methodology of the book is, as I have tried to point out, basically wrong. If—and that is arguable—so detailed a biographical study of Beckett is necessary to permit a true critical evaluation and study of his work, the whole task will have to be freshly undertaken. A book so abounding in misconceptions will be more of a hindrance than a help; it perpetuates legends and makes it necessary to disprove each erroneous statement or wrongly interpreted interview. Quite apart from all this, it is simply untrue that the best Beckett criticism—from Hugh Kenner, Ruby Cohn, John Fletcher, Lawrence Harvey, James Knowlson, John Pilling, Raymond Federman, Melvin Friedman, to name but a few— either tries to press Beckett's works into a preconceived system or, indeed, suffers from an insufficient knowledge of his biography. Many of the people concerned know Beckett well personally and know much more about him as a person—and indeed about his life—than Ms. Bair could ever find out. And what is more, they have enough human sympathy and understanding of Beckett's personality to refrain from wanting to publicize their friend's private life. The justification for the book's genesis is thus as spurious as its methodology.

It is this supposed *raison d'être* for the book which finally reveals its author's basic inability to grapple with its subject. Anyone who has seriously studied Beckett and his *oeuvre* must know that one of his basic convictions and cherished principles is the self-sufficiency and integrity of the work of art. A work of art, whether a play or a poem or a novel or a painting, must stand for itself. If it needs an *explanation* in order to be understood there is something wrong with it. As Beckett has stressed over and over again, if he knew who Godot was and whether he would actually come, he would have had to put it into the play. Anything else would have been cheating. This is not to say that there should not be criticism, exegesis, discussion. They constitute the *response* to the work of art, the expression of the experience of its public; and as such are quite legitimate. But the response does not complete the work of art; it is related to it, but not part of it. To say that a work of art cannot be understood unless one knows whether the author loved or loathed his mother is nonsense. We know no such thing about Sophocles or Shakespeare, and yet we write criticism, we can respond.

In Beckett's case the matter is even clearer. He is a writer who probes his own consciousness to unprecedented depths and with ruthless honesty. Many of the elements which make up Beckett's inner world into which he introduces us with total frankness are fragments of his real world; many more are imaginary—fantasy or fragments of his erudition. To have read Dante (which Ms. Bair obviously has not: she thinks that the Belacqua episode in the *Purgatorio* contains a Latin quotation) is thus much more important for getting the sense of a passage in Beckett than some biographical trivia. In Ms. Bair's case these biographical facts positively hinder her at times from understanding even the barest outline of Beckett's works. What relevance, for example, has it when she points out that the old prostitute with whom the 69-year-old Krapp has some painful senile intercourse bears the name of his Aunt Cissie who was nicknamed Fanny? Are we to suppose that Beckett is suggesting that his old aunt was a prostitute? Or that he had intercourse with her? And are there not more obvious reasons why an old prostitute should bear the by no means unusual, even suggestive name, Fanny?

This is but one, glaringly obvious, example of the naïvety of the basic concept behind a book of this kind. Ms. Bair is only too eager to detect autobiographical elements in everything Beckett has written. What she overlooks is the fact that in one sense all literature is ultimately autobiography simply because the total contents of any writer's—or any human being's—mind are part of his life-experience. The question that interests the literary critic, however, is precisely the validity of this material as an independent creation existing in its own right.

This is not to say that biography is of no value for the understanding of a writer's *oeuvre*. Far from it: it is one element that has to be taken into account. But the key concept here is "understanding." A biography so insensitive, so wrongly conceived, and written by someone so obviously unfamiliar with even the most basic intellectual, cultural, and historical background to its subject, cannot approach even the threshold of aesthetic insight.

There remains the dismaying fact that well-known critics, academics, and men of letters have given the book at least halfhearted approval. Reading some of these reviews, I had the impression that the stress was on how "fascinating" a story the book tells: "Se non è vero è ben trovato." True, perhaps, for spicy anecdotes, juicy gossip. It does not strike me as a particularly valid criterion for a doctoral dissertation loudly claiming to represent "responsible scholarship."

THE MEDIA

The Mind as a Stage—Radio Drama

There is, on the surface, a striking analogy between radio and the silent cinema—both dramatic media which lack one vital element of drama: the silent film, words, sounds, and music; radio, the whole gamut of visual information. The silent cinema died when sound was introduced; should not radio drama have died when television added the visual component to broadcasting? Yet radio drama continues to flourish, at least in those countries enlightened enough not to have allowed their mass communications media to fall entirely into the hands of advertising agencies (as in the United States, where radio drama has practically died—not for artistic reasons; merely because it costs more to produce than a succession of pop records).

Where does the analogy between the silent cinema and "blind" broadcasting break down? The eye certainly is as powerful an organ as the ear. Yet it is through the ear that *words* are primarily communicated; and words communicate concepts, thought, information on a more abstract level than the images of the world the eye takes in. (Of course, words can also be visually communicated—by reading, but at a further remove. Reading a play is not the same as witnessing it—there is no immediacy; the experience is without involvement, the illusion of being present and identified with the action; for, as Aristotle has it, the narrative form—and hence all that is read—takes place in the epic *past*; the drama in an eternal *present*.) The silent cinema, therefore, could communicate only situations and landscapes: for motivation and information of an abstract nature it had to rely on the

171

written word—captions. Radio, on the other hand, can evoke the visual element by suggestion alone. The dialogue can carry the scenery and the costume within it and the human voice can powerfully suggest human appearance.

This, paradoxically, is due to the fact that man is, above all, a creature of the eye and that our minds automatically translate most information we receive into visual terms: the smell of olive oil will evoke a picture of the streets of Seville; the touch of velvet alone, the rich textures and colors of the garment; and similarly, the sound of a voice will conjure up the picture of a face and the mere mention of a place name, its image. No wonder, then, that Marshall McLuhan classifies radio as a visual medium, while regarding television, with its reliance on close-ups and the action of the scanning eye, as a tactile medium. Seeing the lip movements of the characters in the silent cinema could not stimulate the audience to great feats of imaginative effort in reconstructing what the dialogue they were missing might have sounded like; in radio drama the slightest verbal, musical or sound hint *does* powerfully activate the visual imagination.

And as imagined pictures may be more beautiful and powerful than actual ones, the absence of the visual component in this form of drama may well be a considerable asset. On the stage, battle scenes, for example, will always be less than wholly satisfactory: twenty or fifty or even a hundred men cannot evoke armies of many thousands. In radio the mere sound of a vast crowd easily suggests these multitudes. And which producer, in casting Helen of Troy or Venus herself, can ever be certain that he will find an actress who will be regarded by each member of the audience as the final and perfect embodiment of female beauty? In radio each listener will automatically see *his* ideal before his mind's eye and thus be satisfied.

Radio, thus, must be regarded as a perfectly adequate medium for the performance of dramatic works. This having been said, an important distinction must, however, be made; like all the mass media radio has a dual nature. It is, first of all, a mechanized technique for the transmission of preexisting material, just as printing, when first invented, was above all seen as a new mechanical device for the rapid reproduction of manuscripts, or the cinema as a means for preserving and mass-distributing stage performances. It is only at one remove that fine printing and the production of beautiful books was recognized as an art form in its own right, that the cinema developed its own aesthetic and artistic techniques.

Of all the mass media radio is the cheapest and fastest. A full-length stage play can be adequately produced on radio in three or four days of work in the studio and, even today in Britain, reaches on its first performance on, say, a Saturday night and its repeat performance on the following Monday afternoon an audience of between 1½ and 2 million people—the equivalent, that is, of a run of between 1500 and 2000 sold-out performances in a theatre holding a thousand people— a run of more than five years! Merely seen from the point of view of the ease of diffusion and the sheer efficiency and economy of bringing entertainment to large numbers of listeners this is impressive. And as most critical writing on radio and its aesthetic tends to concentrate on the more esoteric aspects of material especially conceived for radio, it is an aspect that should be stressed, and neither despised nor treated as negligible.

In a public service radio organization like the BBC, the medium's ability to diffuse material written for the stage rapidly, cheaply, and relatively widely must obviously receive its due consideration. For here is an obvious opportunity to increase a wide audience's knowledge of drama, to acquaint the country with important dramatic material which otherwise would have had to wait a long time before it attracted the money required to launch a production in the commercial theatre or even on television (where production costs are between ten and twenty times higher and where immense mass audiences automatically exclude material which requires any specialized knowledge or appeals to an intellectual minority). A public service organization like the BBC, or the French, German, Italian, and Scandinavian broadcasting bodies, can act as a patron of the arts and commission translations of important foreign plays: many European dramatists for example who eventually succeeded in reaching the live theatre and television, only became known in Britain because BBC radio had commissioned translations and broadcast them. Once a translation is available it becomes accessible to those who are unable to read German, French, Spanish, or Italian (and that includes most of the theatrical managements and television script editors). Thus, BBC radio launched Anouilh, Brecht, Ugo Betti, and Ionesco onto the English stage. Translations of plays like Max Frisch's *Andorra* (which was produced by the National Theatre at the Old Vic) or Vaclav Havel's masterly satire on totalitarian bureaucracy, *The Memorandum* (later produced by BBC television), were first commissioned by BBC radio.

Low production costs—and the insatiable demands of the medium for material: the BBC broadcasts some one thousand radio plays every year—also make it possible on radio, and on radio alone, to keep the whole corpus of standard classical drama, and the tried successes of the more recent repertoire, constantly before the public. It is the stated policy of the BBC's radio drama department to enable each generation growing up to hear the bulk of classical drama, from the Greek tragedians and Aristophanes to the Elizabethans, Restoration comedy, the great nineteenth century realists, Ibsen, Chekhov, Strindberg, Shaw, right down to Brecht and Beckett; this means that the standard masterpieces are regularly revived in a recurring cycle of about ten years' duration. The same, in the field of popular entertainment, though less systematically, is the case with the established successes of the West End stage.

Far more important, however, than the reproduction of existing dramatic material, is the impetus radio gives to the *writing* of drama, even in the humble sphere of pure entertainment. Most plays broadcast to help bored motorists or housewives bent on their routine chores to while away the time are in the field of straightforward, realistic storytelling, and unencumbered by any high-flown considerations of the aesthetics peculiar to the medium as an art form in its own right. Nevertheless, the freedom which the radio medium gives to writers to develop a plot and the ease with which such plays can be "staged" without any of the material difficulties of the live theatre have often enabled authors to try out their ideas and to lay the foundations for later stage successes. (Agatha Christie's *The Mousetrap*, for example, started on its career as a short radio play called *Three Blind Mice*; Robert Bolt's *A Man for all Seasons* was also launched on its course as a radio play—and these are merely two outstanding instances in a very long list indeed.)

Radio drama, relying as it does almost entirely on *words*, is preeminently a *writer's* medium. It gives the writer enormous scope and, by forcing him to rely mainly on dialogue, also is a splendid school for budding dramatists. The structure of the BBC's radio drama department gives it a unique position in the country in this respect: this is the only institution which as a matter of course scrutinizes all manuscripts that reach it unsolicited and channels them towards the various outlets in the different radio networks. The BBC's television drama department works on a different principle: here each series ("Play of the Month," "Thirty Minute Theatre," "Play for Today.") has its own editorial staff, which means that manuscripts that are sent in to these script editors may have to make the rounds until they find their proper place. And indeed, as a result, a far higher proportion of plays broadcast by BBC television are specially commissioned by the script editors of the different series, and thus made to order.

Moreover, the scope of radio drama is far larger than that of the television play, for radio, unlike television, can cater to relatively small minority audiences, among them the all-important and none-too-numerous community of people interested in avant-garde and truly experimental work (which is placed on Radio 3, formerly the Third Programme), and the literary gourmets who go in for recondite lesser classics or rare foreign works. The audiences for such minority drama in radio may be no larger than about fifty thousand people for a single performance, still the equivalent of a respectable run in a small theatre, but far too small to be considered economical in television.

This is why, to this day, radio drama has been a valuable training ground for young dramatists. The list of writers who have emerged into the theatre, television or films from radio is long and impressive. Among the present generation of leading dramatists it includes figures like John Arden (whose first play to receive public acclaim was a radio work, *The Life of Man*, entered in a North Region Play Competition in 1956), Giles Cooper, Bill Naughton (whose world-famous *Alfie* started life as a radio play), Alun Owen, Robert Bolt, Willis Hall, Henry Livings, Tom Stoppard, and many others. Dylan Thomas not only wrote

Under Milk Wood for radio, he also supported himself for many years almost entirely as a radio writer and performer (he was a superb poetry reader). Harold Pinter wrote three radio plays after the failure of *The Birthday Party* at the Lyric, Hammersmith, in 1958.

The existence of the BBC's radio drama script unit has always played an important part in the development of new writing talent: a public service institution that is actively devoted to the nurturing of writers. Relatively few of the hundreds of unsolicited scripts which are received each month are immediately usable. But those that show talent are criticized at length by letter or personal interview with the writer, discussed, rewritten, recriticized until they have assumed a standard which allows them to be performed. This constant dialogue between young writers and script editors, who are often joined by the prospective producer of the play, amounts to a veritable university of dramatic writing. In addition, the script department organizes one-day seminars for writers who have already had at least one play performed, but who might profit by a course in elementary radio writing techniques. Among the two to three hundred new plays specially written for radio that are performed by the BBC each year, there is an average of about fifty by writers who have not previously had a play performed. Even if only two or three among these eventually become important writers, in a period of ten years this would amount to an impressive and, indeed, amazing total.

Another aspect of radio's economy and speed as a publications medium is its ability to popularize works of narrative literature through dramatization. The serialization of classical novels, for example, has played an important part in reestablishing the reputations of their authors: the vogue of Trollope during the war and the immediate postwar period, to quote but one instance, owed much to such serialization. Another case in point is that of the *Forsyte Saga*, which had been broadcast twice in the late forties and fifties as a serial in forty-eight parts, before television took up the idea and widened the audience from a few million to tens of millions.

Most of this work remains in the comparatively modest sphere of the diffusion of preexisting material by a new, fast, efficient means of propagation or the provision of entertainment for people who may well be occupied with manual tasks while listening to the radio. What then of the more elevated region of radio: radio as an art form in itself?

There has, throughout the history of radio drama (which is a long one: the first play specially written for the medium, Richard Hughes's *Danger* was first broadcast on January 15, 1924), been a great deal of discussion about the true nature of the art form. And while there has never been a complete consensus of opinion on the subject, a certain number of basic facts are now generally accepted.

First of all: physically, the performance of a radio play takes place in a studio, but to the listener this fact is immaterial, in the true sense of the word: the play comes to life in the listener's own imagination, so the *stage* on which it is performed *is the listener's own mind*. He himself, by having to provide the visual component, which is undeniably present in any true dramatic experience transmitted by radio, is an active collaborator with the producer. In this respect he is in exactly the same position as the reader of a book who has to imagine the action in his mind's eye. The difference, however, is that the voices, music, and sounds of the radio play are of a far greater immediacy, have an infinitely more powerful emotional and sensuous impact in themselves, than the abstract symbols of print on the page. The "information" transmitted to the listener is far more specific than that which the reader of a novel or poem receives: the verse is scanned, the emotional charge of a line emerges from the tone of voice of the character who speaks it, and music and sound have an immediately powerful impact. Concentrated listening to a radio play is, thus, more akin to the experience one undergoes when *dreaming* than to that of the reader of a novel: the mind is turned inwards to a field of internal vision. This is the starting point of most of the best work that can lay claim to use the radio medium as an art form in its own right.

Listening to a radio play is also essentially a *solitary* experience: in the theatre the whole audience sees the same picture, but in radio, even if a group of people are gathered round a set, each of them carries his own visual complement to the action in his own mind. Here too we are in a region akin to the world of the dream. No wonder that dreams—and daydreams— are the favorite subject of the radio play proper and the internal monologue its ideal form. For if the listener

177

experiences the radio play essentially inside his own mind, the writer of the play also can project his own solitary vision more immediately, more directly and more completely in radio than in any other medium. Of course, the internal monologue can be polyphonous: there are, for example, a multitude of voices in *Under Milk Wood*, but they are the voices of fellow townspeople that one person, the poet Dylan Thomas, hears in his mind when he thinks back on the little place where he spent his youth. Or to take another, and seemingly diametrically opposed case: the bitter, grotesque stories about little men trying to escape from the humdrum routine of their lives, which are the subject matter of Giles Cooper's masterly radio plays, may at first sight appear as characters in naturalistic storytelling. But, on closer reflection, they can also be seen as the daydreams of one man, their author—or if not daydreams, then *nightmares*. They have the relentless inner logic of the nightmare, the mounting terror of the bad dream; one need only think of the little man in *The Disagreeable Oyster*, stripped naked by a crowd of hostile ladies and begging the taxi driver to take him to a place where he can get clothes, only to be dropped on the premises of a nudists' club. These events happen as swiftly and as inevitably as in a nightmare.

The radio play thus came at a particularly appropriate moment in the development of modern literature: both in the novel and in drama the reaction against naturalism led to an increasing subjectivization and internalization of subject matter. Proust, Joyce, and Kafka took the novel from the description of the surface of life into the inner landscape of the soul; for they had discovered that it is impossible to fix an objective outline of external reality, as reality cannot but be seen through the eyes, the moods and the desires, dreams and imaginings of a single, specific individual. In drama Strindberg took an analogous step when he put, in *The Dream Play* or *Ghost Sonata*, his own dreams on the stage. Artaud, the surrealists, and the playwrights who followed their lead—Beckett, Ionesco, Adamov, Genet, Mrozek, Gombrowicz, Havel—also peopled the stage with the concretized images of their dreams and nightmares.

The radio play can deal with the same subject matter without the disillusioning heavy materiality of flesh-and-blood actors and paint-

and-canvas sets. Radio, indeed, is an ideal medium for the most highly subjective poetic drama which deals, to quote the title of an experimental radio play by Frederick Bradnum, with private dreams and public nightmares.

The range of radio drama of this type is immense: Louis McNeice's *The Dark Tower* projects an artist's search for his own identity in the form of poetic drama; Laurie Lee's *The Voyage of Magellan* makes us see the great voyage of circumnavigation through the inner eye of a blind old seaman; while Samuel Beckett's great radio plays, *All That Fall*, *Embers*, *Words and Music*, and *Cascando*, take us into a bleak world of regret and bitter memory. It was in a radio play, *The Trial of Lucullus*, that Brecht depicted the futility of war through a vision of the great Roman general's descent into Hades, and in a radio play that John Arden expressed his perplexity about the artist's political commitment in the form of a dream allegory, directly derived from Langland and Bunyan (*The Bagman, or The Impromptu of Muswell Hill*, 1970).

Both the subject matter and the material from which radio plays are built being, therefore, ultimately the process of imagining and thinking itself—truly such stuff as dreams are made on—the writer's, director's, and actor's craftsmanship must be both firm and delicate. The more potentially amorphous and shapeless the material, the firmer must be the structure that holds it in shape. Radio is a form of oral literature and therefore obeys some of the ancient principles that govern preliterate genres: the sermons of religious leaders like the Buddha, the long epic poems recited by Greek bards, or the short and pithy Scottish ballads. Structure, for example, can be imparted to such material by *repetition* in the form of recurring lines, refrains as in the French *ballade* form, or stereotype formulae as in the Homeric poems; by rhyme itself, the firm shape of the stanza form, and strong rhythm; by careful "signposting" of the structure itself (on the pattern of "there are three sins to avoid and the first of these is . . . the second of the three is . . . and the third of the three is"), so that the listener always knows exactly where he stands within the structure at any given moment. In the subtle art of the radio dramatist all these devices will be present, although probably not immediately visible to the

naked eye—or rather, ear. Clarity and transparency of structure, however, will always be basic; in a stage play, for example, if we look away
from the stage for a moment, the set is still there when we look back
and we can see which actors are still present. In a radio play, if a detail
is missed through lack of clarity, or if the listener's attention wanders
for a moment, he may have missed that the scene has changed, or that
one or the other of the characters is no longer present, and he has
no means of catching up with the action once the detail has been
missed—unless, that is, the structure of the play is so firm, its progression so clearly indicated throughout, that the balance can be re-
dressed, flagging attention brought up to date, almost immediately.

The volatile nature of the medium, moreover, and the ease with
which the attention can stray, or indeed, the set be switched off, if it
has flagged altogether, make it imperative to grab the listener's interest
and attention immediately and never to let go of it. This is a matter of
arousing expectation and suspense while at the same time remaining
extremely clear: one cannot count on the suspense of confusion,
which sometimes works on the stage when the audience is held by the
desire to see the confused situation being sorted out. In radio, too
much confusion would be deadly.

That is not to say that the lack of visual definition, the "blindness"
of the medium, does not have definite dramatic advantages. In Pinter's
radio play A Slight Ache, one of the characters is the mysterious
matchseller whom Edward and Flora ask into their home and to
whom they open their hearts. This character, who eventually takes the
husband's place in the home, never speaks; he is no more than a silence. It thus remains doubtful whether he does, in fact, exist in a material sense: perhaps he is merely the emanation of the two other characters' subconscious, a figment of their hidden fears and desires. It is
this unresolved ambiguity that constitutes the play's poetic force, its
hypnotic power. When the same play was performed on the stage, and
later on television, the presence of an old man in a shaggy coat completely destroyed that ambiguity. There was no doubt any longer that
the matchseller existed. His silence merely suggested that he was an
idiot, or a deaf-mute; he lacked all mystery, and the hysterical way
in which Edward and Flora addressed him even became somewhat
embarrassing.

Similarly, in Ingmar Bergman's radio play *A Painting on Wood*, the figure of Death in a Dance of Death is represented by silence. Death, being mere nothingness, mere absence, is here most effectively and realistically depicted. When Bergman made a film of his radio play— *The Seventh Seal*—Death became a medieval lay figure in a black costume, and thus far less terrifying, far less true to Death's real nature— the void; no more, in fact, than a character in a play impersonated by a handsome actor.

Silence is thus undoubtedly one of the most powerful elements in radio drama. But silence has to be most delicately handled. It must be led up to, built up towards a climax. A sudden and abrupt cessation of all sound would merely lead the listener to assume that his set had suddenly failed. Only when, as in the case of a character who is presumed to be present, who has been asked a question, who is about to answer, the certain expectation of such an answer is disappointed, only then can silence have that impact. Or to put it differently: the radio play is a continuum of sound; and only when that continuum is firmly established and clearly structured will the sudden gap in it become emotionally valid and make its point.

Radio writing, and writing for radio drama in particular, is thus, even more perhaps than the writing of stage dialogue, a matter of delicate timing—not only the sudden disappointment of an expectation of a speech to come, but also the unexpected turn of phrase, the surprising word at the end of a sentence, which will make for the release of suspense, emotion, or laughter.

Radio as an art form is essentially a matter of carefully timed pauses, rhythm, and pace. Monotony is the deadly enemy, for it lulls the mind and induces boredom. Therefore, the rhythm of the writing, the rhythm of the action must be subtly varied, like the best of dramatic blank verse; and so must the pace: fast scenes must follow slow ones, slow ones fast ones, short scenes long ones, and vice versa.

From all this it will be seen that the radio play approximates musical form—which is not surprising as both have sounds in time as their raw material. A good radio dramatist will have an overall formal concept of his piece: he will know where his slow movement will be and where his scherzo, where he can pull out the stops and where the soft passages will come.

Equally, in approaching his characters the radio dramatist must think musically: their voices are the instruments at his disposal; how will he orchestrate them? In the BBC's archives there is a long letter from Bernard Shaw in which that old music critic advises a producer how to cast a radio performance of *Saint Joan*: this character is a baritone, that one a light tenor, and a third a contralto. And there is a good practical sense in that approach: nothing will confuse the listener more than two characters with very similar voices.

Of course, there are other and subtler ways of characterization as well: in radio more than in any other kind of dialogue the speech patterns, vocabulary, accent, and linguistic idiosyncrasy of each character is the hallmark of the good writer. The most primitive way to achieve such linguistic characterization is the introduction of regional accents: hence the Scottish housekeeper, the cockney bus driver, the exaggeratedly well-spoken butler are the clichés of radio drama. But in the hands of the best writers, like Pinter or Arden, the differentiation of characters by their language is on an altogether different level. Certainly, writing for radio is an excellent training for any dramatist: it prevents him from relying lazily on his actors' appearances or personalities to save him from characterizing his creatures by endowing each of them with his own peculiar way of speaking.

Yet in radio drama, language has to carry a far heavier burden than that of mere characterization—it must evoke the visual background of the action and suggest the appearance of the characters themselves. In this it is comparable to those types of stage drama which could not rely on a great deal of scenery—such as the Elizabethan theatre. Obvious indulgence in long descriptive passages would clearly hold up the action and be thoroughly undramatic. The visual suggestion must therefore be subtly built into the dialogue at the same time as it carries the action. From a few telling strokes a skilled radio dramatist will be able to conjure up even more than merely the visual aspect of the scene—the very smell, the heat, the dustiness of a landscape can become powerfully felt in good radio.

And what about sound effects? Excessive reliance on sound effects is a sure indication of radio drama at a fairly primitive level. The trouble with the sounds we hear in nature or in daily life is that, being often associated with visual impressions, they are not always easy to recognize when merely heard. One often comes across radio scripts from beginners which try to locate the action of a play by, for example, starting with "Sounds of a cotton mill." The author thinks that this will be sufficient to tell all his listeners that the action takes place in such a factory. Yet a cotton mill probably sounds exactly the same as a toy factory or, indeed, a threshing machine, or the engines of an ocean liner. Most sound effects of this kind only come to dramatic life *after* the listener has been *told* what they represent.

There are exceptions, of course. Seagulls always suggest the sea (but probably only because repeated use in radio plays has made them into an aural chiché, an acoustic ideogram!) Curiously enough, so strong is the suggestive power of the word, that a hint in the dialogue often does more than the actual sound effect. It has happened to me that listeners have complimented me on the marvelous sound effects of the sea or the woods in a play I produced, when in fact I had not used any sound effects at all, but the dialogue had referred to the roar of the waves or the song of the birds.

Nevertheless, sound effects can be used most tellingly in radio drama, but only if they have been orchestrated into the total structural pattern, if they play the part of a refrain, a recurring image, or punctuate the dramatic climaxes of the action. Hearing doors being opened or closed each time a character enters a room is tedious and often unnecessary for the listener. Yet at the moment when the wife finally deserts her husband, the angry son leaves his father's house, a slammed door has an immense and immediate dramatic and symbolic impact.

The same considerations apply to music: any reliance on mood music for cheap effect is vulgar and a cliché, worse than the proverbial celestial choirs in the last minutes of Hollywood films. Moreover, the visual imagination of the listener must be considered; an intimate love scene accompanied by a symphony orchestra playing a Tchaikovsky symphony may well conjure up in the listener's mind not only the lovers but the orchestra as well—and in the same room: quite the wrong image.

Yet music, judiciously used, can also become an integral part of the overall sound structure of radio drama. It can punctuate climaxes, suggest moments when the action takes wing into dream or reminiscence, and provide a psychological counterpoint to the text (as, indeed, it should do in opera). And not only traditional music can serve these ends; radio has developed its own forms of music: electronic music and *musique concrète*, pure sounds produced electronically or sounds taken from nature and subjected to the infinite variety of treatment made possible by electronic filters and other devices that modify sounds, and the techniques of tape recording, which allow sounds to be speeded up or slowed down, played backwards, compressed, multiplied, heightened, or cut up into fragments.

Stereophonic broadcasting has added a further dimension to the technical resources of radio drama. Yet the aesthetic implications of the new technique are by no means clear at this moment. Stereophonic reception is, doubtless, better sound reception, it allows the ear to separate different strands of sound far more efficiently than monaural listening: background music can be clearly put behind the spoken dialogue; in crowd scenes it becomes possible to distinguish the drift of several focal points of action or conversation. But—by locating the characters in an arc from left to right, stereo in radio drama also deprives it of its special advantage as an immaterial medium not definitely located in space, able to move between dream and reality, the inner world of the mind and the outer world of concrete objects. So great is the suggestive power of the visual imagination that a room stereophonically put before an audience becomes firmly fixed in their minds, so that, if the next scene takes place, say, in a landscape, it will seem to them that a river has started to flow where the settee used to be, or a car now runs over chairs and tables. Moreover, twin channel stereo only allows horizontal movement: it is still difficult to suggest up and down, and the space thus evoked lacks a vital dimension. Experiments are on the way with four-track stereo, which will put the listener into the center of the action, but this will surely create new problems for drama by making all radio plays theatre in the round.

As long as the producer remains aware of the problems created by stereo, he can, however, overcome them: by, for example, treating a stereo play like a monaural one, that is, emanating from just one spot in space, but having it, as it were, surrounded by music.

The immense possibilities created by the infinite capacity of magnetic tape to be manipulated, by radiophonic sounds and music and

184

by stereo, have led to a resurgence of experiments towards more abstract forms of radio drama: montages of pure sound, pure language, fragments of reality filtered through electronics and collages of sound patterns. It is particularly in Germany where this new experimental form—*das neue Hörspiel* (*new radio drama* on the analogy of *le nouveau roman*)—has caused considerable activity and excitement. Some very fascinating works have emerged from this kind of experimentation; the question remains whether they can be classed as radio drama, or should not rather be regarded as a new form altogether— poetry of pure sound and linguistic experimentation, closely related to *poésie concrète*.

Be that as it may, the work of the director in radio drama remains a highly technical one, precisely because the elements he can play with are relatively few. Even the monaural microphone can suggest a variety of spatial perspectives. One of the director's main tasks in any radio play is to determine from whose point of view each scene should be played, so that the main character occupies the center of the picture while the others move in relation to him. This is just one of the many technical aspects of production which the director has to determine. His main task, however, lies outside the field of mere technique: the work on the preparation (which invariably means editing) of the text, which is the backbone and the essence of his material. Editing of a text for radio always means clarification, the ability to put oneself in the place of a listener who does *not* know the play and is in danger of getting lost in its complications. All great radio drama producers, like D. G. Bridson, Francis Dillon, Val Gielgud, Donald McWhinnie, Douglas Cleverdon, Archie Campbell, Raymond Raikes, Charles Lefeaux, are above all outstanding textual editors. Their work with the actors in the studio only becomes effective on the sure foundation of a totally elucidated, and therefore totally lucid, text.

Radio acting is an art in itself. The microphone is far nearer to the listener than a live actor can ever come even to the first row of the audience. The radio actor's art is thus among the most intimate kinds of acting. The problem is how to combine intensity and emotional impact without becoming overloud, overhysterical (to be two feet away from a raving hysteric is far from pleasant), ranting, theatrical. Characterization by the voice alone is also a very delicate and mysterious

185

matter: there is a kind of aural imagination that certain supreme radio actors possess which enables them to embody a character's appearance, gait, and gestures in subtle nuances of voice, intonation, or accent.

An actor portraying a policeman or a parlor maid on the stage has most of the basic task of characterization done for him by the costume he wears. But how do you talk so that everybody knows you must be a policeman? It seems impossible, yet it has been done again and again by superb radio acting. If one analyzes such a performance, one will find that the effect is based on the closest observation of real life and the imaginative use of such things as accent, pitch, and slowness of delivery. And this kind of primitive, primary characterization is merely the lowest rung of a ladder that leads up to the highest pinnacles of emotion and human truth.

Many outstanding stage actors have benefited from radio training. But this is not to say that all exceptionally successful stage actors will be equally successful in radio (they may compensate for a thin or colorless voice by a commanding physical presence, sparkling eyes, and expressive body on the stage) or, indeed, that the best radio actors will necessarily be impressive on the stage. Their approach may be too intimate and they may lack physical presence.

As radio drama nears the completion of its first half century we may well ask whether, in the television age, it still has a function and therefore a future. One would have to be a prophet to give a definite answer. At present the evidence points to a continued interest in radio plays, both as entertainment, which has now become omnipresent through the transistor set (which is much more mobile than television), and also as a vehicle for a serious poetic exploration of the human mind, a minority art form with great potential depth of insight and width of imaginative range.

Much will depend on factors outside the control of the artists involved: the politics of mass media control and finance may well wipe out an art form—as radio drama has, indeed, been virtually wiped out in the United States—much also on a modicum of critical interest in the press. It is one of the tragedies of a mass medium like radio that a play that may have one hundred thousand listeners—a thousand times more than say, the audience in an experimental theatre—will get far less critical attention than any Soho lunchtime production. At present, in Britain and on the continent of Europe, radio drama still gets a certain amount of reviewing (in Britain the quality papers and some of the weeklies have occasional radio reviews, though some of these, owing to lack of space, must necessarily be pretty perfunctory). Should this modest level of public reaction disappear, writing for radio would become unbearably frustrating. As it is at present, good writers are still attracted to radio, which, though less rewarding in fame or money than writing for television, gives far greater freedom of invention and does not suffer from the intellectual restrictions of a mass medium for the millions.

In a rationally organized civilization, therefore, there should be a place for radio drama just as there is one for chamber music or art cinemas. Radio drama can look back on an impressive record of achievement, both as regards sheer entertainment and the popularization of important stage plays. There is no reason why the future should not hold out the prospect of continued achievement in these spheres.

Television—Mass Demand and Quality

Television is the mass medium par excellence: consumed by a vast number of people in large quantities and requiring a vast supply of material for diffusion. Never, therefore, in the whole of human history, have the products which television diffuses—news, views, entertainments, drama, human personality—been ingested in such enormous quantities by such large masses of human beings. This observation points up the most obvious quantitative aspect of the phenomenon of television: in Great Britain—the first country in the world to introduce (in 1936) a regular television service and thus one of the most highly developed television areas in the world—the average viewing audience consists of between one-quarter and one-third of the total population. It is, of course, much higher during the peak viewing hours in the evening, when it can reach between 40 and 50 percent of the total population.

There are three different program channels at present available at peak time in most areas of Britain. Nevertheless, it can well happen that one of the most popular programs will be watched by more than one-third of the total population—an audience of sixteen to seventeen million people for a single play, light entertainment show, or serial. These figures must be viewed in relation to the sizes of audiences for a single event or artistic presentation in pre-mass-media epochs: one hundred thousand spectators for a football match or, assuming a theatre of a capacity of a thousand spectators giving eight performances a week, about one million spectators for a play that runs for more than two years to packed houses.

A single popular television play in Britian thus reaches an audience that corresponds to a run of more than thirty years in a theatre! And this happens not just exceptionally, but almost every day, and sometimes even several times in the same evening!

If we look at this phenomenon from a slightly different angle, its implications become even more staggering. Walking through any town or village in Britain on a summer evening when the windows are open, one can see the bluish sheen of the television screen in almost any house. It is therefore easily possible, if one knows which programs are at that moment being broadcast on the three available channels, to know what are the only three possible contents at that moment occupying the minds of the people inside the houses in that street. In times past another person's thoughts were one of the greatest of mysteries. Today, during television peak hours in one of the more highly developed countries, the contents of a very high proportion of other people's minds have become highly predictable.

Indeed, if we regard the continuous stream of thought and emotion which constitutes a human being's conscious mental processes as the most private sphere of his individuality, we might express the effect of this mass communications medium by saying that for a given number of hours a day—in the United Kingdom between two and two and a half hours—twentieth-century man switches his mind from private to collective consciousness. It is a staggering and, in the literal sense of the word, awful thought.

The above considerations are based on figures for television viewing in Britain, where more than 95 percent of all households possess a television set. While other countries may not yet have reached this state of saturation, the likelihood that they eventually will is extremely high, almost to the point of certainty.

Three different channels are available in Britain; in many countries there are fewer; in some, like the United States, where up to ten or more different channels may be available to viewers in the bigger metropolitan areas, there are more. Television in the United States is operated by private enterprise and supported by advertising, in contrast to most countries, where it is a public monopoly operated by an agency of the government. Taking the United States as an example, it would then appear that commercial television, offering more channels, provides the viewer with much more variety. Paradoxically, this is not the case.

The availability of more channels in a commercially operated system, like the American one, seems rather to restrict than to increase the choice for the viewer. This is true because market research is extensively used to determine what kind of program will appeal to the maximum number of viewers at a given time. As a result, there tend to be the same kinds of programs on all the channels—situation-comedy series next to other situation-comedy series, western against western, football (American variety) against football. This results in even greater uniformity in the type and level of material offered than in the British or German systems where at least two of the three channels are planned to provide genuine alternatives: serious against light material, arts against sports, intellectually demanding against popular fare.

Seen in such terms—millions of viewers hooked into the same stream of consciousness at a given moment—the quantitative aspect of the cultural revolution that the advent of television constitutes seems staggering enough. Yet, it might be argued, there is another, and even more staggering, even more revolutionary aspect to the matter. This, it seems to me, lies in the fact that the material of television— music-hall show or play or football game—is available *continuously* in an uninterrupted flow, on tap like piped water or electricity.

Admittedly, with the exception of the United States, the continuous stream of programs does not yet, in most parts of the world, cover all the hours of the day and night. However, even in those countries where television hours are still restricted to afternoons and evenings, they cover the periods when most people are at leisure to switch on; and, it seems to me, the extension of program hours to cover the whole day will eventually become inevitable. Already the continuous availability of this alternative collective consciousness is regarded as a basic human right by increasing numbers of people, so it will surely eventually be seen as highly unjust that people who work unusual hours—for instance, evening or night shifts—should be denied it.

Be that as it may. Even though in many countries the availability of a continuous stream of programs does not extend round the clock, the effects of broad availability are nevertheless fully apparent. What are these effects?

The main consequence of the continuous stream of material which television provides—continuousness being a quantitative aspect—is that it juxtaposes, and tends to reduce to the same level in the consumer's mind, very different kinds and categories of viewing matter, different not only in the superficial qualitative sense that some of it is better, some worse—and these terms will have to be more closely defined later—but in a far more basic regard. The viewer has come to see as *one kind of thing*—television programs—what is in fact an amalgam of very heterogeneous material, in a far deeper qualitative sense.

Unlike the theatre or the arts of painting and sculpture, television and its mass media similars, radio and the cinema, are primarily mechanical means of transmission and reproduction: they merely transmit material which is put before them, regardless of its nature. One can arrange the material transmissible by television in a spectrum ranging from total reality at the one end to total irreality (fictitiousness) at the other. Thus, we can begin with events totally unrelated to any planning done by the television industry, *e.g.* news films of a war or a natural disaster. Next are events that are still real, but foreseeable, so that they can be planned and in some degree preprocessed by the television producers, *e.g.* a coronation, a military parade, a sports event like the Olympic games. Then there is a range of events that are still real in the sense that they involve people in their real personalities, but are already structured and preplanned as entertainment, *e.g.* parlor games in which members of the public answer questions to win prizes, or studio discussions between well-known personalities. And finally, at the other extreme end of the spectrum are the totally fictitious events: a play, a serial, a feature film.

The effect of the continuousness with which this material is presented for entertainment is that it tends to blur the qualitative distinctions between the different kinds of material. A scene from the fighting in Vietnam which shows real soldiers really dying may precede or follow a scene from a war play with actors simulating war; a politician trying to raise real issues on which the population is to make up its mind may precede or follow a comedian who is merely using his personality to amuse an audience.

What is significant is that, to the audience as a whole, television is basically a medium of relaxation and entertainment. It is inevitable, therefore, that the distinctions between the real and the artificial tend to become blurred, at least subconsciously. But the critical consequence of this is that even by those who are quite clear in their minds as to what is reality and what is fiction, the ultimate qualitative judgement—was this good or bad television?—is made on the basis of *entertainment values*. Thus it may well happen—indeed will happen almost inevitably—that the real soldiers really dying in Vietnam will be judged as either more or less moving, absorbing, entertaining than the actors in the war play, and the politician by whether his performance was as entertaining as that of the comedian.

No wonder that comedians and other television personalities become figures of national importance and influence on a par with politicians, that politicians are judged by the electorate on the basis of their abilities as comedians or television pundits. The child who, on seeing the live television pictures of the first moon landing, remarked that he had seen more exciting television treatment of the same event in a science fiction serial a long time ago highlighted a very real problem with, in the very long run, very alarming consequences.

For the events which happen unexpectedly and spontaneously, the most real events of all, are the ones that are most outside the control and planning of the television producer and, therefore, tend to produce less good—in the sense of less entertaining, less skillful—television. The closer an event lies to the other end of the spectrum, the irrealistic end, the more manageable it becomes from the television producer's point of view. The quantitative aspect of continuousness thus acts to encourage fiction to invade reality: for example, a wrestling match that is entirely fair and therefore unpredictable will tend to make less entertaining television than one that is fixed beforehand according to a "scenario." Does this lead to more fixed wrestling matches? One does not have to answer the question: to put it is sufficient to highlight the problem.

The organizers of a demonstration who inform television news organizations beforehand that there will be violence that will provide good filmed news material are making use of the same basic problem of television. Because it is possible to film the event with a greater degree of planning and preparation, it assumes far greater importance in the minds of the viewers as a piece of news than it may well deserve.

The French dramatist, Claude Ollier, highlighted this disturbing aspect of the mass media in a radio play in which the assassination of a head of state ultimately turned out to have been prearranged by a broadcasting organization in need of really gripping firsthand news reporting. Reports that appear from time to time about executions held up or even arranged for the benefit of television cameramen in an African civil war show that the satirist, in this case, was by no means exaggerating.

The increasing theatricalization of public life and politics, the selection of candidates by their faces' aptitude to take makeup, the conduct of election campaigns according to the televisual potential of issues rather than their real relevance—all these are ultimately a consequence of the medium's insatiable demand for entertainment material, its consumers' insistence on being agreeably diverted at any time they feel in need of switching their minds from their personal to the collective consciousness.

On the other hand, the positive, beneficial effects of the vast quantity of material on real, semireal, and pseudoreal events that television pours out must not be overlooked. By the very fact that politics and public affairs have become a branch of the entertainment industry they have been brought nearer to millions and millions of people who never previously gave them a thought. The candidate for office may be selected according to the same criteria by which a film star is promoted, but he will also have become as familiar a personality as a film star to vast masses of electors whose interest would have remained dormant in the pretelevision age. And the sheer quantity of news films about an event like the war in Vietnam has, it can be very convincingly though never wholly conclusively argued, transformed American public opinion about it.

All this occurs at the most real end of the spectrum of television material. What of the middle ground of events involving real people but staged and stage-managed by television? This is an area which is of

193

immense importance to television producers precisely because of the medium's vast appetite for material.

Whereas real events are hard to capture and plan for, the wholly fictional program requires a very scarce commodity—writers and performers of outstanding ability—quite apart from being the most costly type of production because it needs long rehearsal and expensive sets and costumes. On the other hand, the pseudoevent, such as the parlor game, the talk show with its confrontation between interviewer and public personality, and a multitude of variations of the same pattern, is both plannable and relatively inexpensive to stage in terms of rehearsal time and sets, while still containing enough of the elements of the real and the spontaneous to make it absorbing viewing.

The greater the quantity of material a television system has to provide, the larger will this element have to loom in its output. It is for this reason that vast stretches of time on American television in the mornings and afternoons are filled by guessing and other games.

From a cultural point of view this material is the least positive aspect of television. It is entertaining but little else. Neither information nor edification are conveyed by it. In addition, by exposing members of the public to the lure of large prizes it contains an element of manipulation, of the exploitation of greed and of the longing for notoriety, which makes it less than just harmless amusement. The same applies to interview shows where one guest after the other is paraded before the audience, exposed to more or less searching questioning and then involved in general and fairly trivial conversation. Empty air time is here, literally, filled with vacuousness: the viewer switching off his consciousness and switching it on to material of this kind is replacing his own thoughts by a spiritual and intellectual vacuum.

Nonetheless, in the search for material to fill empty spaces by foreseeable and plannable events, television has occasionally performed socially useful acts. Thus, relatively little known kinds of sport—in Britain, for example, show jumping—which are exciting and spectacular to watch have been televised and have, in consequence, become highly popular.

Even the parlor game occasionally can provide information and excite new interests. To cite another example from the United Kingdom, a program of the parlor-game type, in which archaeologists were asked to guess the origin, nature, and age of objects supplied by museums, led to a vast expansion of interest in archaeology, a quickening of amateur exploration of the local past, and a rise in the sale of books on the subject.

It will have been noticed that the concept of "quality" has appeared with a variety of different meanings in this discussion. I have said that any program on this mass medium can be seen as good or bad from the point of view of the consumer, whose primary test, a short-term one, is whether it is entertaining or boring. I have also indicated that, from the point of view of the detached observer considering the effects of television in the long-term context of its impact on a society or culture, a program will be good if socially beneficial, bad if it tends, in the long run, to debase the cultural level of the society or to have harmful effects on its political health.

Now, in passing to the area of the wholly premeditated, planned type of television program, which is also the area where the mass medium conveys artistic values and may itself become something like an art, the concept of quality appears in a third form. Good or bad here means artistically successful or unsuccessful.

It is by no means certain that the quality of a program of this nature will be apparent to the viewer, who is, above all, preoccupied by entertainment value. The very profusion of quantity in television creates innumerable dilemmas of evaluation: the silliest parlor game may be infinitely more entertaining than an artistic masterpiece which—and here is the rub, and the measure of the dilemma—may in fifty years' time be appreciated as an immortal work.

The trouble is that, indeed, only time can reveal the really great artistic success. Who, fifty years ago, would have guessed that the silent film comedies of Chaplin and Buster Keaton would today be generally acclaimed as among the finest masterpieces of twentieth-century art, on a par with Proust and Picasso?

Television's appetite for skills of an artistic—or pseudoartistic—nature is literally insatiable. Whereas, before the advent of this mass medium, a country's theatre demanded no more than, say, one hundred or two hundred new plays from its dramatists each year, today a

195

country with three television channels may well present six or more dramatic programs (plays, serials, comedies) each evening and thus demand something like two thousand new dramatic scripts a year. Any look at actual television schedules will show that this is a highly conservative estimate.

The same—remaining in the relatively restricted and therefore comparatively easily surveyable field of drama—applies to the performers. Before the advent of this mass medium an actor who learned a new part could, if the play proved successful, count on appearing in it a hundred times or more in one theatre, and then afterwards touring in it to other parts of the country. On television a single performance practically saturates the entire population of the country. The public cannot accept the same actor in a multitude of parts within a short span of time, so the demand for actors also has vastly increased.

How many playwrights, how many actors of outstanding talent can a country produce? How many does it need to provide enough material for a full television service? The supply of talent cannot be unlimited. So here quantity directly creates a problem of quality.

This point has major cultural consequences in the case of the smaller countries or language areas. A country of three or four million inhabitants may simply not possess enough actors or playwrights to provide even a fraction of the material demanded by television. So the answer is found in the mass import of foreign material, dubbed or with subtitles, and this in the long run poses a serious threat to the cultural identity of the country concerned. One can say that the mass medium tends to create the large cultural unit.

In the case of large language areas, like those of the English- and Spanish-speaking countries, this cultural impact is at least part of a process of organic change, even though some of its effects—for example, the increasing Americanization of areas like Australia or New Zealand—may be viewed with distaste by some of those affected. In the case of smaller national cultures, however, the long-term effects may well be both much more far-reaching and more deplorable. This is particularly the case in countries that are not only small in area, but bordered by powerful neighbors—like Switzerland, where German, French, and Italian television can be received in considerable areas speaking the same language as the neighboring larger unit. Such countries are faced with powerful outside competition for loyalty, and this can generate potentially explosive centrifugal forces.

If the importing of television material is having such an impact on highly developed European countries, in the developing world, where television is often a prestige symbol of newly independent states, having neither a tradition of the skills required nor a reservoir of trained performers, these effects may be disastrously magnified—and surely will in the near future. It will require great insight and skill on the part of those in charge of television programming in these countries to avoid, or at least minimize, a really catastrophic development: the loss of their own cultural identities. Perhaps this can be done by judiciously mixing imports from very different areas and by concentrating on manifestations of the local culture which may be unspectacular—the local storyteller or folksinger—but which are firmly based in the national tradition.

It would be wrong, however, to regard the effects of the mass demand for drama, situation comedy, and spectacular musical and dance shows—at least in the larger culture areas—as wholly detrimental. A large demand stimulates talent. Indeed, throughout the history of art the highest achievements have always sprung from situations where many craftsmen or artists were engaged in satisfying a large demand: Rembrandt's artistic production was based on the widespread demand for portraits among the rich burghers of Holland, which evoked a numerically strong guild of painters; Shakespeare and Marlowe, Calderón and Lope de Vega, Racine and Molière were the peaks of a broadly based culture, which created a considerable demand for dramatists.

The same is true in the field of television of the artistic skills which spring directly from the production process. There can never have been as many highly skilled film directors and cameramen as we find today in countries like the United States, the United Kingdom, the Federal Republic of Germany, or France.

The effects of this on related arts, such as the cinema, are obvious. Many of the best filmmakers started their careers in television. And the cinema—it must perhaps be stressed—will in all likelihood emerge as the highest and most characteristic artistic achievement of our century when viewed from the vantage point of history.

The same is true of dramatists, at least in certain countries like the United Kingdom or the Federal Republic of Germany. The large demand for television drama is, without doubt, one of the reasons for the current flowering of dramatic talent in Britain. Many of the best playwrights—such as John Arden, David Mercer, and Harold Pinter—achieved their first successes in television.

In the United States, by contrast, the commercial nature of television has been detrimental to the development of drama: plays are too costly to produce relative to the size of the audience they can command, which in turn determines the advertising revenue. In many European countries the public-service concept behind the organization of the mass media has been able to counteract this tendency to make size of audience all-determining.

Precisely in the field of television drama, the quantitative demand has created certain characteristic forms, which have their strong negative aspects side by side with some positive ones.

The dramatic series, in which the same set of characters reappears in self-contained episode after self-contained episode, is perhaps the most characteristic feature of television. It is also one of the most formidable cultural phenomena of our time. These series are undoubtedly among the most popular features of television in the major countries and the characters they create become mythological figures with their own lives and personalities, which far transcend the relatively modest confines of their original *raison d'être*. They are the archetypes of twentieth-century man's collective consciousness and, perforce, also of his collective unconscious.[1]

Such series are the sagas of the twentieth century. They correspond almost exactly to the stories that, in primitive communities, bards and ballad singers used to provide, always about nearly identical exploits of the tribal heroes. The western series in particular here provide an uncannily apt parallel.

The mass demand, which, for the first time since man emerged from the primitive tribe, enables every member of the community in societies with freedom of communication and market research on the

1. For a fuller discussion of this phenomenon, see the next chapter.

response to the media, to have a say in the creation of its cultural material—whereas in every culture since antiquity, cultural creation always responded to the requirements of a small élite minority—and the annihilation of all physical distance through the electronic mass media (which Marshall McLuhan has rightly called the creation of the electronic village), have thus literally re-created something like the cultural situation of primitive man. The chief can once again speak directly to his people and can be instantly recognized by every member of the community, and the whole community again shares in the exploits of the heroes: real—the soldiers at the war front one sees in the newsreel, or the wise television pundits who are the medicine men of our societies; or legendary—the neomythological figures of the fiction serials.

The analogy is complete, but does it reveal a situation that is frightening or one that is reassuring? Neither, I think. For it has great positive as well as negative aspects: after all from primitive man's myths about heroes sprang such immortal works as the *Iliad* and the *Odyssey*. Television is, or can at least become, the great folk art of modern man. The huge quantity of material it produces, the vast number of human beings on which it has to draw do give it the character of genuine folk art—based on the demands of the mass rather than on the tastes of a few élitist figures.

The negative aspect of the above situation follows from the fact that while there is a true analogy with the primitive man in his tribe and his village, modern man is not a primitive and his world is a village only in the electronic, not in the literal sense. Clearly the possibilities of mass manipulation through television—commercial manipulation in some free-enterprise societies, political manipulation in collectivist countries—are truly frightening.

It seems to me, however, that the very quantity of television carries its own built-in safety valve. Television commercials may be effective sales devices, yet in the long run surely they must immunize their audience. The time will come when the law of diminishing returns sets in. The same is true—and even more so—of political propaganda using the mass media. And the same, surely, will be true of the less overt manipulation that is done simply by presenting the implicit moral and social values contained in entertainment programs, plays, and popular songs.

The very quantity of the material poured out to the electronic village must, over the generations, the decades, the centuries, produce a highly critical and sophisticated tribe, a community hardened and immunized against both the overt and the hidden manipulators. And such resistance to manipulation and criticism is also, I believe, the immediate task of those aware and informed enough to be able to think in the long term.

Criticism and judicious evaluation of material offered on the mass media must surely become one of the principal subjects treated in the education of future citizens in any truly democratic community. Since anyone who is familiar with the technical problems and procedures behind the scenes of the medium develops a trained eye to detect the concealed manipulation, surely generations of children who have grown up with television and become familiar with its techniques will no longer be as credulous and as naïve as their elders who first encountered it as a new toy when they were already adults. They will certainly develop their own almost automatic evaluation of the different kinds of material offered to them, will become able to distinguish between the real and the manufactured event, between the genuine and the synthetic personality, between the true work of art and the spurious hack product.

Television may have reduced our culture to the status of the primitive tribe, but that tribe will soon comprise the whole of humanity, without distinction of race, creed, or social class. That tribe will then, if external circumstances remain favorable, have vast opportunities of development—development towards mass sophistication, mass wisdom, and a genuine mass culture. These opportunities are made available, for the first time in history, by an electronic communications medium, which is able to bring the whole of human wisdom to every human being.

In the long term perhaps quantity will have become the foundation of a great leap forward in the overall quality of human culture and through it of human life itself.

The Television Series—The Modern Folk Epic

The most revolutionary aspect of the electronic mass media of communication is their continuous availability, even more so than their ubiquitousness. Never before in the history of mankind has there been a continuous stream of collective consciousness into which—in the advanced Western societies—every member of the community can at will at any time of the day or night plug himself in, thus filling his individual consciousness with the thought and emotional content shared at that instant by several million of his fellow citizens. In considering the sociology and aesthetics of the electronic mass media this is the principal and paramount factor to be kept in mind. Television critics tend to treat single programs in isolation as though they were individual works of art. In some sense they may be that, yet many other and more decisive aspects of their impact and, indeed, aesthetic ground rules will be lost by such a consideration.

For example, as the program-builders are intent on stopping people switching off when one item ends, the opening minutes, even seconds, of the next item are of crucial importance; for it is through these that the viewer's decision whether to switch off, or over to another channel, will be determined. If the first few seconds of the new item arouse expectation of something really good or thrilling to come, he may stay with the transmission; if not, he is irrevocably lost. Hence, no consideration of the structure of a television broadcast, whether dramatic or documentary, can dispense with a consideration of this iron law of program-building. In American television, where commercials are bound to intrude all too frequently, the same consideration applies every few minutes. Before each commercial break the viewer must be left hooked and expectant as to how the program will continue. Hence the dramaturgy of most American television plays or series will inevitably have to consist of a sequence of short-term cliff-hangers and climaxes.

But the consequences of this continual electronic media flow go even deeper. With the loss of a sense of occasion that accompanies a visit to the theatre or even cinema-going and the ease with which one can enter and leave the continuous stream of mass consciousness, one of the prime objectives of the program builder who wants to attract the maximum audience for the maximum length of time, must be to shape that amorphous continuity, to create fixed points that stick in the mind of the audience, to condition the audience into regular habits of viewing. Fixed points, which articulate the time-flow for each day (*e.g.* fixed times for news and weather reports) and for each day of the week (sports on Saturday or Sunday and a certain star's variety show each Thursday), are essential to enable the audience to build up expectations, to make them turn to this channel or that with some regularity. This is one of the prime reasons why the electronic mass media thrive on repetition and recurrence.

Another reason, no less potent, is the all-devouring nature of a medium that has to churn out material without interruption practically forever. A stage playwright may labor over a single work for years; if he gets it performed and it is successful, it will remain accessible for years, in its first long run, then on tour, then perhaps in revivals. The material of the mass media is instantly consumed. A piece of dramatic writing, once performed and seen by millions may perhaps get one or two repeats much later, but once broadcast, it is, to all intents and purposes, finished. The program planner sees an endless expanse of hours, days, months, years in front of him that must, relentlessly, be filled. It is clearly quite impossible (as is still possible in the theatre or even the cinema) to wait for good material to turn up and then to plan on the basis of what one has found. What if nothing good, or good enough, does turn up? Here too the regular fixed item is the answer to the planner's nightmare. A regular series every Monday followed by a regular series every Tuesday, Wednesday, and on through the week, assuages his *horror vacui*. Television planning is planning in strips: a fixed sequence vertically through the hours of the day (news, parlor game, chat show, dramatic series, variety series) and horizontally through the week (the same show every Monday at eight, another every Tuesday at eight and so on through the days of the week, month, and year). Only thus can the amorphousness of an unending timeflow be structured into a fixed roster of predictable items, which can then be varied to allow the once-off prestige show or classical play.

The planner's needs coincide with the viewer's urge. Anyone who has worked in mass communications knows that familiarity is not a handicap; the masses delight in the pleasures of recognition—of the familiar face, the familiar character, the familiar tune. Once they have found a hero in a play, they would like him to return and appear in a different adventure, different enough in detail from the last to have the suspense of the unknown, yet familiar enough in pattern to recapture the pleasure of the previous one. When faced with a completely new dramatic work the viewer has to undergo the difficult and intellectually demanding process of decoding a new exposition: who are the characters? how related? in what period of history? where do they live? All these questions have to be answered anew for each new play. The television series relieves the viewer of this recurring intellectual burden. He already knows the principal characters and their situation. Thus the exposition can be confined to presenting the particulars of just that one episode; and here too most of the work has been done beforehand: knowing the hero to be, let us say, a detective working in Los Angeles and knowing the pattern of the series in question, everything falls instantly into place.

That is why television drama, properly speaking, has practically disappeared from the commercial television screen in the United States, and why it has to fight an embittered rearguard action in the more fortunate European countries which have public service networks.

It is important to remember that there is not merely a difference in degree between television drama in the sense of a "single play" (as the TV jargon in England has it: there is a flavor of oddity in the term which sets the exception apart from the rule, which is the series) and the television series. The latter is a new genre, different in *kind* and obeying different aesthetic laws. If the single play is a product of *craftsmanship*, the series is an *industrial product*, mass-produced.

Series are planned in multiples of 13 (13 weeks are a quarter of the calendar year and television planning is done in quarters). Thus, even the least extensive series will need at least 13 scripts, but it is far more likely that 26, 39, 52, or if the series manages to run for years, 104, 208, 306 scripts will be needed. No author can write 13 plays about the same character within a reasonable time (and series must go out at weekly intervals), let alone 306 or 408. Hence, the necessity for series to be mass-produced by teams of writers.

Teams of writers must be centrally briefed and directed. (We are here in an industrial mass-production process with high initial investment). An idea is mooted, a pilot program written, discussed, produced, and market-researched. The result is a *format*, *i.e.* a number of recurring characters in a recurring pattern of situations: the lawyer who is also a detective, the sheriff in a western town and his sidekick, the spy, the spaceship with its astronauts, the silly ass husband and his resourceful wife in the situation comedy. The characters have descriptions which can be handed to the scriptwriters of different episodes; the structural pattern is mapped out once and for all. It remains only to decide on the nature of individual episodes in the series—there must be sufficient variation. The spy, for example, cannot operate in South American countries two or three weeks running, so an episode in South America must be followed by one in Eastern Europe or the Arctic and that, to get maximum variation, by one in the Far East; a very gruesome episode must be followed by a more lighthearted one; and there must be one with a lot of love-interest after one which was confined to conflict between hard-faced men. All the permutations of such variation must be gone through before a viable sequence is centrally determined—it is only after this that the writers can be commissioned and briefed and supplied with their do-it-yourself kits: "Here are your characters; here is your basic structural pattern (*e.g.* there must be a chase, or suspense sequence toward the end of each episode); and here is your basic situation. Now go away and write your episode!" There may be variations on this model of the production process, but basically this is how it must be set up.

Is this then the point at which we throw up our hands in horror at the death of individual creativeness, the degradation of art, the cynical manipulation of the masses by commercial interests and greedy exploiters? Possibly. Yet we should perhaps also pause and see the matter in perspective. From the point of view of nineteenth-century aesthetics (largely romantic in origin and basic viewpoint) this situation is indeed horrifying—the death of individuality, the end of art as a means of individual expression of individual emotion and experience. Yet there are possible standpoints which differ from the nineteenth-century romantic and individualist one. Elizabethan drama was written rapidly by teams of collaborators hurrying to supply material that was needed to vary the program. Here too the entrepreneurs farmed out predigested material to teams of hack writers (and yet many masterpieces resulted from this production process). And if we go back into the period of purely oral literature (and McLuhan is right in postulating a return to a period of electronically disseminated preliterate literature) we find very similar situations: bards spontaneously making up episodes in the lives of stereotyped heroes by using stereotyped elements (lines, situations, villains) for purely mercenary motives (to please the ruler who had summoned them to entertain his guests or to flatter his family). The literature of the folk epic is anonymous, does not express the author's individual emotions, uses prefabricated material—and yet it has produced some of the greatest works known to man.

How could this come about? The advocates of romantic aesthetics have their romantic answer: these works were not written by individuals, true enough, but they are the products of the soul of a whole people. Each individual bard has improved one or two lines as he repeated them, has adapted his material to the sensibility of his audience, so that ultimately the works in question were written by the nations that produced them, retaining the passages and episodes that pleased, forgetting those that proved unpopular.

How could we compare the products of calculating businessmen with the sacred distillation of a great nation's storehouse of folk myth? The answer, paradoxically, lies in the commercial motivation of the producers. As Kracauer has rightly pointed out in his study of the German film before Hitler, the cinema, by being responsive for commercial motives, to public demand, can actually be regarded as the collective dream material of a given culture and can be psychoanalyzed like an individual's dreams. The same, but even more so, is true of television, which is much more sensitive to the psychological needs or cravings of a much wider public (namely virtually the whole nation) simply because its products are consumed more frequently, in larger quantities, than any cinema films produced for showing in movie houses could ever be.

Once the format of a series is worked out, once it is running, the producers are subject to a constant stream of feedback: audience ratings, market research, correspondence. If they want to keep a series going they have to adapt the characters, the situations, the basic pattern to the demands of the public. Unsuccessful series die. But the survivors, as they progress, are ultimately shaped—indeed written—by the audience's subconscious. In my own very practical involvement with radio soap opera I have experienced this process at first hand. A series is launched with a given set of characters. An audience survey is made about the popularity of the main characters. Surprisingly, one of the more secondary characters proves the most popular. Gradually he is pushed into the center. And in the same way a series, once started, responds to the currents of public demand. It is *because* the makers of the series are motivated by their desire to succeed that the series, the longer they run, become more and more the product of the imagination, desires, fears, and dreams of their audience.

This, after all and to establish the historical continuity, was equally true of pulp fiction before the advent of the electronic mass media, of the early cinema, which met similar requirements from a mass audience. (One has only to think of the recurring character personified by Chaplin's Little Man, by Buster Keaton, the Marx Brothers, Laurel and Hardy, but also heroes and heroines like Douglas Fairbanks, Lillian Gish, and Mary Pickford, who, although they appeared in different situations, always portrayed themselves.) Or going back even further in time we recall the folk theatre (harlequinade, pantomime, *commedia dell'arte*) and earlier still the vast oral literature of folk tales (Robin Hood, King Arthur, knights errant) until we finally link up with the oral literature of the epic poetry of ancient Greece or Scandinavia.

This folk literature is the very opposite of individual creativeness: it represents a common meeting ground of the imagination of a people or civilization where its preoccupations and interests are focused. It is no coincidence, for example, that in American popular culture, long before the electronic mass media, the western theme dominated pulp fiction and popular entertainment like the circus (*cf.* the wild west shows). The western is a genuine folk myth; in vastly exaggerated and overdramatized terms it recounts the creation of a new country. The basic themes revolve round the introduction of law and order, the conflict of cattle men versus cereal growers, the conquest of the original inhabitants of the country, and so on. In this way the western myth is thematically analogous to the cycle of stories about the Trojan War which focused on a very similar subject, the conquest of Asia Minor by the Greeks. Similarly, the gangster cycle represents a preoccupation with the problems of the new urban society, and the spy and secret agent cycles show the fears of the cold war period. On the comedy level, innumerable situation comedies highlight the ever-recurring problems and anxieties of family life—the clumsy spouse ruining the party for the boss on whom promotion depends, the unruly children, and so on.

Folk art of this type, springing as it does, directly from the collective subconscious of simple people (including, of course, the vulgar and uneducated entrepreneurs who promote it) will inevitably be mostly crude, vulgar, repetitive, unoriginal, poorly characterized, and sentimental. What we must remember, however, is that the analogous productions of previous ages were probably equally crude and without merit. Of these, after all, only the very greatest have survived. The *Iliad* and the *Odyssey* are distillations of hundreds and thousands of crude episodes that were not worth preserving. And there are whole centuries of such popular products which have not survived at all, because they brought forth nothing worthy of survival.

In the cinema the western, the gangster, and the private eye cycle have already produced a few masterpieces. In a thousand years' time, if they survive at all, these may be the only examples out of many thousands of worthless products of the same thematic cycle that will be known and admired. There is no reason why the television serial should not also produce a few lasting masterpieces out of its many hundreds of thousands of worthless, crudely manufactured episodes.

Viewed in a purely American context therefore, the television series appears as true folk art, however vulgar or crude it may be. The impact of this folk art on Europe—and the rest of the world—is far more problematical.

The size of America as a market for this folk art, which enables its products to be sold cheaply to other parts of the world as a kind of bonus to their producers, means that the products of the collective subconscious of one nation are inundating the consciousness of other nations, whose problems may be completely different. One of the many revolutionary aspects of the continuous nature of the electronic media, particularly television, is that small nations are simply unable to mobilize the talent that would enable them to fill the endless hours of transmission time with indigenously produced material. Hence the inevitable invasion of the television screens of the world by material from those cultural units which are numerically strong enough to produce sufficient material. The United States and, to a lesser degree, Great Britain are the prime source of such material in the Western world. As far as the English-speaking countries are concerned, their screens are even more easily inundated by American television material. But all the other countries of Western Europe also import vast quantities, which they show dubbed or with subtitles.

We thus have the paradoxical situation of the folk art of one very specialized and particular culture invading the consciousness of the members of very different cultures; or, to put it at a different level of impact, the subconscious preoccupations and problems of one highly neurotic part of the world, being used to meet the perhaps very different subconscious needs of other areas and cultures.

The result, in the first instance, is bound to be misunderstanding and confusion. On the conscious plane, there is confusion about the true nature of American society. The country appears to many of the more simpleminded European consumers of mass entertainment as a land of gangsters and cowboys—primitive, lawless, and aggressive. On a deeper level, there is the spread of basic American attitudes and life-styles. There may also be subconscious revulsion and rejection of these life-styles. The anti-Americanism of many of the less sophisticated Europeans may be an outcome of such subconscious rejection of the American attitudes that are constantly dangled before them.

In the long run all this may turn out to be just one aspect of a global process of cultural unification, leveling, or ironing out of cultural differences, a reflection in the superstructure of consciousness of what is already taking place in the economic and social infrastructure. As vast multinational companies divide the markets of the world among them, as the politics of the atomic deterrent erode the autonomy of smaller units, so the iron laws of the technology of electronic entertainment will tend to abolish the cultural and psychological differentiation between the countries of the Western world. It is one of the ironies of this process that Western Europe, which might be the equal of the United States numerically and in economic potential, cannot reciprocate this process in the field of mass entertainment simply because of its cultural and linguistic divisions. If the import of American popular art could be matched by a corresponding export of European folk art to America, the situation would be far healthier. But with the exception of Britain, which does export a large amount of television material, as well as writers, actors, musicians (one only has to think of the Beatles or Rolling Stones) to America, Western Europe seems practically excluded from making an impact on the United States. The traffic here is strictly one-way. No wonder that this creates unease among European intellectuals, and a certain amount of revulsion among the masses.

The process thus seems inevitable. As American breakfast cereals, American soft drinks, American pop music, and American industrial practices spread in Europe, the American folk heroes also, inevitably, take over the fantasy world of Europeans. The conquest of the American West becomes one of the folk myths on which Italian peasants and German steelworkers are reared; Dr. Kildare and the inhabitants of Peyton Place; Ironside and the secret agents of UNCLE, Lucy and Dick Van Dyke, Charlie's Angels and the Fonz become their own folk heroes. One may regret this development, but short of totalitarian suppression (and this would leave large and painful gaps in the material needed by the mass media in Europe), there seems to be no remedy. What is particularly unfortunate in this situation is that by a historical accident the electronic mass media fell from the very beginning into the hands of the advertising industry in America, while in Europe the concept of public service broadcasting mitigated some of the more deplorable aspects that distort popular entertainment in the United States. Perhaps the success of some of the efforts to correct this imbalance in America by promoting at least one public service television network there provides some hope for the future. That programs like *Sesame Street* are now among those American television series that begin to have an impact on Europe may be a sign of better things to come. For, while there is nothing wrong with popular entertainment consisting of folk art, what is needed more than anything in the cultural impasse of our time is a bridge between the world of crude folk art and that of consciously cultivated high art. The deep division between the two spheres, which is so painfully manifest in the United States, is unhealthy and dangerous. Only conscious control of the electronic mass media, not in a totalitarian sense, but to provide a better admixture of material for the important culturally conscious minority and a chance for the masses to sample such material and to develop their tastes toward it, can counteract the dangerous tendencies towards a polarization of masses and élites, which are only too apparent in the United States today.

Television—The Social Impact

That the emergence of the electronic mass media, above all television, is effecting fundamental changes in politics and society is by now a truism of overwhelming obviousness. Yet the debate about the whys, wherefores, and possible corrective measures seems to me barren and unhelpful in the extreme. On the one hand it is being conducted on a strictly practical and pragmatic level (Is there too much violence on TV? Are interviewers too rude or not rude enough? Is there too much or too little time devoted to current affairs?) and, on the other hand, on a level of theoretical abstraction, which seems to me to miss many of the fundamental questions altogether. This applies to the prophetic visions of a Marshall McLuhan as much as to the severely "factual" and "scientific" sociological, statistical, semiotic, and other studies which are usually conducted in a jargon that seems impenetrable but soon reveals itself as merely a pretentious smoke screen masking banalities.

One of the chief failings of all this discussion, paradoxically in a field supposedly universal and tending to transform the world into a global village, is its parochialism. Vast theoretical structures are built on the strengths or shortcomings of the particular radio or television services in the authors' own countries, world-shaking generalizations are spun out of the personal idiosyncrasies of the presenters of *Panorama* or *News at Ten* in Britain, the twitchings of Walter Cronkite's moustache in New York, or the inane gigglings of Johnny Carson in California. It might, therefore, I thought, be of some interest to look at

211

the discussion about the media in a completely different linguistic and cultural context; and so I have been spending some time reading some of the products of German "*Medienkritik*" of the last few years. And while this made for even more dispiriting reading, it might have had the result of making one look at the familiar arguments from a slightly different standpoint.

It is in the nature of the present intellectual situation in West Germany that the three, fairly typical, products of *Medienkritik* that I used for this purpose are all "Marxist" in approach. It would lead too far, were one to try to account for this vogue of a modish but mostly misunderstood Marxism among German intellectuals in detail. It could be the effect of the intense and wholly laudable *Nachholbedürfnis* (need to catch up) which has dominated German cultural life in the last thirty years and has now led to German intellectuals reaching the point which the Auden-Isherwood-Spanish-Civil-War generation in England had reached about 1936. Or it might be due to the fact that the only towering intellectual giants writing in German in a period when intellectual life inside Germany had ceased altogether were Bertolt Brecht and Walter Benjamin, while among the returning intellectuals after the war, Max Horkheimer and T. W. Adorno were the most prominent—all Marxists to a man. Or, possibly, the ugliness of the money-grabbing *nouveaux riches* who emerged as the ruling class of West Germany through the *Wirtschaftswunder* has once more alienated the intellectuals into a stance of total opposition to the status quo. In any event "Marxism" in a bewildering variety of shades and colors is still the prevailing orthodoxy among intellectuals in West Germany.

The electronic media are the most attractive and promising field of employment for young intellectuals; hence, among the younger practitioners in radio and television (as in the theatre, in publishing, and in the press) "Marxists" abound. No wonder that frequently the tensions between these young Turks and the establishment of the media, much more directly under the control of the major political parties than in Britain, erupt in various crises and conflicts. That is why the call for a reform of the media is more stridently voiced in the West German Federal Republic than elsewhere. The *Medienkritik* by sociologists and publicists is largely motivated by such demands.

In the class society in an age of mass-communications the rulers
are not content with exploiting the dependent classes. In addition they systematically dominate their consciousness. A critique
of television has to proceed within the framework of this insight.
It has to start from the recognition that neither the communica-
tor nor the medium itself nor the recipient of its message can be
the center of analysis. The process of mental pauperization can
only be understood in the context of the processes of social production, socialization, and communication. Only thus will the
specific function of television in the final phase of capitalism become visible. For a large part of the population the mass media
do not serve as an instrument of communication. In the way they
are used they are comparable with Aladdin's lamp and are a
remedy against anxiety and frustration, an instrument to pro-
cure surrogates for satisfaction and sedation. In such a mental
climate spurious information and panic lie close together. We
shall show that in German television the invasion from Mars is
taking place every evening and that what happened in 1938 is an
exception only because then people rushed, panic-stricken into
the streets, while today it is the perverse rule that all that is silently accepted.

That is the thesis propounded by Götz Dahlmüller, Wulf D. Hund,
and Helmut Kommer in a massive volume.[1] This "handbook against
manipulation" is a product of strict party-line "Marxism" of the most
old-fashioned type of oversimplified *Vulgärmarxismus*. The content
of its 386 pages, for all its prolixity of detail and all its hypertrophy of
inflated jargon, could easily be accommodated on a postage stamp. It
amounts to no more than saying that in a capitalist society *all* institutions are geared to the oppression of the working class, and that you
will not get decent television unless capitalism is overthrown. There is
a curious inner contradiction in writing a long book criticizing details
of television on these lines. For if one believes the thesis, there is no
point in detailed criticism. Even the infiltration of the media by revo-
lutionaries would be ineffective so long as the structure of control by
the oppressive capitalist institutions is, as the authors postulate, quite
incapable of tolerating anything which does not expressly serve the

1. Götz Dahlmüller, Wulf D. Hund, and Helmut Kommer, *Kritik des
Fernsehens, Handbuch gegen Manipulation* (Neuwied: Luchterhand, 1973).

purpose of deceiving and mentally pauperizing the masses. Even the occasional left-wing program that gets by can (and the authors argue this quite specifically) be taken as a particularly Machiavellian device by which the oppressors manage to create the illusion that there is, after all, such a thing as freedom of speech in their system. And wouldn't *that*, by weakening revolutionary fervor, be the cruelest cut, the most dastardly, oppressive, manipulative device of all?

The most outlandish aspect of this curious book is its total un-awareness of the fact that television also exists in the *noncapitalist world*. Surely this is a circumstance that, to anyone with a truly scientific mind, would suggest a wide field of empirical confirmation of the theoretical postulates developed in the authors' argumentation. Take their demonstration that the transmission of football matches is a particularly wicked capitalist manipulative device:

> What, quite rightly, fascinates the audience here is the dialectic between the individual and the collective in the game. The skill and dexterity of the individual players and the manner of their cooperation in the strategy of football, united in a common will, is indeed a fascinating event: above all, *because the individual citizen hardly or never experiences anything like it in his social reality* [my italics].
>
> As a producer of social wealth he is isolated, as the mere bearer of a function separated from the collective work-process, abstractly determined by capitalist exploitative interests. The aggressions and tensions which arise everywhere where isolated producers meet, the low degree of solidarity of which they are capable owing to the fact that their individual striving and their true interests are in contradiction with each other, the absence of any real relationship, as producers, to the goods they produce and their utilization—all this seems as though it was wiped out, when they take in a football match. Here everything that does not work in the reality of society seems to function well: the solidarity of the teams, the insightful relationship of the individual to the collective, the insightful relation of all of them towards the common aim of their efforts, etc.
>
> Up to this point the football match would be an illusionistic vision of social harmony if it were not for the opposing team.

Through it alone does that tension enter the picture that makes it so valuable for the mass media, for it is through it that the game acquires its character of alternate cold and hot baths, which constitutes the insidious canalization of tensions that sport provides. The situation of the teams is determined by the fight they wage against each other and their aims are antagonistic, unrelated to any aim of a higher order, but merely towards victory over the adversary. In this respect football is a reflection of social antagonisms: the interests of the capitalists are incompatible with those of the wage-slaves, the interests of profit-maximization are incompatible with the need for optimal satisfaction of societal needs.

It is this double-bottomed quality above all, its ability on the one hand to reflect social antagonisms, and on the other, to create the semblance of nonalienated labor, which makes professional sport so suitable for canalizing social tensions.

And so on and on for another page. Quite apart from the piquancy of the particular jargon it provides (which may excuse the inordinate length of the quotation), this example poses, surely, a very simple question. If the authors succeed in convincing us that the televising of football matches is an insidious device by which the workers are being relieved of the otherwise unbearable tensions created by the alienated nature of their daily work, what then, pray, is the reason why the same football matches (in the case of, say, the World Cup) are also broadcast in the noncapitalist world and are, moreover, by general consensus, among the most popular broadcasts in those countries? And if, in those happy lands, social antagonisms no longer exist and the fact that the workers can clearly see the purpose and social relevance of their daily toil relieves them of frustration, why do they still revel in the antagonism of opposing teams, which to them must appear as quite unnecessary canalizations of tensions under which they no longer suffer?

A critique of the media so blinkered, so totally devoid of a sense of reality, is no more than an emotional release of the authors' own tensions and frustrations.

Hans Magnus Enzensberger, a poet and essayist of considerable stature, and a far more substantial spokesman of the West German New Left, recognizes this state of affairs, when he remarks in his essay

Baukasten zu einer Theorie der Medien (A Do-It-Yourself-Kit Towards a Theory of the Media), "The manipulation theory of the Left is
basically defensive, and must eventually lead to defeatism. This turn
towards the defensive is grounded, subjectively, on a feeling of impo-
tence. Objectively it is correlated to the entirely correct recognition of
the fact that the all-important means of production are in the hands of
the adversary. But to respond to such a state of affairs with moral in-
dignation is naïve." Enzensberger's essay appears in a volume containing a selection of his writings in English translation,[2] which, however, is barely readable because the translations of most of the essays
in it can only be understood by readers who know enough German to
refer to the original texts to make out what the translator wants to
say.[3] Enzensberger's main point, in dealing with the electronic mass
media, is a plea not to shy away from manipulation. If the ruling class
uses the mass media to manipulate the masses and their conscious-

2. Hans Magnus Enzensberger, *The Consciousness Industry: On Literature, Politics and the Media*, selected and translated by Michael Roloff (New
York: Seabury Press, 1974). This volume contains a selection of essays scattered in three volumes published in Germany by Suhrkamp Verlag of Frankfurt: *Einzelheiten I* (1962), *Einzelheiten II* (1963), and *Palaver* (1974).
3. Here are just a few examples picked out at random. "So now we can
hear it again, the little death nell for literature" (p. 83). Who, we might well
ask is Little Death Nell—a new heroine from Dickens, or a misprint for "the
death of Little Nell"? So we look up the original (p. 41 of Enzensberger, *Palaver*, where this essay, "Gemeinplätze die neueste Literatur betreffend," is re-
printed), and we find: "Jetzt also hören wir es wieder laüten, das Sterbeglöcklein für die Literatur." And now we realize: not a Little Nell, but a little knell
is meant. But what would a *little* knell be? The translator doesn't realize that a
Sterbeglöcklein is a little bell, which tolls a knell; but a knell can be neither
little nor large, merely soft or loud. A bell is a bell, but a knell is the sound
produced by ringing that bell. Elementary, my dear Watson.
In the same essay Enzensberger describes how some artists nowadays are
resolved to make an end of art. "The literati are celebrating the end of literature. . . . *The sculptors produce plastic coffins for their plastics*" (my italics).
Now what would that mean? No one who doesn't know German will ever
discover the answer. To know what that sentence means one must know that
in German *Plastik* means a sculpture, or the art of sculpture. So the sentence:
"Die Bildhauer stellen Plastiksärge her für die Plastik" means "The sculptors
are making plastic coffins for the art of sculpture"! A nice little translator's
carve-up; in French it might even go like a bomb.
Another example, a few lines on: "Almost everyone longs for certainty; and
if indeed it is all over and done with for writing, the fact evidently would be a
soporific." The reader is puzzled (or at least this reader was), so he proceeds to

ness, surely, he argues, the Left should do likewise rather than throw up its hands in moral horror. He wants them to mobilize the masses towards a new and revolutionary use of the media. How is this to happen?

As neither Marx nor Engels knew the electronic mass media and as a reference to sacred texts seems essential for adherents of a pseudo-theology like Marxism, some casual remarks which Brecht made about radio between 1927 and 1932, amounting to no more than some twelve pages in his collected works, have been elevated to the status of scripture. Brecht's main point was that radio should become more than merely a one-way means of communication; he wanted it to be used to enable the masses to get a hearing. This postulate has, in fact, been more than realized by the mounting volume of phone-in programs in the United States and Europe as well as through the copious use of the *vox-populi* type of interviewing on television and radio.

Enzensberger goes much further. He points out that, technically, every transistor radio is a potential radio transmitter and could be turned into one by a small modification. This may be true. But—and here again one is struck by the remoteness from reality that character-

---

the German original: "Nach Gewissheit verlangt es die meisten, und wäre es die, dass es aus und vorbei sei mit dem Schreiben. Auch das wäre offenbar noch eine Art von Beruhigung." Which means "Most people long for certainty, even if it were no more than the certainty that literature is finished. Even such a certainty would obviously bring a measure of relief." The translator here, apart from missing the movement of the thought, has simply mixed up *Beruhigung* (relief, something which restores one's calm) with *Beruhigungsmittel* (a medicine that calms the nerves or, more commonly, puts one to sleep).

And a final example, a few paragraphs on: "Since literature is made by the few for the few, it takes little to disturb this equilibrium." I could not follow the logic of this argument. So I went to the German. What does it say: "Da (die Literatur) von wenigen für wenige gemacht wird, genügen wenige um sie aus dem Gleichgewicht zu bringen." Which is much more logical, for it means, in fact, "As literature is made by few people for few people, a few people are sufficient to throw it out of balance."

And so on and so on. The trouble with the critique of translation is that it is not only boring, but totally meaningless for readers who are not familiar with *both* languages involved. That, alas, is why bad translations are rarely detected by English readers, and even more rarely castigated in the manner they deserve. Only translations so monumentally bad (like the above) that they become incomprehensible are even noticed.

izes such "revolutionary" musings—on what wavelengths would the millionfold transmissions of millions of individuals broadcasting on their transistor-transmitters be accommodated? And, indeed, who would want, or have the time, to hear what such immense numbers of individuals had to say? And would they *have* anything to say at all? In the far more important field of television even Enzensberger has to admit that this is a medium incapable of being used by each individual in a population. And so, after an opening of great pretence to originality and world-shaking, fundamental rethinking, Enzensberger's do-it-yourself kit for a new theory of the media comes down to a demand for the organization of cultural collectives, which should devote themselves to the production of programs that, somehow or other, would be offered to the establishment-run media. This is no more and no less than a plea for "access to the media," a demand that has increasingly been met in Britain in recent years and that, in the United States, is already embodied in the rules governing the running of local radio and television stations.

Access broadcasting of this kind does result in a wide variety of programs produced by pressure groups and collectives of various kinds. But in practice, the experience with access broadcasting highlights the basic dilemma that underlies Enzensberger's position. The views of minority groups will of necessity only appeal to a minority of listeners and viewers. Even if it were technically possible to accommodate multitudes of such minority broadcasts on the wave bands (or perhaps the far more numerous channels available in a cable service), this would lead at best to a fragmentation of the audience. It could diminish the mass appeal of the media and produce a veritable Babel of more or less relevant voices. At best, that is. What is much more likely is that highly professional and polished entertainment and news programs coming from the traditional sources would continue to command the allegiance of the vast majority of listeners and viewers, while the numerous "access" broadcasters would be crying in the wilderness.

Again, the impenetrable parochialism of this kind of universalist theorizing seems remarkable. Enzensberger need only have looked across the northwestern borders of the Federal Republic to see the system he advocates in full operation in Holland. There both radio and television transmitters are put at the disposal of any political or other group which can command the support of more than a certain number of listeners or viewers. The system works, but it works not much better, and perhaps a little worse, than elsewhere. It is significant that recent developments there point towards ever-increasing support for nonpolitical, entertainment-oriented listener and viewer associations at the expense of the more ideologically committed ones.

What Enzensberger's demands ultimately amount to is the wish to transform *mass* media into the equivalent of small-circulation poetry magazines or intellectual quarterlies with which a poet and highbrow pundit like Enzensberger is happiest and most familiar. But the mass media, alas, are and will remain media for the masses. Frank Boeckelmann, a sociologist close to the Frankfurt school, is trying to come to grips with that aspect of the problem.[4] Although written in the obscurantist, pseudophilosophical jargon so beloved by those masters of the Frankfurt school, Adorno and Horkheimer, Boeckelmann's book contains much good sense and a number of valuable insights.

Boeckelmann's starting point is Professor Jürgen Habermas' concept of the structural transformation of the "public domain"—the dissolution of the nineteenth-century liberal concept of a private and a public sphere, which neatly separated the state from society. In the public domain or the political arena, responsible citizens met to debate and give form and shape to public opinion. With the increasing intermingling of the public and private sphere (where, for instance, the welfare state has taken over many of the functions previously exercised within the privacy of the family), public opinion has become more and more institutionalized. It is no longer the product of genuine debate among individuals, formed, as it were, from below, but is imposed from above by the spokesmen of pressure groups like political parties and trade unions. Deprived of any real influence on the formation of public opinion, the individual becomes merely a passive recipient of ready-made standpoints between which, at best, he has a choice. In attempting to fit the mass media into this theoretical framework, Boeckelmann makes a very important point: the mass media certainly have their impact on the population by the way they treat the news they put before the public. But even more decisive is another,

4. Frank Boeckelmann, *Theorie der Massenkommunikation* (Frankfurt: Suhrkamp Verlag, 1975).

and far less obvious, way in which they shape the minds of their passive audience. For they not only give the news they put out their own slant and interpretation, they, above all, also *select*, among the infinite number of occurrences in politics, culture, economics, sport, crime, and other spheres, those they feel ought to be treated. And it is quite true, if one thinks about it for a moment, that the choice of the subjects which are deemed to have *news value* or to be worthy of treatment as features or plays, is very restricted indeed, and seems pretty arbitrary at that. By concentrating on some groups of subjects and excluding others from the vast number of potential topics, the mass media (the press, radio, and television) tend to create an institutionally sanctioned *artificial reality*, a synthetic mental environment for the masses. The themes selected must be able to arouse interest and hold the attention of the public. Boeckelmann lists some of the formal and presentational criteria that are used to arouse attention: personalization of the subject matter; concentration on success and achievement; novelty; aggressiveness; stress on the advantages of normality as against the penalties of abnormality; the appeal of wealth; the appeal of the exotic, bizarre, and unusual.

In a long section of his book Boeckelmann tries to assess the *impact* of the mass media and comes to the conclusion that it is wrong to talk about direct *effects* of the mass media on their audience by, for example, establishing a causal relationship between violence on the media and increased crime in society. Here he touches the central problem of any rational approach to the study of the influence of the mass media and any practical understanding of the ways in which they can be controlled and made to serve society in a positive and constructive manner. Yet, as seems inevitable in a writer so wrapped up in narrow sectarian prejudice and so remote from experience in the actual working of the media, his belief that the selection of topics for the media could be fairly easily improved if it were made by more enlightened individuals is of disarming naïvety. He submits a long list of "neglected" themes which should be treated by the media, and it ranges from "housing problems" and "the life of old people" to "history of the working class movement." Again, the habitual parochialism in the approach of a "social scientist" is most striking. Whether these topics are neglected in West Germany or not, in many other equally capitalistic, equally "class-dominated" countries like Britain, Sweden, Italy, Austria, Finland (to name but a few of whose production I have some firsthand knowledge), they are among the most frequent subjects dealt with in news, features, and drama.

The selection of themes in the mass media may be dull, unskillful, and even injurious to the cultural well-being of a society. But is it as arbitrary as it may appear to a naïve observer? This question cannot be answered by simply looking at the media in isolation. It amounts to more—no less than raising the far larger question of what constitutes the content of a society's collective consciousness, its general framework of knowledge, values, interests. It is not enough to deplore the fact that people are more interested in personalized than abstract news, that their attention is more easily aroused by sex and violence than by aesthetic or intellectual values. One must also ask *why* this is so. A critique of the mass media in any given society must, therefore, be firmly anchored in a consideration of its general cultural level, and of the structures of the emotions and aspirations which lie beneath the surface of its educational institutions. *Why* is it that violence has such a powerful pulling power? *Why* is it that audiences are quite clearly unable to take arguments above a certain level of abstraction? Is it due to purely environmental factors (*e.g.* a low educational level)? Or are there genetic limitations to the number of individuals in any society who have the ability to think abstractly, or would *not* be more easily aroused by sex and violence than by fine musical counterpoint or brilliant philosophical argument?

Yet, these questions probably being beyond a satisfactory answer at present, and things being as they are, are the topics dealt with in the mass media really selected arbitrarily by the individuals who are presumed to be running them? It seems astonishing that sociologists like Boeckelmann pay little attention to the processes by which topics rise to the surface in a society like his own, let alone in societies organized on a different pattern, like those of the Soviet Union or China. In a society with a free press, for example, the competition among newspapers alone will ensure that there can be no question of topics for discussion being arbitrarily chosen by a small clique of manipulators. The criteria by which the inclusion of items in television and radio news bulletins is determined may be—and indeed often are—unimaginative and willful. But the decisive factor in their selection is not the arbitrary whim of a manipulator but a fairly general consensus on what constitutes "news values" in the society in question. And this consensus is based not on some fossilized dogma but on the continuous experience of all engaged in the process. New subjects, ignored by the establishment, continuously seep in from the fringe. Provided the society is free enough to voice minority views, there will be a continuous dialectic between established values and the onrush of views and interests from the fringe of the established sector. The rise of the so-called underground press in the United States and Europe is a case in point. Hitherto taboo subjects were quickly absorbed from it into the established press and acquired "news value," and indeed so were the individual journalistic talents the underground threw up. And who, in the age of urban guerrilla warfare and anarcho-terrorism, would deny that groups outside the establishment have the means by which their concerns, the burning themes they want to endow with news value, can be injected into the store of media topics?

The same considerations operate in the selection of subjects for nonnews programs. The equivalent to the underground press in the Western world is the fringe theatre. Here, too, a continuous process of absorption of topics, writers, actors, and directors is at work. What was off-off-Broadway one day may well be on Broadway the next and actually dominate television and radio the day after. This is true of new trends in pop music as well as in serious drama. In Britain the speed with which the writers, directors, and actors of the fringe theatre are taken up by television is remarkable. One need only think of playwrights like John McGrath, David Edgar, Howard Brenton, David Hare, Howard Barker, whose work for television is not a whit more "establishment-minded" than anything they may have written for the fringe. Nor is this merely so in the "serious" sector of drama. One has only to think of how an antiestablishment fringe author like Johnny Speaight came to the fore in the most popular area of mass entertainment with a series like *Till Death Us Do Part* in Britain, and then even had his basic—and by no means unsubversive idea—transferred to the United States and adapted to conditions there (as *All in the Family*) and then translated, for better or worse, into problem-laden German for television and the stage, to see that the "circulation of the fringe élite" even imposes themes across national frontiers.

In an open society where individuals and small groups retain the possibility of publishing their ideas in little magazines or underground papers, where fringe theatre can still be produced without major capital investment, the system by which topics are selected for the media is, by and large, self-correcting. "News values" and the themes which absorb the public's attention may be perverse, trivial, or obtuse; but they will, taken over all, be a mirror of the society's collective mind. For those who run the mass media, even though they might themselves believe that they are manipulators of the public consciousness, are themselves only exponents of that consciousness (the less outstanding their intelligence and the more average their background and education, the more this holds good). They are subject to the same fluctuations of its interests and preoccupations. They are also, because they want to succeed in holding their audience's attention, under immense pressure to respond to its demands. If they fail, they are bound to lose touch and to diminish their own influence. Ironically, the best evidence for this comes from the totalitarian countries, where the mass media are indeed rigidly manipulated from above and where the emergence of new topics is much more difficult. As the gap between the social reality in the audience's daily lives and that presented by the media widens, their impact also is reduced.

When I visited Georg Lukács in Budapest shortly before he died, he passionately condemned the vicious manipulation of the masses in the West. When I interjected that after all the ceaseless outpourings of propaganda from radio and television in the Eastern countries must also be regarded as a form of mass-manipulation, he dismissed this argument with the casual remark: "That propaganda is utterly harmless because nobody believes a word of it!" And, indeed, in a society where crime or accidents are not reported, where the audience finds that life's daily vexations are completely ignored by the media, their credibility and influence must be greatly reduced. The massive jamming of foreign broadcasts by the Soviet authorities, however, shows that the demand to hear about the topics not selected by the manipulators persists. So does the incessant striving to get the suppressed topics out into the open, whether in *samizdat* publications or in novels and plays written in what Lukács called "Aesopian language."

That the selection of themes in an open society ultimately constitutes a self-correcting system does not mean that the situation could not be improved. It could, indeed, be argued that *more* rather than less manipulation would be needed to improve it. In the United States, where radio and television are largely in the hands of the advertising industry, the service provided is highly unsatisfactory—not because it is undemocratic but because it is far *too* democratic. What market research establishes as the "most popular" material so dominates the TV channels that the needs of important, but numerically small, minorities are not met at all by the commercial operators, and only marginally by the under-capitalized "public service" network. And while a commercial system *does* assimilate new material, even if it originates from strictly antiestablishment sources, this happens only if (like a new wave of popular music) it is likely to appeal to a vast majority. In Europe the public service, or mixed-economy, patterns of control of the mass media *can* result in a conscious effort to meet the needs of minorities as well. Moreover, by not being under a constant compulsion to please the largest possible number, they can experiment with different topics and forms and thus, perhaps, create new demands. There can, after all, be no demand for something which is not as yet known. The dramatic rise in the demand for classical music and serious drama in Britain (still only that of a minority, but one that has grown spectacularly over the last half-century) is a case in point.

The improvement of the systems by which the mass media are operated and above all by which the selectors of the material for the mass media are themselves selected thus remains an important problem. That the excessive influence of political parties in the governing bodies of the broadcasting organizations of West Germany and Italy is a source of considerable weakness is only too obvious. More than that, all "public service" organizations are prone to become self-perpetuating oligarchies. In a period when parliamentary institutions are rapidly losing their prestige and influence, is the arena of politics itself being usurped by the mass media? And does this give the controllers of the media an undue influence?

A continuous discussion of these matters in the media themselves and in the press is, clearly, of the utmost importance. In view of the fact that the media are themselves dependent on the general cultural and educational climate of a society, it is equally imperative that the gap which at present exists between the media and education should be filled. Not only do children tend to learn more from television than they ever learn at school; the lessons they absorb from these two sources are frequently in direct contradiction. The educational system should, as a matter of the highest priority, teach its pupils the art of watching and interpreting the media, developing a critical sense, and thus immunize them against the worst abuses of addiction to television.

All this, of course, presupposes that the media are effective in dominating the mind of society. But there is an immense amount of confusion as to how and to what extent such a domination actually occurs. Political parties and antiporn crusaders seem to believe in an immediate short-term impact of anything that is said on the media. In fact, experience tends to show that this kind of impact is minimal. In populations exposed to innumerable news broadcasts, only a tiny minority can ever be relied upon to know the names of even a few of the important politicians, regular "talking heads" on the home screen. The extensive exposure of the pros and cons of the Common Market during the referendum campaign in Britain signally failed to create genuine understanding of even the most simple basic facts among the vast majority of the British public. This may be due to the fact that the visual image of television communicates personality and external appearance more effectively than concepts verbally communicated. It could also be that the circumstances under which television is received do not favor concentration but induce an almost semiconscious state of relaxed half-attention. Yet television commercials have an immediate, and statistically measurable, direct short-term impact on the sales of the products they advertise. But these are visual and often musical rather than mainly verbal. They are very short, are frequently repeated, and contain slogans and jingles which stick in the memory through rhythm and rhyme rather than rational argument.

For the short-term communication of *messages* television seems a fairly inefficient medium. Marshall McLuhan's slogan that the medium *is* the message, although overstated as behooves the prophetic stance of that great stimulator of ideas, comes far nearer to the true state of affairs. What television brings about, above all, is a fundamental change in the life-style and habits of its audience. Beyond that there is only a slow and gradual change in attitudes and the general content of their consciousness. It is precisely the passive, semialert state of mind in which television is watched that ensures that nonverbal contents—images—which consciousness itself perhaps never knowingly perceived, are subliminally absorbed. And these are more powerful than the much more obvious surface content of a news bulletin or play.

It is this, incidentally, which makes conscious manipulation of populations by television so difficult. The makers of the program themselves will largely be unaware of the aspects of their work which will have such subliminal impacts. They may thus transmit their own subconscious impulses far more efficiently than their conscious intentions. For example: the news-reader who is earnestly striving to make the white paper he is talking about as lucid and comprehensible as possible may merely be transmitting his taste in ties or hairstyles to the audience. Or, over a long period of time, the only lasting effect of months and months of watching and listening to the media may be the adoption of a new habit of speech which will remain operative in the audience long after the conceptual content of what they heard is evaporated and forgotten. The "manipulators" are thus, to a large extent, unaware of what they are actually achieving, and they are quite unable to control it.

In itself, this is nothing new. The spirit of an age, as embodied in its literature, painting, or architecture, discloses only to later generations what it was really about. *We* can see what motivated styles like the gothic or baroque, literary movements like romanticism or expressionism and what it *really* was that they tended to express, while the artists (and their audiences) concerned remained unaware of the deeper, subconscious implications of their work. If Siegfried Kracauer in his famous book *From Caligari to Hitler* was able to isolate the roots of future Nazi violence in the early German cinema, the films of the 1920s (even those produced by completely unpolitical or anti-Fascist directors and writers), this was due to the fact that these films expressed the subconscious attitudes of the producers as well as the audiences. Ultimately the producers and the audiences belong to the same cultural milieu and respond to the same impulses. The idea that there is a rigid dividing line between the "manipulators" and the audiences of the mass media, with wholly conscious operators working on the wholly passive minds of helpless victims, is a fallacy. If, as the "access" programs show, the recipients of the message change places with those who usually transmit it, the difference in basic approach is minimal. What is noticeable is merely the difference in professional skill.

In an open society, therefore, the mass media must be seen as intimately and indissolubly linked with the general fabric of society, its psychological cravings, subconscious wishes, its interests and instinctive drives as well as the conceptual content of its culture, the topics it discusses, the matters it wants to know about. The truly dangerous aspect of the electronic mass media is the fact that their technology—the scarcity of wavelengths, the vast cost of production of television programs—limits the number of outlets and thus compels monopolistic or oligopolistic forms of organization. In the present state of technology there is no easy way round this situation. But it is clear that the less totalitarian the system of control and organization of the media, the better it ensures their receptivity to the true tendencies and movements of society's conscious and subconscious states of mind—and the more acceptable they will be. Nor must it ever be forgotten that a free movement of ideas and artistic impulses outside the field of the media is essential for the well-being and healthy functioning of the media themselves. In a totalitarian society they will, of necessity, be out of touch with social reality. In an open society the public will get the media it deserves, but at least, in getting no better than it deserves it will be able to become more conscious of its own shortcomings and enable individuals who respond to these shortcomings to contribute to their exposure and eventual transcendence. In that sense the media—in an open society in which they are rationally and flexibly organized—can, in the long run perhaps, raise the level of self-awareness of that society, and gradually contribute to an improvement in the quality of life it offers.

Aristotle and the Advertisers—The Television Commercial as Drama

We have all seen it a hundred times, and in dozens of variations: that short sequence of images in which a husband expresses disappointment and distress at his wife's inability to provide him with a decent cup of coffee and seems inclined to seek a better tasting potion outside the home, perhaps even at the bosom of another lady; the anxious consultation, which ensues between the wife and her mother or an experienced and trusted friend, who counsels the use of another brand of coffee; and finally, the idyllic tableau of the husband astonished and surprised by the excellence of his wife's new coffee, demanding a second—or even a third!—cup of the miraculously effective product.

A television commercial. And, doubtless, it includes elements of drama, yet is it not too short, too trivial, too contemptible altogether to deserve serious consideration? That seems the generally accepted opinion. But in an age when, through the newly discovered technologies of mechanical reproduction and dissemination, drama has become one of the chief instruments of human expression, communication, and indeed, thought, all uses of the dramatic form surely deserve study. If the television commercial could be shown to be drama, it would be among the most ubiquitous and the most influential of its forms and hence deserve the attention of the serious critics and theoreticians of that art, most of whom paradoxically still seem to be spellbound by types of drama (such as tragedy) that are hallowed by age and tradition, though practically extinct today. And surely, in a civilization in which drama, through the mass media, has become an omnipresent, all-pervasive, continuously available, and unending stream of entertainment for the vast majority of individuals in the so-called developed world, a comprehensive theory, morphology, and typology of drama is urgently needed. Such a theory would have to take cognizance of the fact that the bulk of drama today is to be found not on the stage but in the mechanized mass media, the cinema, television, and in most civilized countries, radio; that, both on the stage and in the mass media, drama exists in a multitude of new forms, which might even deserve to be considered genres unknown to Aristotle—from mime to musicals, from police serials to science fiction, from westerns to soap opera, from improvisational theatre to happenings—and that, among all these, the television commercial might well be both unprecedented and highly significant.

The coffee commercial cited above, albeit a mere thirty to fifty seconds in length, certainly exhibits attributes of drama. Yet to what extent is it typical of the television commercial in general? Not all TV commercials use plot, character, and spoken dialogue to the same extent. Nevertheless, I think it can be shown that most, if not all, TV commercials are essentially dramatic, because basically they use mimetic action to produce a semblance of real life, and the basic ingredients of drama—character and a story line—are present in the great majority of them, either manifestly or by implication.

Take another frequently occurring type: a beautiful girl who tells us that her hair used to be lifeless and stringy, while now, as she proudly displays, it is radiantly vital and fluffy. Is this not just a bare announcement, flat and undramatic? I should argue that, in fact, there is drama in it, implied in the clearly fictitious character who is telling us her story. What captures our interest and imagination is the radiant girl, and what she tells us is an event which marked a turning point in her life. Before she discovered the miraculous new shampoo she was destined to live in obscurity and neglect, but now she has become beautiful and radiant with bliss. Are we not, therefore, here in the presence of that traditional form of drama in which a seemingly static display of character and atmosphere evokes highly charged, decisive events of the past that are now implicit in the present—the type of drama, in fact, of which Ibsen's *Ghosts* is a frequently cited specimen?

What, though, if the lady in question is a well-known show business or sporting personality and hence a *real* rather than a fictitious character? Do we not then enter the realm of reality rather than fictional drama? I feel that there are very strong grounds for arguing the opposite: for film stars, pop singers, and even famous sporting personalities project not their real selves but a carefully tailored fictional image. There has always, throughout the history of drama, been the great actor who essentially displayed no more than a single, continuous personality rather than a series of differing characters (witness the harlequins and other permanent character types of the *commedia dell'arte*; great melodrama performers like Frédéric Lemaître; great comics like Chaplin, Buster Keaton, Laurel and Hardy, or the Marx Brothers; or indeed, great film stars like Marilyn Monroe or John Wayne—to name but a very few). Such actors do not enact parts so much as lend their highly wrought and artistically crafted fictitious personality to a succession of roles that exist merely to display that splendid artifact. Hence if Bob Hope or John Wayne appear as spokesmen for banking institutions, or Karl Malden as the advocate of a credit card, no one is seriously asked to believe that they are informing us of their real experience with these institutions; we all know that they are speaking a preestablished, carefully polished text, which, however brief it may be, has been composed by a team of highly skilled professional writers, and that they are merely lending them the charisma of their long-established—and fictional—urbanity, sturdiness, or sincerity.

There remains, admittedly, a residue of nondramatic TV commercials: those which are no more than newspaper advertisements displaying a text and a symbol, with a voice merely reading it out to the less literate members of the audience, and those in which the local car or carpet salesman more or less successfully tries to reel off a folksy appeal to his customers. But these commercials tend to be the local stations' fill-up material. The bulk of the major, nationally shown commercials are profoundly dramatic and exhibit, in their own peculiar way, in minimal length and maximum compression, the basic characteristics of the dramatic mode of expression in a state of particular purity—precisely because here it approaches the point of zero extension, as though the TV commercial were a kind of differential calculus of the aesthetics of drama.

Let us return to our initial example: the coffee playlet. Its three-beat basic structure can be found again and again. In the first beat the exposition is made and the problem posed. Always disaster threatens: persistent headaches endanger the love relationship or success at work of the heroine or hero (or for headaches read constipation, body odor, uncomfortable sanitary pads, ill-fitting dentures, hemorrhoids, lost credit cards, inefficient detergents that bring disgrace on the housewife). In the second beat a wise friend or confidant suggests a solution. And this invariably culminates in a moment of insight, of conversion, in fact the classical anagnorisis that leads to dianoia and thus to the peripeteia, the turning point of the action. The third beat shows the happy conclusion to what was a potentially tragic situation. For it is always and invariably the hero's or heroine's ultimate happiness that is at stake: his health or job or domestic peace. In most cases there is even the equivalent of the chorus of ancient tragedy in the form of an unseen voice, or indeed, a choral song, summing up the moral lesson of the action and generalizing it into a universally applicable principle. And this is, almost invariably, accompanied by a visual epiphany of the product's symbol, container, trademark, or logo—in other words the allegorical or symbolic representation of the beneficent power that has brought about the fortunate outcome and averted the ultimate disaster; the close analogy to the *deus ex machina* of classical tragedy is inescapable.

All this is compressed into a span of from thirty to fifty seconds. Moreover such a mini-drama contains distinctly drawn characters, who, while representing easily recognizable human types (as so many characters of traditional drama), are yet individualized in subtle ways, through the personalities of the actors portraying them, the way they are dressed, the way they speak. The setting of the action, however briefly it may be glimpsed, also greatly contributes to the solidity of characterization: the tasteful furnishings of the home, not too opulent, but neat, tidy, and pretty enough to evoke admiring sympathy and empathy; the suburban scene visible through the living room or kitchen window, the breakfast table that bears witness to the housewifely skills of the heroine—and all subtly underlined by mood music rising to a dramatic climax at the moment of anagnorisis and swelling to a triumphant coda at the fortunate conclusion of the action. Of all the art forms only drama can communicate such an immense amount of information on so many levels simultaneously within the span of a few seconds. That all this has to be taken in instantaneously, moreover, ensures that most of the impact will be subliminal—tremendously suggestive while hardly ever rising to the level of full consciousness. It is this which explains the great effectiveness of the TV commercial and the inevitability of its increasing employment of dramatic techniques. Drama does not simply translate the abstract idea into concrete terms. It literally incarnates the abstract message by bringing it to life in a human personality and a human situation. Thus it activates powerful subconscious drives and the deep animal magnetisms that dominate the lives of men and women who are always interested in and attracted by other human beings, their looks, their charm, their mystery.

"A message translated into terms of personality"—that, certainly, is one of the focal points around which TV commercials turn: the housewife, attractive but anonymous, who appears in such a commercial, exudes all the hidden attraction and interest she can command. Each of these mini-playlets stands by itself. Each is analogous to a complete play in conventional drama. It can be shown repeatedly and can have a long run, but then the characters in it are spent. There is another form, however, even more characteristic of television drama—the serial. The series of plays featuring a recurring set of characters is the most successful dramatic format of television. No wonder, then, that the TV commercial mini-drama also resorts to the recurring personality, be he or she fictional; real-life-synthetic, like the film stars or sporting heroes mentioned above; or allegorical, like the sweet little lady who embodies the spirit of relief from stomach acids and miraculously appears with her pills to bring comfort to a succession of truck drivers, longshoremen, or crane operators suffering from upset tummies.

The free interchangeability of real and fictional experts in this context once again underlines the essentially fictitious character even of the "real" people involved and shows clearly that we are dealing with a form of drama. The kindly pharmacist who recommends the headache powder, the thoughtful bespectacled doctor who recounts the successes of a toothpaste, the crusty small-town lady grocer who praises her coffee beans with the air of experience based on decades of wise counseling are manifestly actors, carefully typecast; yet their authority is not a whit less weighty than that of the rare actual experts who may occasionally appear. The actor on the stage who plays Faust or Hamlet does not, after all, have to be as wise as the one or as noble as the other: it suffices that he can *appear* as wise or as noble. And the same is true of the dramatized advertisement: since illusion is the essence of drama, the illusion of authority is far more valuable in the dramatized commercial than any real authority. The fact that an actor like Robert Young has established himself as a medical character in an evening series enables him to exude redoubled authority when he appears in a long series of commercials as a doctor recommending caffeine-free coffee. It need not even be mentioned any longer that he is playing a doctor. Everybody recognizes him as a doctor while also remaining completely aware that he is an actor. (It is Genet, among modern playwrights, who has recognized the role of illusion as a source of authority in our society. His play *The Balcony* deals with precisely that subject: the insignificant people who have merely assumed the trappings of bishop, judge, or general in that house of illusions, the brothel, can, in the hour of need, be used to convince the masses that those authorities are still present. Many TV commercials are, in fact, mini-versions of *The Balcony*.)

The creation of authority figures—in a world where they are conspicuously absent in reality—can thus be seen as one of the essential features and endeavors of the TV commercial. That these authority figures are essentially creations of fiction gives us another important indication as to the nature of the drama we are dealing with: for these authority figures, whether fictional or not, are perceived as real in a higher sense. Fictions, however, which embody the essential, lived reality of a culture and society, will readily be recognized as falling within the strict definition of *myth*. The TV commercial, no less than Greek tragedy, deals with the myths at the basis of a culture.

This allows us to see the authority figures that populate the world of the TV commercial as analogous to the characters of a mythical universe: they form an ascending series that starts with the wise confidant who imparts to the heroine the secret of better coffee (a Ulysses or Nestor) and leads via the all-knowing initiate (pharmacist, grocer, doctor, or crusty father figure—corresponding to a Tiresias, a Calchas, or the priestess of the Delphic oracle) into the realm of the great film stars and sporting personalities who are not less but even more mythical in their nature, being the true models for the emulation of the society, the incarnation of its ideals of success and the good life, and immensely rich and powerful to boot. The very fact that a bank, a cosmetics firm, or a manufacturer of breakfast foods has been able to buy their services is proof of that corporation's immense wealth and influence. These great figures—Bob Hope, John Wayne, John Travolta, Farrah Fawcett-Majors—on the one hand, lend their charisma to the businesses with whom they have become identified, and on the other, they prove the power and effectiveness of those concerns. In exactly the same way, a priest derives prestige from the greatness of the deity he serves, while at the same time proving his own potency by his ability to command the effective delivery of the benefits his deity provides to the community. The great personalities of the TV commercial universe can thus be seen as the demigods and mythical heroes of our society, conferring the blessings of their archetypal fictional personality image upon the products they endorse and through them upon mankind in general, so that John Wayne becomes, as it were, the Hercules, Bob Hope the Ulysses, John Travolta the Dionysos, and Farrah Fawcett-Majors the Aphrodite of our contemporary pantheon. Their presence in the TV commercial underlines its basic character as ritual drama (however debased it may appear in comparison to that of earlier civilizations).

From these still partially realistic demigods the next step up the ladder of authority figures is only logical: we now enter the realm of the wholly allegorical characters, either still invested with human form, like the aforementioned Mother Tums, a spirit assuming human shape to help humans as Athene does when she appears as a shepherd or Wotan as the Wanderer, or openly supernatural like the talking salad that longs to be eaten with a certain salad dressing, the syrup bottle that sings the praises of its contents, the little man of dough who incarnates the power of baking powder, the tiny pink and naked figure who projects the living image of the softness of a toilet tissue, or the animated figures of the triumphant knights (drawing on the imagery of Saint George and the Dragon) who fight, resplendent in shining armor, endless but ever victorious battles against the demons of disease, dirt, or engine corrosion—a nasty crew of ugly devils with leering, malicious faces and corrosive voices.

The superhuman is closely akin to the merely extrahuman. The talking and dancing animals who appear in the commercials for dog and cat foods are clearly denizens of a realm of the miraculous and thus also ingredients of myth; so, in a sense, are the objects that merely lure us by their lusciousness and magnetic beauty: the car lit up by flashes of lightning which symbolize its great power, the steaks and pizzas that visibly melt in the mouth. They, too, are like those trees and flowers of mythical forests that lure the traveler ever deeper into their thickets, because they are more splendid, more colorful, more magnetic than any object could ever be in real life.

Into this category, by extension, also fall the enlarged versions of the symbolic representation of products and corporations: those soft drink bottles the size of the Eiffel tower, those trademarks which suddenly assume gigantic three-dimensional shape so that they tower above the landscape and the people inhabiting it like mountain ranges, the long lines of dominoes that collapse in an immense chain reaction to form the logotype of a company. Here the drama of character has been reduced to a minimum and we are at the other end of the spectrum of theatrical expression, the one contained in the word itself—*theatron*—pure spectacle, the dominant element being the production of memorable images.

Like all drama, the TV commercial can be comprehended as lying between the two extremes of a spectrum: at one end the drama of character and at the other the drama of pure image. In traditional drama one extreme might be exemplified by the psychological drama-of-character of playwrights like Molière, Racine, Ibsen, or Chekhov; the other extreme by the drama of pure image like Ionesco's *Amédée*, Beckett's *Happy Days* or *Not I*. On a slightly less ambitious plane, these extremes are represented by the French bedroom comedy and the Broadway spectacular. At one extreme, ideas and concepts are translated into personality, at the other, the abstract idea itself is being made visible—and audible.

It is significant, in this context, that the more abstract the imagery of the TV commercial becomes, the more extensively it relies on music: around the giant soft drink bottle revolves a chorus of dancing singers; the mountain range of a trademark is surrounded by a choir of devoted singing worshippers. The higher the degree of abstraction and pure symbolism, the nearer the spectacle approaches ritual forms. If the Eucharist can be seen as ritual drama combining a high degree of abstraction in the visual sphere with an equally powerful element of music, this type of TV commercial approaches a secular act of worship: often, literally, a dance around the golden calf.

Between the extremes, which represent the purest forms at the two ends of the spectrum, are ranged, of course, innumerable combinations of both main elements. The character-based mini-drama of the coffee playlet includes important subliminal visual ingredients, and the crowd singing around the superlifesize symbol contains an immense amount of instantaneous characterization as the faces of the singers come into focus when the camera sweeps over them: they will always be representative of the maximum number of different types—men, women, children, blacks, Asians, the young, and the old—and their pleasant appearance will emphasize the desirable effects of being a worshipper of that particular product.

The reliance on character and image as against the two other main ingredients of drama—plot and dialogue—is clearly the consequence of the TV commercial's ineluctable need for brevity. Both character and image are instantly perceived on a multitude of levels, while dialogue and plot—even the simple plot of the coffee playlet—require time and a certain amount of concentration. Yet the verbal element can never be entirely dispensed with. Still, all possible ways of making it stick in the memory must be employed: foremost among these is the jingle, which combines an easily memorized, rhymed, verbal component with a melody, which, if it fulfills its purpose, will fix the words in the brain with compulsive power. Equally important is the spoken catchphrase, which, always emanating from a memorable personality and authority figure, can be briefer than the jingle and will achieve a growing impact by being repeated over and over until the audience is actually conditioned to complete it automatically whenever they see the character or hear the first syllable spoken.

Brecht, the great theoretician of the didactic play (*Lehrstück*), was the first to emphasize the need for drama to be "quotable" and to convey its message by easily remembered and reproduced phrases, gestures, and images. His idea that the gist of each scene should be summed up in one memorable *Grundgestus* (a basic, gestural, and visual as well as verbal, instantly reproducible—quotable—compound of sound, vision, and gesture) has found its ideal fulfillment in the dramaturgy of the TV commercial. And no wonder: Brecht was a fervent adherent of behaviorist psychology and the TV commercial is the only form of drama that owes its actual practice to the systematic and scientifically controlled application of the findings of precisely that school of psychological thought. Compared with the TV commercial, Brecht's own efforts to create a type of drama that could effectively influence human behavior and contribute to the shaping of society must appear as highly amateurish fumbling. Brecht wanted to turn drama into a powerful tool of social engineering. In that sense the TV commercial, paradoxically and ironically, is the very culmination and triumphant realization of his ideas.

From the point of view of its *form*, the range of TV commercial drama can thus be seen as very large indeed: it extends from the chamber play to the grand spectacular musical; from the realistic to the utmost bounds of the allegorical, fantastical, and abstract. It is in the nature of things that, as regards content, its scope should be far more restricted. The main theme of this mini-species of drama—and I hope that by now the claim that it constitutes such will appear justified—is the attainment of happiness through the use or consumption of specific goods or services. The outcome (with the exception of a few noncommercial commercials, that is, public service commercials warning against the dangers of alcoholism or reckless driving) is always a happy one. But, as I suggested above, there is always an implied element of tragedy. For the absence of the advertised product or service is always seen as fatal to the attainment of peace of mind, well-being, or successful human relationships. The basic genre of TV commercial drama thus seems to be that of melodrama in which a potentially tragic situation is resolved by a last-minute miraculous intervention from above. It may seem surprising that there is a relative scarcity of comedy in the world of the TV commercial. Occasionally comedy appears in the form of a witty catchphrase or a mini-drama concentrating on a faintly comic character, like that of the fisherman who urges his companions to abandon their breakfast cereal lest they miss the best hour for fishing and who, when induced to taste the cereal, is so overwhelmed by its excellence that he forgets about the fishing altogether. But comedy requires concentration and a certain time span for its development and is thus less instantly perceivable than the simpler melodramatic situation, or the implied tragedy in the mere sight of a character who has already escaped disaster and can merely inform us of his newfound happiness, thus leaving the tragic situation wholly implicit in. the past. The worshippers dancing around the gigantic symbol of the product clearly also belong in this category: they have reached a state of ecstatic happiness through the consumption of the drink, the use of the lipstick concerned, and their hymnic incantations show us the degree of tragic misfortune they have thus avoided or escaped. There is even an implication of tragedy in the straight exhortation uttered by one of the tutelary demigods simply to use the product or service in question. For failure to obey the precepts uttered by mythic deities must inevitably have tragic results. Nonfulfillment of such commandments involves a grave risk of disaster.

And always, behind the action, there hovers the power that can bring it to its satisfactory conclusion, made manifest through its symbol, praised and hymned by unseen voices in prose or verse, speech, or song. There can be no doubt about it: the TV commercial, exactly as the oldest known types of theatre, is essentially a religious form of drama which shows us human beings as living in a world controlled by a multitude of powerful forces that shape our lives. We have free will, we can choose whether we follow their precepts or not, but woe betide those who make the wrong choice!

The moral universe, therefore, portrayed in what I for one regard as the most widespread and influential art form of our time, is essentially that of a polytheistic religion. It is a world dominated by a sheer numberless pantheon of powerful forces, which literally reside in every article of use or consumption, in every institution of daily life. If the winds and waters, the trees and brooks of ancient Greece were inhabited by a vast host of nymphs, dryads, satyrs, and other local and specific deities, so is the universe of the TV commercial. The polytheism that confronts us here is thus a fairly primitive one, closely akin to animistic and fetishistic beliefs.

We may not be conscious of it, but this *is* the religion by which most of us actually live, whatever our more consciously and explicitly held beliefs and religious persuasions may be. This is the actual religion that is being absorbed by our children from almost the day of their birth.

And no wonder—if Marshall McLuhan is right, as he surely is, that in the age of the mass media we have turned away from a civilization based on reading, linear rational thought, and chains of logical reasoning; if we have reverted to a nonverbal mode of perception, based on the simultaneous ingestion of subliminally perceived visual and aural images; if the abolition of space has made us live again in the electronic equivalent of the tribal settlement expanded into a global village—then the reversion to a form of animism is merely logical. Nor should we forget that the rational culture of the Gutenberg galaxy never extended beyond the very narrow confines of an educated minority élite and that the vast majority of mankind, even in the developed countries, and even after the introduction of universal education and literacy, remained on a fairly primitive level of intellectual development. The limits of the rational culture are shown only too clearly in the reliance on pictorial material and highly simplified texts by the popular press that grew up in the period between the spread of literacy and the onset of the electronic mass media. Even the Christianity of more primitive people, relying as it did on a multitude of saints, each specializing in a particular field of rescue, was basically animistic. And so was—and is—the literalism of fundamentalist forms of puritan Protestantism.

Television has not created this state of affairs; it has merely made it more visible. For here the operation of the market has, probably for the first time in human history, led to a vast scientific effort to establish, by intensive psychological research, the real reactions, and hence also the implicit mechanisms of belief, displayed by the overwhelming majority of the population. The TV commercial has evolved to its present dramaturgy through a process of empirical research, a constant dialectic of trial and error. Indeed, it would be wrong to blame the individuals who control and operate the advertising industry as wicked manipulators of mass psychology. Ultimately the dramaturgy and content of the TV commercial universe is the outcrop of the fan-

239

tasies and implied beliefs of those masses themselves; it is they who create the scenarios of the commercials through the continuous feedback of reactions between the makers of the artifacts concerned and the viewers' responses.

It would be wholly erroneous to assume that the populations of countries without TV commercials exist on a higher level of implied religious beliefs. In the countries of the Communist world, for example, where commercials do not exist, the experience of the rulers with the techniques of political persuasion has led to the evolution of a propaganda which, in all details, replicates the universe of the TV commercials. There too the reliance is on incantation, short memorable catchphrases endlessly repeated, the instant visual imagery of symbols and personality portraits (like the icons of Marx, Engels, and other demigods carried in processions, the red flags, the hammer-and-sickle symbolism) and a whole gamut of similarly structured devices that carry the hallmark of a wholly analogous primitive animism and fetishism. It is surely highly significant that a sophisticated philosophical system like Marxism should have had to be translated into the terms of a tribal religion in order to reach and influence the behavior of the mass populations of countries under the domination of parties which were originally, in a dim past, actuated by intellectuals who were able to comprehend such a complex philosophy. It is equally significant that citizens of those countries that are deprived of all commercials except political ones become literally mesmerized and addicted to the Western type of TV commercials when they have a chance to see them. There is a vast, unexpressed, subconscious yearning in these people not only for the consumer goods concerned, but also for the hidden forces and the miraculous action of the spirits inhabiting them.

In the light of the above considerations, it appears that not only must the TV commercial be regarded as a species of drama, but that, indeed, it comes very close to the most basic forms of the theatre, near its very roots. For the connection between myth and its manifestation and collective incarnation in dramatized ritual has always been recognized as being both close and organic. The myth of a society is collectively experienced in its dramatic rituals. And the TV commercial, it seems to me, is the ritual manifestation of the basic myth of our society and, as such, not only its most ubiquitous, but also its most significant form of folk drama.

What conclusions are we to draw from that insight (if it were granted that it amounts to one)? Can we manipulate the subconscious psyche of the population by trying to raise the level of commercials? Or should we ban them altogether?

Surely the collective subconscious that tends to operate on the level of animistic imagery cannot be transformed by any short-term measures, however drastic. For here we are dealing with the deepest levels of human nature itself that can change only on a secular time scale— the time scale of evolutionary progress itself. Nor would the banning of TV commercials contribute anything to such a type of change.

What we can do, however, is become aware of the fact that we are, here, in the presence of a phenomenon that is by no means contemptible or unimportant, but on the contrary, basic to an understanding of the true nature of our civilization and its problems. Awareness of subconscious urges is, in itself, a first step towards liberation or at least control. Education and the systematic cultivation of rational and conscious modes of perception and thought might, over the long run, change the reaction of audiences who have grown more sophisticated and thus raise the visual and conceptual level of this form of folk drama. A recognition of the impact of such a powerful ritual force and its myths on children should lead to efforts to build an ability to deal with it into the educational process itself. That, at present, is almost wholly neglected.

And a recognition of the true nature of the phenomenon might also lead to a more rational regulation of its application. In those countries where the frequency of use of TV commercials and their positioning in breaks between programs rather than within them is fairly strictly regulated (Germany, Britain, Scandinavia, for instance), TV commercials have lost none of their efficacy and impact but have become less all-pervasive, thus allowing alternative forms of drama—on a higher intellectual, artistic, and moral level—to exercise a counterbalancing impact. Higher forms of drama, which require greater length to develop more individualized character, more rationally devised story lines, more complex and profound imagery, might ultimately produce a feedback into the world of the commercial. Once the commercial has ceased to be—as it is at present—the best produced, most lavishly financed, technically most perfect ingredient of the whole television package, once it has to compete with material that is more intelligent and more accomplished, it might well raise its own level of intelligence and rationality.

These, admittedly, may be no more than pious hopes, whistling in the dark. Of one thing, however, I am certain: awareness, consciousness, the ability to see a phenomenon for what it is, must be an important first step towards solving any problem. Hence the neglect of the truly popular forms of drama—of which the TV commercial is the most obvious and most blatant example—by the serious critics and theoreticians of that immensely important form of human expression seems highly regrettable. The TV commercial—and all the other forms of dramatic mass entertainment and mass manipulation—not only deserve serious study; a theory of drama that neglects them seems to me elitist, pretentious, and out of touch with the reality of its subject matter.

A Note on Sources

The essays in this volume appeared originally, in somewhat different form, in the following publications:

Reinhardt—Creator of the Modern German Theatre, *Drama Review* (June, 1977).

Brecht—The Icon and the Self-portrait, *Encounter* (December, 1977).

Brecht in Chinese Garb, *Encounter* (August, 1966).

Brecht's Poetry in English, *Books and Bookmen* (August, 1976).

Beckett and His Interpreters, as the introduction in *Samuel Beckett: A Collection of Critical Essays.* Edited by Martin Esslin. Englewood Cliffs, N.J.: Prentice-Hall, 1965.

Beckett's Novels, in *The Novelist as Philosopher.* Edited by John Cruickshank. London: Oxford University Press, 1962.

Beckett's Poems—Some Random Notes, in *Beckett at Sixty.* Edited by John Calder. London: John Calder, 1967.

A Theatre of Stasis—Beckett's Late Plays, *Gambit,* vol. VII, no. 28, 1976.

Samuel Beckett and the Art of Broadcasting, *Encounter* (September, 1975), incorporates an article, "Beckett's Rough for Radio," *Journal of Modern Literature* (February, 1977).

The Unnamable Pursued by the Unspeakable, *Encounter* (March, 1979).

A NOTE ON SOURCES

The Mind as a Stage—Radio Drama, *Theatre Quarterly,* vol. I, no.
   3, 1971.
Television—Mass Demand and Quality, *Impact of Science on So-
   ciety,* vol. XX, no. 3, 1970.
The Television Series—The Modern Folk Epic, in *Superculture:
   American Popular Culture in Europe.* Edited by C. W. Bigsby.
   London: Paul Elek, 1975.
Television—The Social Impact, *Encounter* (February, 1976).
Aristotle and the Advertisers—The Television Commercial as Drama,
   Kenyon Review (Fall, 1974).

Index

INDEX

Kafka, Franz, 80, 93, 98, 178
Keaton, Buster, 195, 206, 230
Kierkegaard, Sören, 80–84, 90, 91
Kommer, Helmut, 213–14
Korsch, Karl, 59, 60
Krapp's Last Tape (Beckett), 119, 125, 134, 136

Laurel and Hardy, 206, 230
Lee, Laurie, 179
Lessness (Beckett), 140–41
Leventhal, A. J., 155–56, 164
Literary criticism. *See* Critism
Livings, Henry, 175

McLuhan, Marshall, 131, 172, 199, 205, 211, 225–26, 239
MacNeice, Louis, 179
McWhinnie, Donald, 128–30, 132–37 *passim*
Malacoda (Beckett), 112–13
Malone Dies (Beckett), 100, 102–103, 113, 134
Marx Brothers, 206, 230
Marxism: and Brecht, 4, 41–43, 52–53, 54–60, 72; critique of television, 212–17
Mass media: access broadcasting, 218–19; impact, 219–22, 227; open vs. closed societies, 221–24, 227. *See also* Radio; Television
Media. *See* Mass media; Radio; Television
Meditation, The (Beckett), 133
Mercer, David, 198
Merchant of Venice (Shakespeare), 19, 20, 29
Me-ti (Brecht), 40, 54–64
Midsummer Night's Dream, A (Shakespeare), 14–15, 19, 29
Molloy (Beckett), 84, 100–102, 108, 133, 134
More Pricks Than Kicks (Beckett), 89, 95–96
Murphy (Beckett), 79, 96–97, 98
Music: in Beckett's works, 135–36, 147; in radio plays, 181–84; in television commercials, 235–36

Naughton, Bill, 175
Netherlands, 218–19
Newby, P. H., 125–26
Nihilism, 84–85
Not I (Beckett), 118, 120–21, 123, 124, 146, 152, 235

Old Tune, The (Pinget), 137–38
Ollier, Claude, 193
Owen, Alun, 175

Picasso, Pablo, 195
Pickford, Mary, 206
Pinter, Harold, 142, 176, 180, 182, 198
Play (Beckett), 83, 89, 117–18, 138–39, 140
Plays for radio. *See* Radio drama; and titles of specific plays
Plays for television. *See* Television drama; and titles of specific plays
Playwrights. *See* Radio drama; Television drama; and names of playwrights
Poetry: Brecht, 61, 65–72; Beckett, 107, 109, 111–16, 123
Proust, Marcel, 78, 81, 89, 94, 178, 195

Radio: technical aspects, 129, 182–85; nature of medium for drama, 130–32, 134, 172–87; Beckett's imagery, 146; compared with silent movies, 171–72; compared with television, 173, 175; promotion of arts, 173–76; in Netherlands, 218–19. *See also* Mass media
Radio I (Beckett), 142–44, 146–48
Radio II (Beckett), 142, 146–50
Radio drama: Beckett, 108, 109, 123–50, 174, 178, 179; Brecht, 174, 179; specific playwrights, 174–76, 178–81; as art form, 177–84; and music, 181–84; use of sound effects, 182–83; role of director, 185; actors, 185–86; future of, 186–87

247